GCSE

Physics

Practice, practice practice — that's the key to doing well in Grade 9-1 GCSE Physics. And that's where this excellent CGP book can help.

It's simply bursting with realistic exam-style questions on every topic. All the key practicals are covered too and there are plenty of targeted analysis questions to test those tricky AO3 skills.

There's even a section of mixed questions which test different topics, just like in the real exams. You'll find complete answers to every question at the back. Enjoy!

Exam Practice Workbook

Higher Level

Contents

Use the tick boxes to check off the topics you've completed.

You can find some useful information about What to Expect in the Exams and other exam tips at cgpbooks.co.uk/GCSEPhysicsHigher/Exams

Published by CGP

Editors:
Emily Garrett, Rob Hayman, Duncan Lindsay, Sarah Williams and George Wright.

Contributors:
Mark A. Edwards, Barbara Mascetti, Brian Mills and Jonathan Schofield.

With thanks to Mark A. Edwards and Glenn Rogers for the proofreading.

With thanks to Emily Smith for the copyright research.

Data on page 92 contains public sector information licensed under the Open Government Licence v3.0.
http://www.nationalarchives.gov.uk/doc/open-government-licence/version/3/

Clipart from Corel®
Illustrations by: Sandy Gardner Artist, email sandy@sandygardner.co.uk
Printed by Elanders Ltd, Newcastle upon Tyne

Based on the classic CGP style created by Richard Parsons.

How to Use This Book

- Hold the book upright, approximately 50 cm from your face, ensuring that the text looks like this, not sıɥʇ. Alternatively, place the book on a horizontal surface (e.g. a table or desk) and sit adjacent to the book, at a distance which doesn't make the text too small to read.
- Before attempting to use this book, familiarise yourself with the following safety information:

Fluid Pressure

There are warm-up questions for the trickier sub-topics, to ease you in and get you thinking along the right lines.

Warm-Up

Choose from the labels on the left to fill in the blanks on the right.
You do not need to use all of the words.

parallel gases volume solids perpendicular parsecs area pascals

Liquids and .... are both fluids.
Fluid pressure is the force exerted .... to a surface, per unit ....
The unit of pressure is ....

These grade stamps help to show how difficult the questions are. Remember, to get a top grade you need to be able to answer all the questions, not just the hardest ones.

In the real exams, some questions will be marked using a 'levels of response' mark scheme. In this book, these questions are marked with an asterisk (*). You'll be marked on the overall quality of your answer, so make sure you give a full, detailed answer that is logical and coherent.

3 A student uses the apparatus in **Figure 1** to calculate the densities of different rings to determine what materials they are made from. (Grade 6-7)

PRACTICAL

Figure 1

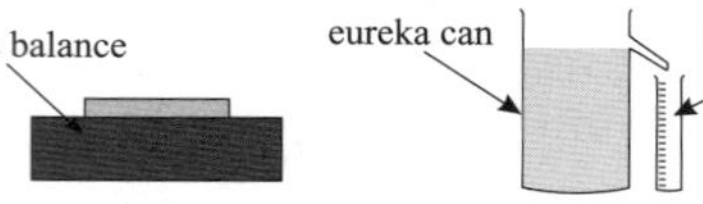

3.1* A eureka can is a beaker with a spout through which overflowing water can escape. The can is filled up to the spout so that when an object is placed in the can the displaced water flows into the measuring cylinder.
Describe the procedure for determining the density of an object using the apparatus in **Figure 1**.

....

....

....

....

....

[4]

You'll have done some 'required practical activities' as part of your course, and you could be asked about any of them in your exams. Whenever one of the required practical activities crops up in this book, it's marked up like this.

You're told how many marks each question part is worth, and then the total for the whole question.

20% of marks in the real exams test analytical skills that come under Assessment Objective 3 (AO3). AO3 skills include evaluating data, drawing conclusions and suggesting ways to improve procedures. The skills needed to earn these precious AO3 marks are easily overlooked, so sections targeting these skills are marked up like this.

Target AO3

4 A student is doing an experiment to determine the gravitational field strength on Earth. (Grade 6-7)

To do this, the student intends to measure the weight of a set of iron standard masses. Each standard mass is labelled with its mass, which is used as the value of mass in the experiment.

Exam Tips give you hints to help with answering exam questions.

Exam Tip

Don't get excited and rush straight into plugging numbers into an equation. Examiners love to sneak values in that are given in the wrong units. Take the time to spot any non-SI units, like minutes, that are hiding in the question.

☐ ☐ ☐

Topic 5 — Forces

Tick the box that matches how confident you feel with the questions in each sub-topic. This should help show you where you need to focus your revision.

- There's also an Equations List at the back of this book — you'll probably be given these equations in your exam. You can look up equations on this list to help you answer some of the questions in this book.

Energy Stores and Systems

1 **Figure 1** shows an apple on a tree. **Figure 2** shows a filament bulb connected to a battery. Both **Figure 1** and **Figure 2** show systems.

Grade 4-6

Figure 1

Figure 2

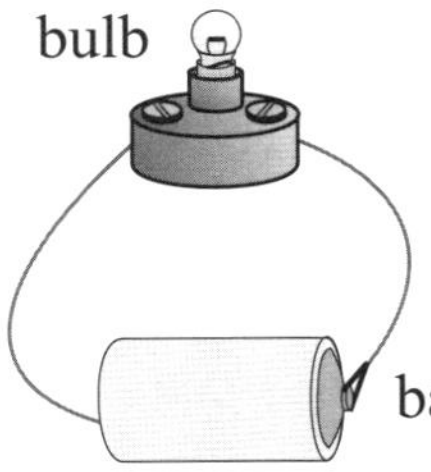

1.1 Define the term 'system'.

....

[1]

1.2 The apple in **Figure 1** falls from the tree.
Give **two** energy stores that energy is transferred between when this happens.

Energy is transferred from: ....

Energy is transferred to: ....

[2]

1.3 In **Figure 2**, energy is transferred from the chemical energy store of the battery to the thermal energy store of the bulb. State how energy is transferred between these two stores.

....

....

[1]

[Total 4 marks]

2* A cyclist allows his bike to roll down a hill without pedalling. Towards the bottom of the hill he applies his brakes. The bike comes to a stop. Applying the brakes causes the brakes to warm up. Describe the energy transfers that have occurred. State the forces doing work that cause each of these energy transfers. You can ignore any friction between the bike and the ground and any air resistance.

Grade 6-7

....

....

....

....

....

[Total 4 marks]

Exam Tip

Make sure you know the different types of energy store and remember that energy transfers can occur mechanically (because of a force doing work, like above), electrically, by heating or by radiation (e.g. light and sound waves).

Kinetic and Potential Energy Stores

1 A student is tuning his guitar. He stretches the string by 10 mm so it produces the right note when played. The string has a spring constant of 20 N/m. (Grade 6-7)

Calculate the energy stored in the elastic potential energy store of the string as it is stretched. You can assume that the limit of proportionality was not exceeded whilst it was being stretched. Use an equation from the Equations List.

Energy = ... J

[Total 2 marks]

2 A 0.1 kg toy contains a compressed spring. When the spring is released, the toy flies 0.45 m upwards from ground level, before falling back down to the ground. (Grade 6-7)

Assuming there's no air resistance, calculate the speed of the toy when it hits the ground. Gravitational field strength = 9.8 N/kg.

Speed = ... m/s

[Total 5 marks]

3 Two children, A and B, fire identical 10.0 g ball bearings from a catapult. The elastic band of each catapult is elastically extended by 0.10 m and then released to fire the ball bearings. (Grade 7-9)

3.1 Child A's elastic band has a spring constant of 144 N/m. Calculate the energy transferred to the kinetic energy store of child A's ball bearing. Use an equation from the Equations List.

Energy = ... J

[2]

3.2 The initial speed of child B's ball bearing is twice as fast as child A's ball bearing. Calculate the spring constant of child B's elastic band. Give your answer to 2 significant figures.

Spring constant = ... N/m

[5]

[Total 7 marks]

Specific Heat Capacity

Warm-Up

Which of the following is the correct definition of specific heat capacity? Tick **one** box.

- The energy transferred when an object is burnt. ☐
- The maximum amount of energy an object can store before it melts. ☐
- The energy needed to raise 1 kg of a substance by 10 °C. ☐
- The energy needed to raise 1 kg of a substance by 1 °C. ☐

PRACTICAL

1 **Figure 1** shows the apparatus used by a student to investigate the specific heat capacities of various liquids. She measured out 0.30 kg of each substance, then supplied 15 kJ of energy to each sample using an immersion heater. She then recorded her results, shown in **Table 1**.

Grade 6-7

Figure 1

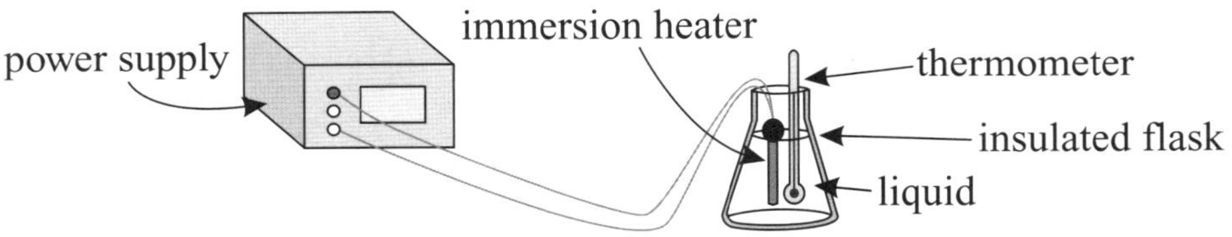

Table 1

Liquid	Mass (kg)	Temperature change (°C)	Specific heat capacity (J/kg °C)
A	0.30	12	4200
B	0.30	23	2200
C	0.30	25	....

1.1 Complete **Table 1** by calculating the specific heat capacity of Liquid C.
Use an equation from the Equations List.

[3]

1.2 Describe the energy transfers that occur when a liquid is heated using the equipment in **Figure 1**.

....

....

....

....

[4]

[Total 7 marks]

Exam Tip

You may be asked about experiments you've never seen before in an exam, but don't panic. Take your time to read the experiment carefully and work out what's going on before attempting any questions to get full marks.

Target AO3

2 A student is testing three materials, A, B and C, to find their specific heat capacities. Grade 7-9

He heats a 100 g block of each material using an electric heater. The heater is connected to a joulemeter, which measures the amount of energy transferred to the block. The student measures the temperature of each block for every 250 J of energy transferred. Each block of material is wrapped in a layer of silicone foam while it is heated.

2.1 The student says, "Putting foam around the blocks while they are heated will improve the accuracy of my results." State whether the student is correct. Explain your answer.

....

....

....

[2]

A graph of the student's results for the three materials is shown in **Figure 3**.

Figure 3

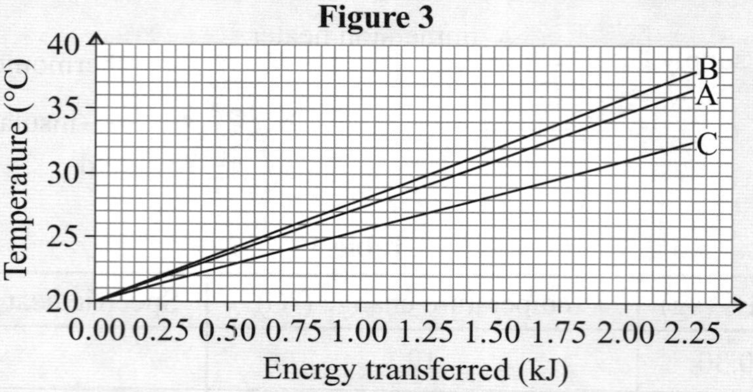

2.2 Using the graph, determine the material with the greatest specific heat capacity. Explain your answer.

....

....

....

....

....

[3]

2.3 Explain how the student can determine whether his results are valid.

....

....

....

[2]

[Total 7 marks]

Exam Tip

You may be asked to analyse the effect that using a particular piece of equipment, or method of measurement, will have on the quality of the experiment. It might help to think through how you've seen it used in other experiments.

Conservation of Energy and Power

Warm-Up

Choose from the words on the left to fill in the blanks in the sentences on the right. You do not need to use all of the words.

joules   work done   total   minimum   energy lost   rate of   watts

Power is the .... energy transfer or .... It is measured in ....

1 An electric fan wastes some energy by transferring it to the thermal energy stores of its surroundings. Describe what is meant by 'wasted energy'.

Grade 4-6

....

....

....

[Total 1 mark]

2 **Figure 1** shows a rechargeable battery-powered shaver. The shaver transfers some energy to useful energy stores and wastes some energy.

Grade 4-6

Figure 1

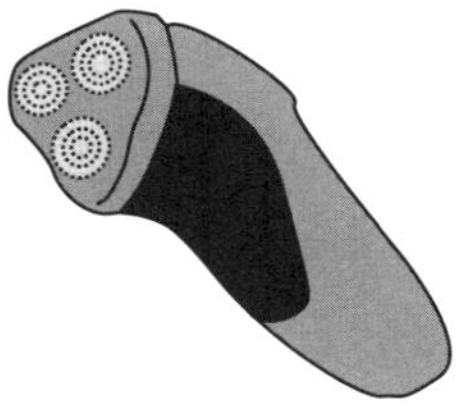

2.1 Which statements about energy are false? Tick **two** boxes.

Energy can be transferred usefully. ☐

Energy can be created. ☐

Energy can be stored. ☐

Energy can be dissipated. ☐

Energy can be destroyed. ☐

[1]

2.2 Give **one** example of a useful energy store and **one** of a wasted energy store that the shaver transfers energy to.

Useful energy store: ....

Wasted energy store: ....

[2]

2.3 Describe what effect increasing the power of the shaver would have on the shaver's battery life.

....

[1]

[Total 4 marks]

3 A student is investigating the insulating properties of various materials. He surrounds a beaker of water with each material, before heating the water using an electric immersion heater with a constant power of 35 W. Grade 6-7

3.1 Write down the equation that links power, work done and time.

....

[1]

3.2 Calculate the work done by the immersion heater when it is operated for 600 s.

Work done = ... J

[2]

3.3 Whilst investigating the insulating properties of cotton wool, the student forgets to measure the time that he leaves the immersion heater on for. Calculate the time that the heater was on for, if it transferred 16 800 J of energy to the system.

Time = ... s

[2]

[Total 5 marks]

4 A car contains a worn out engine with a power of 32 000 W. The car takes 9.0 s to accelerate from rest to 15 m/s. A mechanic replaces the engine with a more powerful but otherwise identical one. The new engine has a power of 62 000 W. Grade 7-9

4.1 Explain how the new engine will affect the time it takes for the car to accelerate from rest to 15 m/s.

....

....

....

....

[3]

4.2 Calculate how long it will take for the car to accelerate to 15 m/s now. You can assume that the total amount of energy wasted whilst the car is accelerating is the same for both engines.

Time = ... s

[4]

[Total 7 marks]

Exam Tip

For really big powers, you might see the unit kW, which stands for kilowatt. Don't let this put you off though, you just need to remember that 1000 W = 1 kW. You might see this in a few other units too, for example 1000 m = 1 km.

Conduction and Convection

1 Use words from the box below to complete the passage. You can only use each word **once** and you do not need to use all of the words. Grade 4-6

solids	**density**	**liquids**	**volume**	**gases**	**hotter**	**cooler**

Convection occurs in .... and ....

It is where a change in .... causes particles to move from

.... to .... regions.

[Total 3 marks]

2 A student uses the apparatus in **Figure 1** to investigate conduction. She heats blocks of different materials, shown in **Figure 2**, and uses a stopwatch to measure the time it takes for the upper surface of the block to increase in temperature by 2 °C. Grade 6-7

Figure 1

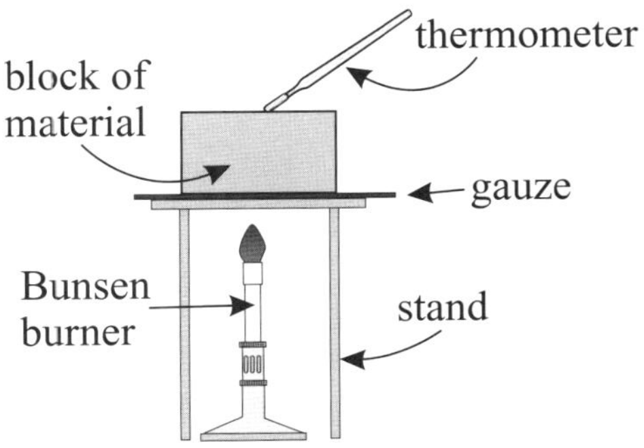

Figure 2

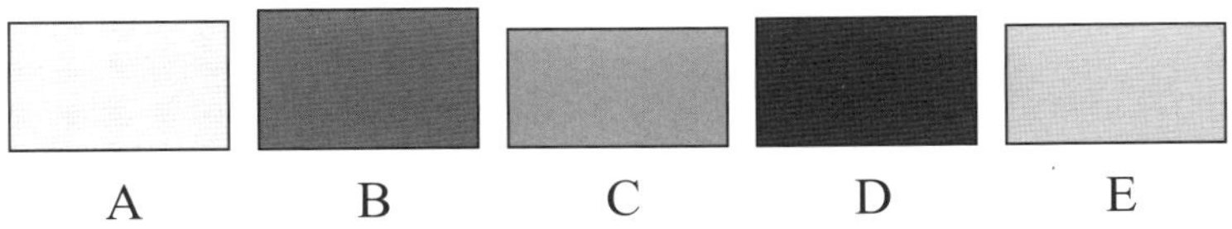

2.1 Suggest **one** way to improve the student's experiment.

....

[1]

2.2 Describe, in terms of particles, the energy transfers that take place within a block as it is heated.

....

....

....

....

[3]

Table 1

Block	A	B	C	D	E
Time taken (s)	83	37	74	97	86

2.3 **Table 1** shows the student's results.
Suggest a conclusion you can make about block B, compared to the other blocks.

....

[1]

[Total 5 marks]

Reducing Unwanted Energy Transfers

Warm-Up

Which of the following options would reduce the air resistance acting on a cyclist? Circle **one** box.

Wearing clothes that are more thermally insulating	Lubricating the bicycle's wheels	Changing the colour of his clothes	Wearing a more streamlined helmet

1 Which of the following statements are true? Tick **two** boxes. Grade 4-6

The thickness of a house's walls does not affect the rate at which it loses energy. ☐

Thicker walls decrease the rate of energy lost from a house. ☐

Thicker walls increase the rate of energy lost from a house. ☐

Bricks with a higher thermal conductivity transfer energy at a faster rate. ☐

[Total 1 mark]

2 **Figure 1** shows a thermal image of a house. Different parts of the outside of the house are at different temperatures. The owner wants to keep the inside of the house as warm as possible. Grade 4-6

Figure 1

2.1 Suggest where the highest rate of unwanted energy transfer occurs in the house.

....

[1]

2.2 Suggest **one** way to reduce this unwanted energy transfer.

....

....

[1]

2.3 A second house is tested and it is found that the majority of its unwanted energy transfers occur around the doors and windows. Suggest **two** ways to reduce these energy transfers.

1. ....

2. ....

[2]

[Total 4 marks]

Exam Tip

Some questions, like those in Question 2, will ask you to give a specific number of answers to that question. It's worth remembering that you won't get more marks for giving extra information. Give the answers you need to and move on.

3 **Figure 2** shows an old-fashioned well. The handle is turned, which rotates the axle. This causes the rope attached to the bucket to wrap around the axle, raising the bucket from the well.

Grade 6-7

Figure 2

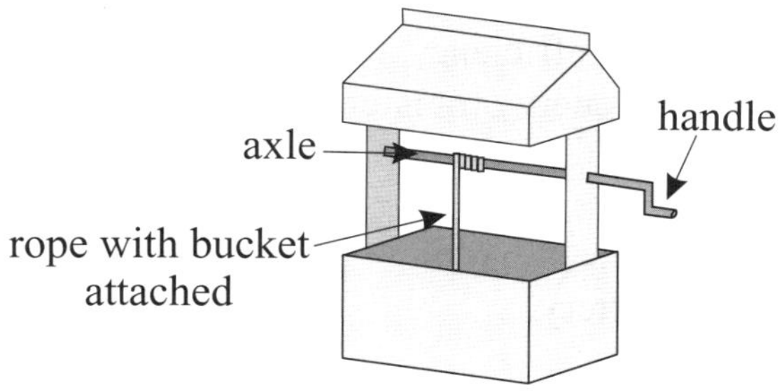

A student measures the time taken to raise a bucket of water from the well. After lubricating the axle of the well, the student repeats the test and finds the time taken is shorter. Explain why.

....

....

....

....

....

[Total 3 marks]

PRACTICAL

4 A student investigates which type of window is the best at reducing unwanted energy transfers. The student places different samples of windows on a hot plate and measures how long it takes for the top surface of the window sample to reach 30 °C.

Grade 7-9

Figure 3

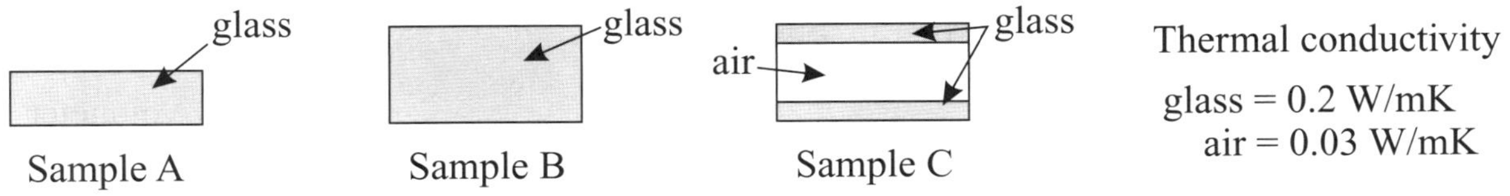

Figure 3 shows the cross-sections of each window sample. Rank them from best to worst for reducing unwanted energy transfers from a house and explain your choices.

Best: .... Second best: .... Worst: ....

....

....

....

....

....

....

[Total 5 marks]

Efficiency

1 20 kJ of energy is transferred to a mobile phone battery to fully charge it once it has lost all charge. It transfers 16 kJ of useful energy during use until it needs to be recharged. Grade 4-6

1.1 Write down the equation that links efficiency, total input energy transfer and useful output energy transfer.

....

[1]

1.2 Calculate the efficiency of the battery.

Efficiency = ...

[2]

[Total 3 marks]

2 An electric motor has a useful power output of 57 W and an efficiency of 75%. Calculate the total power input for the motor. Use an equation from the Equations List. Grade 4-6

Input power = ... W

[Total 3 marks]

3 A student investigates the efficiency of a scale model of an electricity generating wind turbine using the equipment in **Figure 1**. Grade 6-7

The student changes the number of sails on the turbine and measures the power output from the turbine's generator. The air blower is supplied with 533 W and has an efficiency of 0.62.

Figure 1

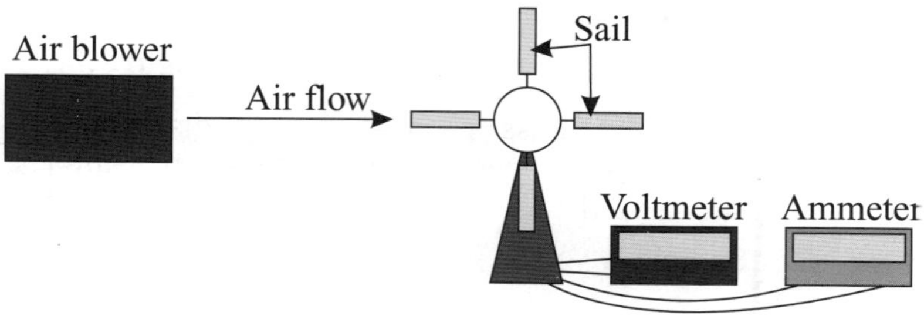

3.1 When using two sails, the efficiency of the turbine was 13%. Calculate the power generated. Give your answer to 2 significant figures.

Output power = ... W

[4]

3.2 Suggest **two** ways the student could increase the efficiency of the turbine.

1. ....

2. ....

[2]

[Total 6 marks]

Target AO3

4 A student is investigating whether the efficiency of a kettle varies with the volume of water in the kettle. Grade 7-9

The kettle automatically switches off when the water in the kettle reaches its boiling point. The student carries out the following method:

1. Fill the kettle with 500 ml of 20 °C water.
2. Calculate the mass of the water, and calculate the energy that should be required to raise the temperature of the water from 20 °C to 100 °C (the useful energy output).
3. Turn on the kettle, and allow it to boil the water and automatically switch off.
4. Measure and record the energy transferred to the kettle whilst it was on using a joulemeter.
5. Allow the kettle to cool, and then repeat steps 1-4 for different volumes of water.

4.1 Suggest **one** way the student could improve the experiment.

....

....

[1]

4.2 At one point during the experiment, the student forgets to allow the kettle to cool before carrying out a measurement for a new volume of water. Explain how this will affect their results.

....

....

....

[2]

The student records the useful energy output from the kettle for each volume of water and the energy transferred to the kettle (the total energy input) in **Table 1**.

Table 1

Volume of water (cm^3)	660	1000	1330	1660	2000
Total energy input (MJ)	0.212	0.302	0.388	0.474	0.547
Useful energy output (MJ)	0.168	0.252	0.336	0.420	0.504

4.3 Before the experiment, the student predicted that the kettle would be more efficient for smaller volumes of water. Are the results consistent with this prediction? Explain your answer.

....

....

....

....

....

[4]

[Total 7 marks]

Exam Tip

For experiments with a detailed method, take the time to read through the individual steps before you tackle the question. You might also find it helpful to underline key information and data so that you can find it more easily later on.

Energy Resources and Their Uses

Warm-Up

Write the resources below in the correct place in the table to show whether they are renewable or non-renewable energy resources.

bio-fuel oil coal hydroelectricity solar wind nuclear fuel tidal geothermal wave power gas

Renewable	Non-renewable

1 Describe the difference between renewable and non-renewable energy resources. Grade 4-6

....

....

[Total 2 marks]

2 Most cars run on petrol or diesel, which are both derived from fossil fuels. Grade 4-6

2.1 Name the **three** fossil fuels.

....

[1]

2.2 Give **two** other everyday uses for fossil fuels.

1. ....

2. ....

[2]

2.3 Some modern cars are made to run on bio-fuels. What are bio-fuels?

....

....

[1]

2.4 Suggest **one** reason why car manufacturers are developing cars that run on alternative fuels to petrol and diesel.

....

....

[1]

[Total 5 marks]

3 A UK university is considering ways to reduce their energy bills. They are considering building either a single wind turbine nearby, or installing solar panels on top of their buildings. By commenting on the change of seasons throughout the year, suggest why the university may decide to install both wind turbines and solar panels.

Grade 6-7

....

....

....

....

[Total 5 marks]

4 An energy provider is looking to replace their old fossil fuel power plant. They are eligible for a government grant, so the initial building costs are negligible.

Grade 7-9

4.1* The energy provider is interested in building a power plant that uses renewable energy resources. They have narrowed their choice to either a hydroelectric power plant or a tidal barrage. Compare generating electricity from hydroelectricity and tides, commenting on their reliability and their impact on the environment.

....

....

....

....

....

....

[4]

4.2* An alternative is replacing the old power plant with a new power plant that is run on fossil fuels. Discuss the advantages and disadvantages of using fossil fuels to generate electricity.

....

....

....

....

....

....

....

....

....

....

[6]

[Total 10 marks]

Trends in Energy Resource Use

1 **Figure 1** shows the energy resources used to generate electricity in a country. Grade 4-6

Figure 1

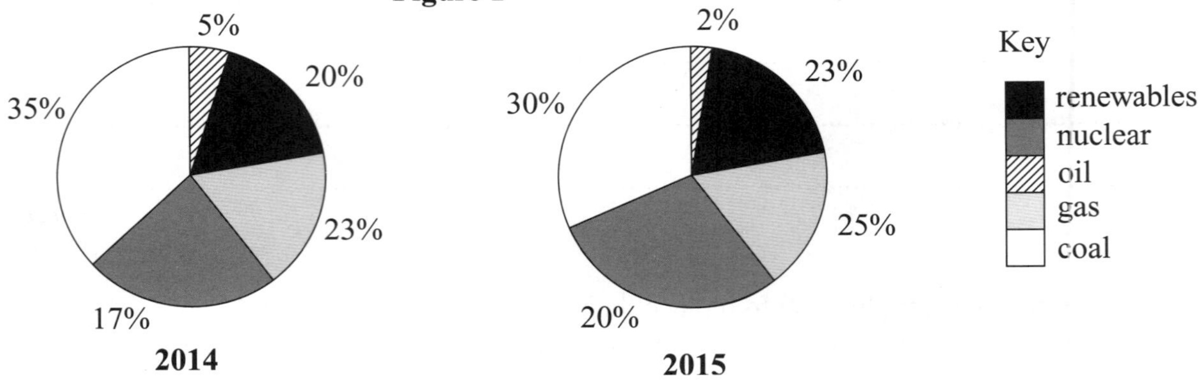

1.1 Determine what percentage of the country's electricity was generated by fossil fuels in 2014.

.........................%

[2]

1.2 Suggest **one** trend you can determine from the graphs in **Figure 1**.

....

[1]

[Total 3 marks]

2* In the UK, the use of renewable energy resources is increasing, but many say it is not increasing at a fast enough rate. Suggest reasons for this increase in the use of renewable energy resources. Suggest and explain the factors that may affect the speed at which we use more renewable energy resources. Grade 7-9

....

....

....

....

....

....

....

....

....

....

....

[Total 6 marks]

Current and Circuit Symbols

Warm-Up

Draw lines to match circuit symbols A-D to their correct names.

switch   filament lamp   fuse   cell

1 **Figure 1** shows a simple circuit, featuring a 10 Ω resistor. Grade 4-6

Figure 1

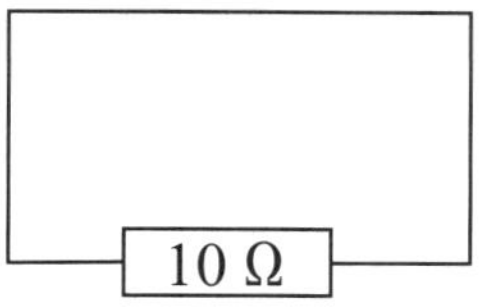

1.1 Explain why there is no current in the circuit.

....

[1]

1.2 Use a word from the following list to complete the sentence below:

charge	potential difference	resistance	frequency

Current is the rate of flow of ....

[1]

[Total 2 marks]

2 **Figure 2** shows two ammeters, A_1 and A_2, in a circuit. The reading on A_1 is 0.5 A. Grade 4-6

Figure 2

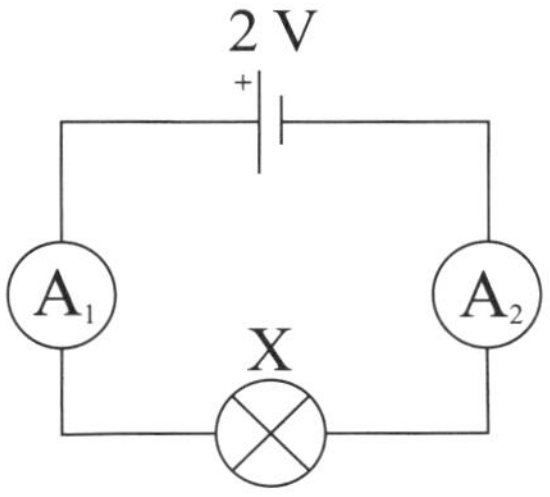

2.1 What is the reading on A_2?

Current = ... A

[1]

2.2 State the equation that links electric charge, time and current.

....

[1]

2.3 Calculate the charge that flows through component **X** in 2 minutes. Give the unit in your answer.

Charge = ... Unit = ...

[3]

[Total 5 marks]

Exam Tip

You'll need to know the basics of how circuits work and the different circuit symbols for most electricity questions.

Resistance and V = IR

1 A current of 3 A flows through a 6 Ω resistor.
Calculate the potential difference across the resistor. Grade 4-6

Potential Difference = ... V
[Total 2 marks]

PRACTICAL

2 A student investigated how the resistance of a piece of wire depends on its length.
The circuit she used is shown in **Figure 1**. Her results are displayed in **Table 1**. Grade 6-7

Figure 1

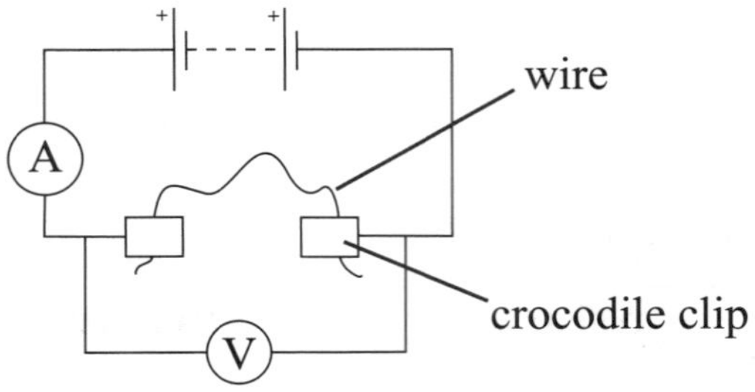

Table 1

Length / cm	Resistance / Ω
10	0.6
20	1.3
30	1.7
40	2.4
50	3.0

2.1 Describe how the student could have used the apparatus in **Figure 1** to obtain the results in **Table 1**.

....

....
[2]

2.2 Plot a graph of the data in **Table 1** on the grid shown in **Figure 2**. Label the axes correctly. Draw a line of best fit on the graph.
[4]

Figure 2

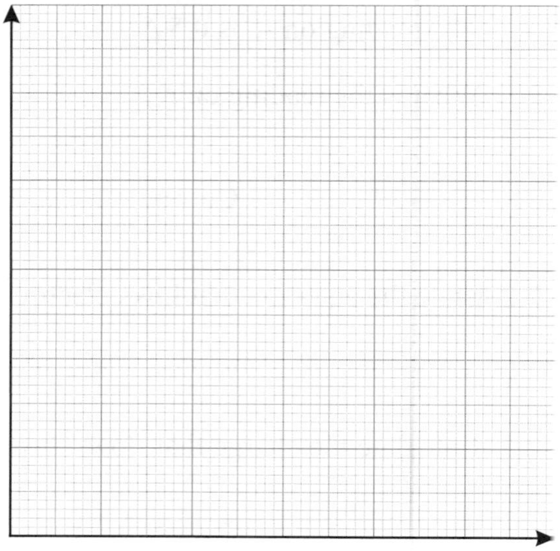

2.3 State **one** conclusion the student can make about the relationship between the resistance of a wire and its length. Explain how **Figure 2** shows this.

....

....

....

....
[2]

[Total 8 marks]

Exam Tip

Always use a sharp pencil to both plot your data and draw your line of best fit. It will make it easier for you to draw your line accurately, as well as making it easier for the examiner to check that all of your points are in the right places.

Resistance and I-V Characteristics

1 **Figure 1** shows some graphs of current against potential difference. Grade 4-6

1.1 Tick the box below the correct graph for a resistor at constant temperature.

Figure 1

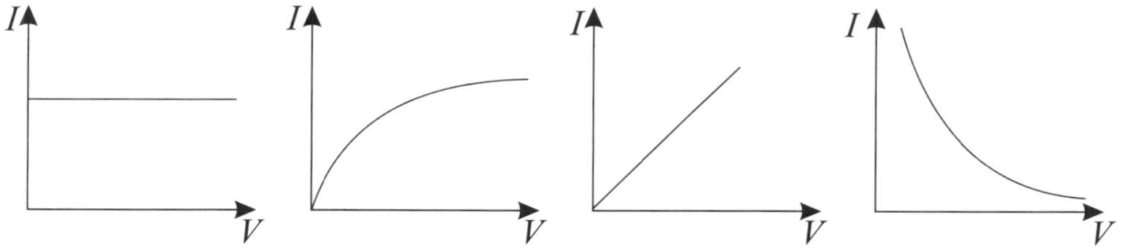

A ☐ B ☐ C ☐ D ☐

[1]

1.2 Name the type of graph shown in **Figure 1**.

....

[1]

1.3 Use words from the following list to complete the sentences below:

linear	**non-linear**	**non-ohmic**	**ohmic**

A resistor at a constant temperature is an example of a(n) ....

conductor. It is also an example of a(n) .... component.

[2]

[Total 4 marks]

2 This question is about diodes. Grade 6-7

2.1 Draw the standard circuit symbol for a diode.

[1]

2.2 An old name for a diode is a valve. A valve in a bicycle pump only lets air flow through it in one direction. In what way do diodes behave in a similar way to valves?

....

[1]

2.3 A student measured the resistance of a diode using an electric circuit. He found the resistance to be 0.02 Ω. The next day he measured the diode again. This time he measured the resistance to be 100 MΩ. Suggest why the student's measurements were so different.
You may assume that the circuit is working perfectly on both occasions.

....

....

[2]

[Total 4 marks]

PRACTICAL

3 A student used the circuit in **Figure 2** to find the *I-V* characteristic of a filament lamp. Grade 6-7

3.1 Explain the purpose of the variable resistor in the circuit.

....

....

....

....
[2]

Figure 2

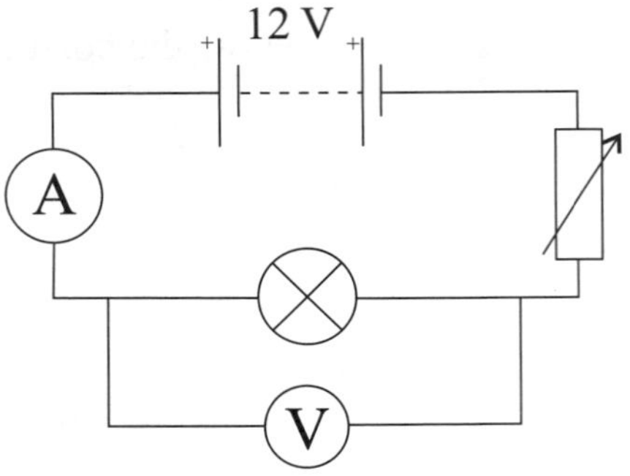

3.2 The student obtained the graph displayed in **Figure 3**.
Use the graph to find the resistance of the lamp at 3 A.

Figure 3

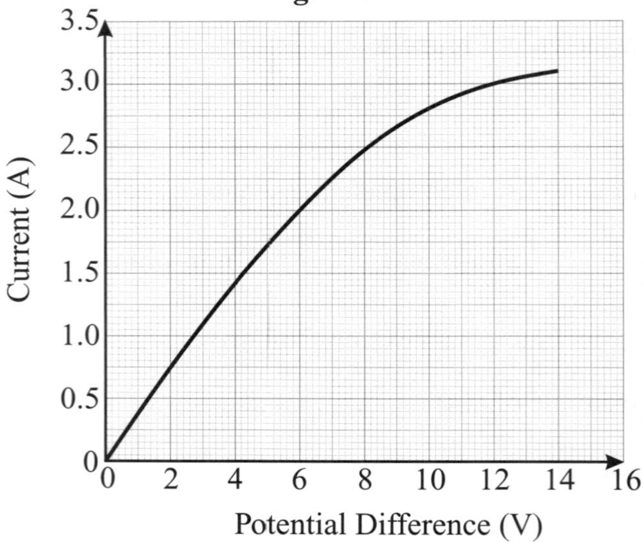

Resistance = ... Ω
[4]

3.3 What does the graph tell you about the lamp's resistance as the current increases?
Explain why the resistance behaves in this way.

....

....
[2]

3.4 The student states that the lamp behaves as an ohmic conductor up to a potential difference of approximately 3.5 V. Explain what has led the student to this conclusion.

....

....
[2]

[Total 10 marks]

Exam Tip

If you're asked a question about a required practical, think about how you would conduct that experiment in real life. It won't always be just the method you need to think about too. You should also consider how the experiment should be set up, what safety precautions you might need to take, or what errors you need to account for as part of the experiment.

Target AO3

4 A student creates a test circuit containing a diode, as shown in **Figure 4**. Grade 6-7

Figure 4

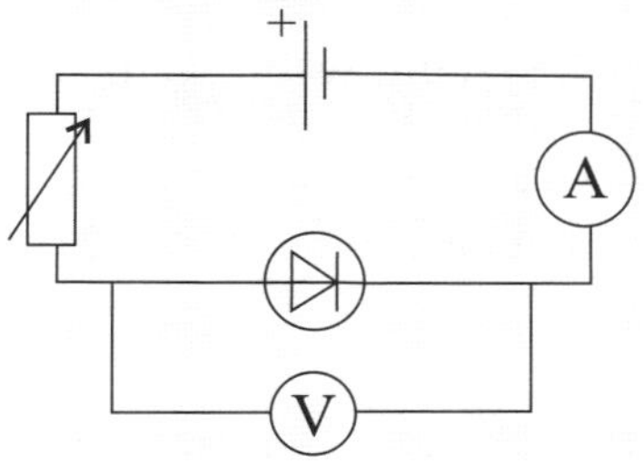

4.1 Describe a method the student could use to investigate how the resistance of the diode changes with current.

....

....

....

....

....

....

....

....

[3]

The student carries out the experiment and plots her results on a graph, shown in **Figure 5**.

Figure 5

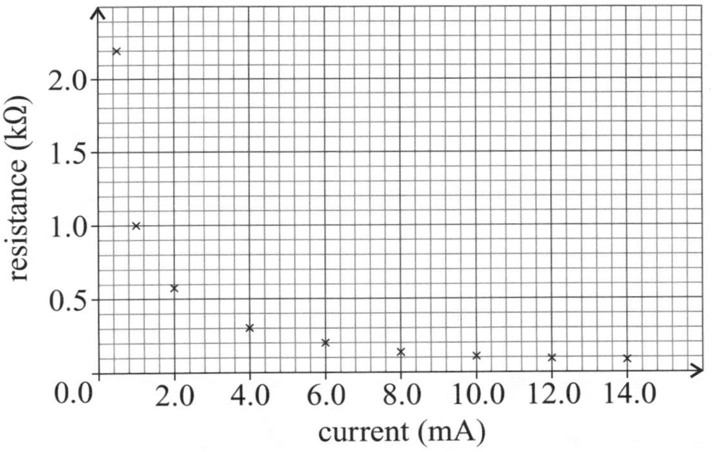

4.2 Draw a curve of best fit on **Figure 5**.

[1]

4.3 The student states, "From my results, I can conclude that the greater the magnitude of the current through the diode, the lower the resistance." Explain why the student cannot make this conclusion from her results.

....

....

....

....

[2]

[Total 6 marks]

Circuit Devices

1 A student wants to measure the resistance of a light dependent resistor. Grade 4-6

1.1 Draw a circuit diagram (including an ammeter and a voltmeter) that can be used to measure the resistance of an LDR.

[3]

The resistance of an LDR changes depending on its surroundings.

1.2 State what happens to the resistance of an LDR as the surrounding light intensity increases.

....

[1]

1.3 Give **one** example of a device that uses a light dependent resistor.

....

[1]

[Total 5 marks]

2 **Figure 1** shows a circuit that can be used for a light that lights up when the surface of a cooker is hot. Describe how the circuit works. Grade 7-9

Figure 1

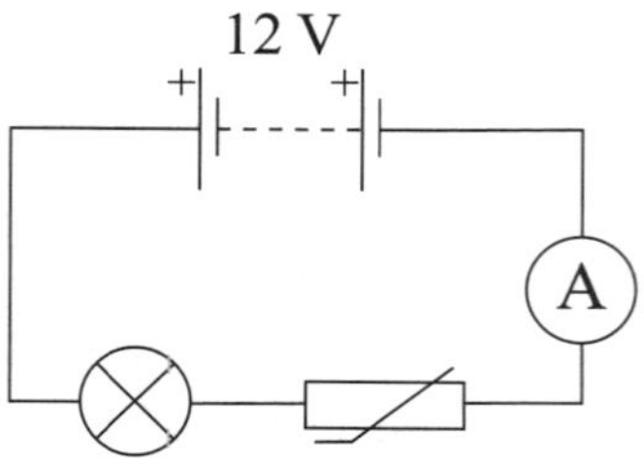

....

....

....

....

....

[Total 4 marks]

Exam Tip

You may be asked to interpret the resistance graph of an LDR or thermistor. Remember the graph starts steep and then levels out. So for an LDR at low light intensities, a small change in light intensity will cause a large change in resistance.

Series Circuits

1 **Figure 1** shows a number of circuits.
Tick the box below the diagram that shows **all** the components connected in **series**.

Grade 4-6

Figure 1

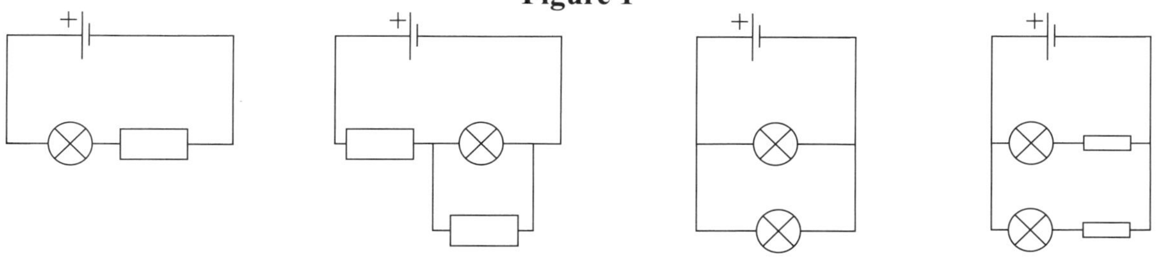

A ☐ B ☐ C ☐ D ☐

[Total 1 mark]

2 In the circuit in **Figure 2**, the reading on the ammeter is 75 mA.

Grade 6-7

Figure 2

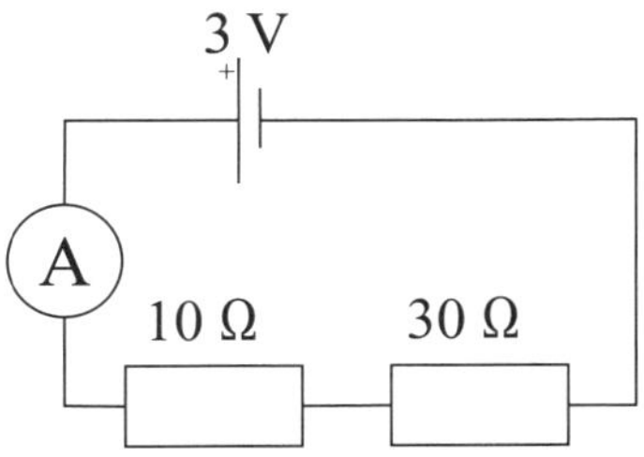

2.1 Calculate the total resistance of the two resistors.

Resistance = ... Ω

[1]

2.2 Find the potential difference across the 30 Ω resistor.

Potential Difference = ... V

[2]

[Total 3 marks]

3 In the circuit in **Figure 3**, the reading on the voltmeter is 2 V.
Component R is a resistor. Find the resistance of R.

Grade 7-9

Figure 3

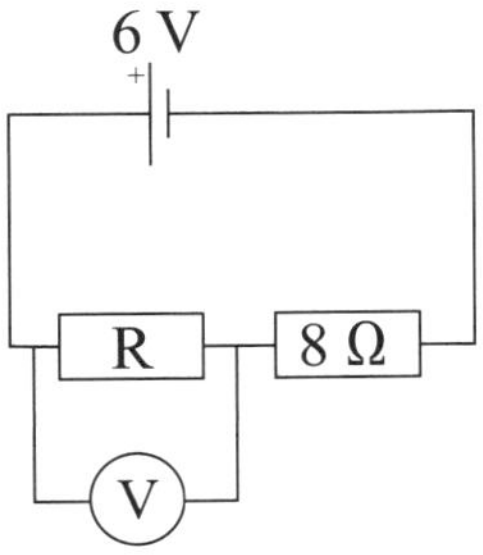

Resistance = ... Ω

[Total 5 marks]

☐ ☐ ☐

Parallel Circuits

1 Draw a circuit diagram consisting of a cell and two filament lamps connected in parallel. Grade 4-6

[Total 1 mark]

2 **Figure 1** shows a circuit with a 6 V supply and 4 Ω and 12 Ω resistors connected in parallel. There are also three ammeters and two voltmeters in the circuit. Grade 6-7

Figure 1

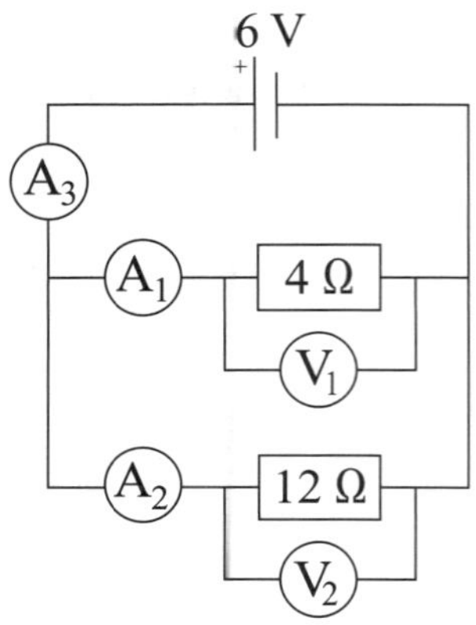

2.1 Determine the readings on voltmeters V_1 and V_2.

Potential difference = ... V
[1]

2.2 Calculate the currents through A_1 and A_2.

A_1 current = ... A, A_2 current = ... A
[5]

2.3 Calculate the current from the supply as measured by A_3.

A_3 = ... A
[1]
[Total 7 marks]

3* Explain why adding resistors in series increases the total resistance, whilst adding resistors in parallel decreases the total resistance. Grade 7-9

....

....

....

....

....

....

....

[Total 6 marks]

Exam Tip

It's really easy to accidentally hit a wrong key on your calculator when you're under exam conditions. If you've got the time, it's definitely worth having a few goes at each calculation just to check that you get the same answer each time.

Investigating Resistance

PRACTICAL

1 A student is investigating how adding identical fixed resistors in series affects the resistance of the circuit. **Figure 1** shows his results.

Grade 6-7

Figure 1

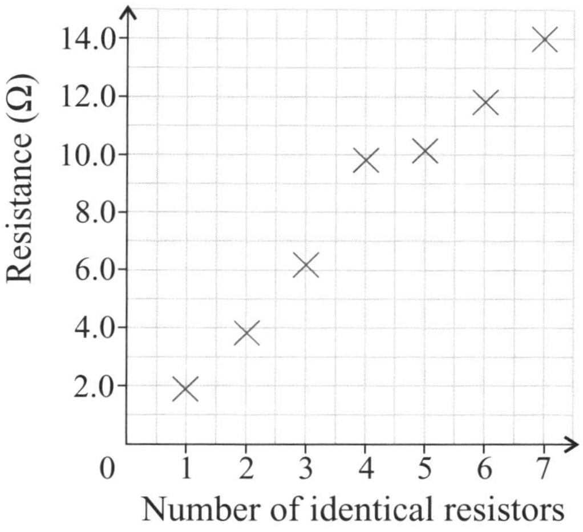

1.1 The student made a mistake when plotting his results. Draw a line of best fit for the student's data on **Figure 1**. Use this to predict the correct resistance for the incorrectly plotted result.

Resistance = ... Ω

[2]

1.2 The student repeats his experiment, this time using 1 Ω resistors.
Draw the predicted line of best fit for the results of this experiment on the axes in **Figure 1**.

[2]

[Total 4 marks]

2* A student wants to investigate how adding fixed resistors in parallel affects the overall resistance of a circuit. Describe an experiment the student could do to investigate this. You may draw a circuit diagram as part of your answer.

Grade 6-7

....

....

....

....

....

....

....

....

[Total 6 marks]

Electricity in the Home

Warm-Up

Use the words given to complete the sentences about the wires in three-core cables.

green and yellow   0   230   brown

The live wire is .... and is at a potential difference of .... V.

The earth wire is .... and is at a potential difference of .... V.

1 A toaster is connected to the mains electricity supply using a three-core cable. Grade 6-7

1.1 State the frequency and potential difference of the UK mains supply.

....

[2]

1.2* The toaster cable has a fault such that the live wire is in electrical contact with the neutral wire. Explain why the toaster will not work while this fault remains.

....

....

....

....

[4]

[Total 6 marks]

2 The cable that connects an iron to the mains supply has become worn with use. There is no insulation covering part of the live wire. The iron is plugged in, but switched off. Grade 6-7

2.1 State **two** purposes of the insulation that covers the live wire.

....

....

[2]

2.2 A man switches on the iron and touches the exposed live wire. He receives an electric shock. With reference to the electrical potential of the man, explain why he receives an electric shock.

....

....

....

[3]

2.3 The socket is switched off and the iron is unplugged. Explain whether there is still a danger of the man receiving an electric shock from the plug socket.

....

....

....

[3]

[Total 8 marks]

Power of Electrical Appliances

1 Use the correct words from the following list to complete the sentences below. Grade 4-6

current	power	in total	per second	potential difference	safety

The .... of an appliance is the energy transferred ....

Energy is transferred because the .... does work against the appliance's resistance.

[Total 3 marks]

2 A child is playing with a toy car. The car is powered by a battery and has two speed settings — fast and slow. Grade 6-7

2.1 The child sets the speed to slow and drives the car for 20 seconds. The power of the car at this speed is 50 W. Write down the formula that links energy, power and time.

....

[1]

2.2 Calculate the energy transferred by the car.

Energy transferred = ... J

[2]

2.3 The child now sets the speed to fast. The power of the car at this speed is 75 W. Explain why the battery runs down more quickly when the car is set at a higher speed.

....

....

[2]

[Total 5 marks]

3 **Table 1** shows some data for two different cycles of a washing machine. Grade 7-9

Table 1

Cycle	Power	Time needed
Standard Mode	600 W	125 minutes
Economy Mode	400 W	160 minutes

3.1 Name the **two** main useful energy transfers that take place in the washing machine.

....

....

[3]

3.2 Calculate the work done by the washing machine per minute when the machine is in Economy Mode.

Work done = ... J

[2]

3.3 Calculate the energy saved per cycle by using Economy Mode instead of Standard Mode.

Energy saved = ... J

[4]

[Total 9 marks]

Target AO3

4 A student wants to measure the useful power output of a motor. Grade 7-9

The student has the following equipment she can use in an experiment:

- a motor, attached to an axle
- a power supply and basic circuitry
- a length of string
- a clamp and clamp stand
- a metre ruler
- a stopwatch
- a 1 kg mass

4.1* Describe an experiment that the student could perform to determine the useful power output of the motor, using the equipment listed.

[4]

Figure 1 shows the display of the stopwatch when the student takes a time measurement during her experiment. The time recorded was 18.5 s.

Figure 1

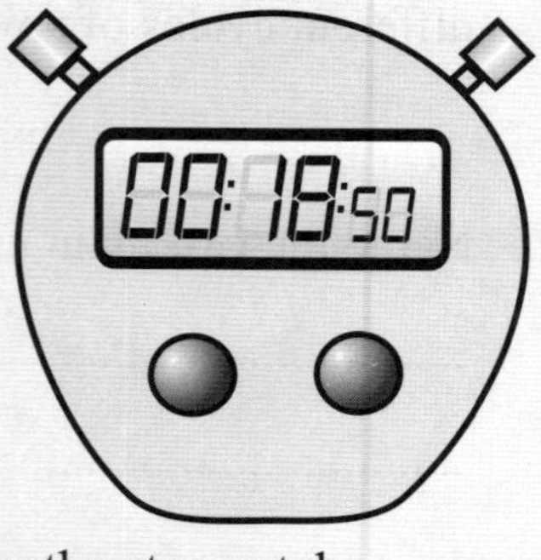

4.2 State the smallest increment of time the stopwatch can measure.

[1]

4.3 Suggest why any errors in the student's time measurements are likely to be larger than the smallest increment of time that can be measured by the stopwatch.

[2]

[Total 7 marks]

Exam Tip

Question 4.1 is an example of a question with different levels of response. These questions tend to be worth more marks than the other questions in the exam, so it's worth learning how to answer them properly. It's a good idea to plan how you're going to structure your answer first rather than jumping straight in, so you make sure you cover all the key points.

More on Power

Warm-Up

Use the words below to fill in the gaps in the passage about energy in a circuit.

work resistance energy decreases

A power source supplies .... to a charge.
When a charge passes through a component with .... ,
it does .... , so the charge's energy ....

1 **Figure 1** shows a circuit. The reading on the voltmeter is 6 V and the reading on the ammeter is 2 A. This means 2 coulombs of electric charge pass through the ammeter every second.

Grade 6-7

Figure 1

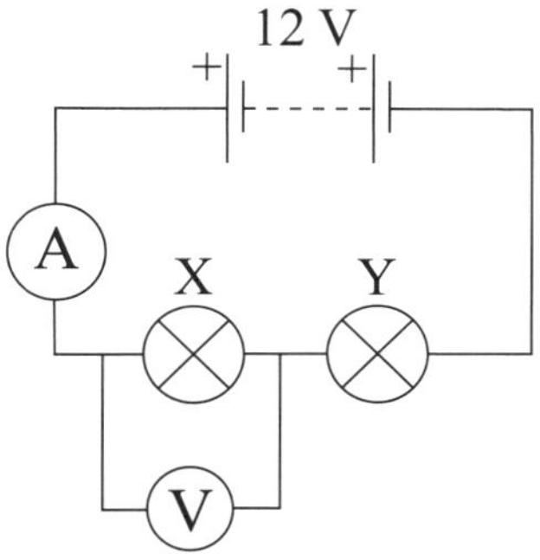

1.1 Write down the equation that links potential difference, charge and energy transferred.

....

[1]

1.2 Calculate the energy transferred to lamp X when 2 C of charge passes through it.

Energy transferred = ... J

[2]

1.3 Explain why multiplying the current through lamp X by the potential difference across it will give you the same value as in 1.2.

....

....

....

[3]

[Total 6 marks]

2 Fans use a motor to turn a set of blades.

Grade 7-9

2.1 A 75 W ceiling fan in an office is powered by the mains supply at 230 V. Calculate the current supplied to the fan.

Current = ... A

[2]

2.2 A smaller fan on someone's desk runs from a computer's USB port. It has a power of 2.5 W, and draws a current of 0.50 A. Calculate its resistance.

Resistance = ... Ω

[2]

[Total 4 marks]

The National Grid

1 The national grid uses **transformers** to transfer energy efficiently. Grade 4-6

1.1 Which **two** of the following quantities are changed by a transformer? (Assume the transformer is 100% efficient.) Put ticks in the boxes next to the correct answers.

☐ Power ☐ Potential Difference ☐ Current ☐ Resistance

[2]

1.2 Describe the difference in the function of a step-up and a step-down transformer.

....

[1]

[Total 3 marks]

2 **Figure 1** shows a diagram of part of the national grid which transfers energy from a power station to a home. Grade 6-7

Figure 1

2.1 What types of transformer are transformers A and B?

Transformer A = ...

Transformer B = ...

[2]

2.2* Explain how transformer A helps to improve the efficiency of the national grid.

....

....

....

....

....

....

[4]

2.3 Explain the purpose of transformer B.

....

....

[2]

[Total 8 marks]

Exam Tip

Read the question carefully before answering any multiple choice questions. Some will ask you for one answer, while others will ask for multiple answers. You might also find questions that ask you to spot which answer is the odd one out.

Static Electricity

1 Two balloons are charged up and attached to a ceiling using thread, as shown in **Figure 1**. Grade 4-6

Figure 1

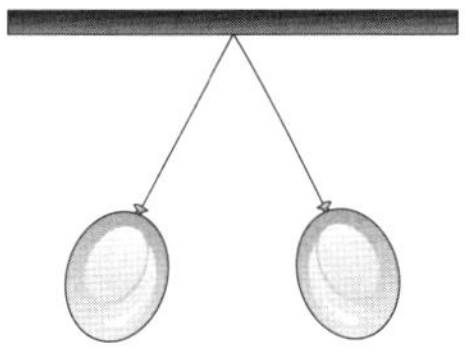

1.1 Using **Figure 1**, describe whether the static charges on the balloons are alike or opposite. Explain your answer.

....

....

[2]

1.2 Suggest how the balloons may have been charged up.

....

[1]

[Total 3 marks]

2 A student rubs a polythene rod with a dusting cloth. The rod becomes negatively charged and the dusting cloth becomes positively charged. Grade 6-7

2.1 Describe what happens to the electrons as the polythene rod is rubbed.

....

....

[2]

2.2 The rod is now suspended from a string tied around its centre. Describe how the student could use this set-up and the dusting cloth to show that opposite charges attract.

....

....

[2]

[Total 4 marks]

3 A man walks up some carpeted stairs. The handrail is made of metal and is electrically connected to earth. When he puts his hand near the rail, there is a spark. Grade 7-9

3.1 The carpet and the man's shoes rub together, making the man electrically charged. Explain why there is a spark between the man's hand and the rail.

....

....

[2]

3.2 Given that the spark leapt from the man to the handrail, was the man positively charged or negatively charged? Explain your answer.

....

....

[3]

[Total 5 marks]

Electric Fields

1 **Figure 1** shows a negatively charged sphere. Grade 6-7

1.1 Draw field lines on **Figure 1** to show the electric field around the sphere.

Figure 1

[1]

1.2 Explain what is meant by an electric field.

....

[1]

1.3 State what happens to the strength of the field as you move away from the charged sphere.

....

[1]

1.4 A second sphere is placed inside the electric field of the first sphere.
This new sphere does not experience an electric force. Suggest why this is the case.

....

[1]

[Total 4 marks]

2 **Figure 2** shows an electric field between two oppositely charged spheres. An air particle is also shown (not to scale). The air particle is made up of both positive and negative charges. It experiences a non-contact force. Grade 6-7

Figure 2

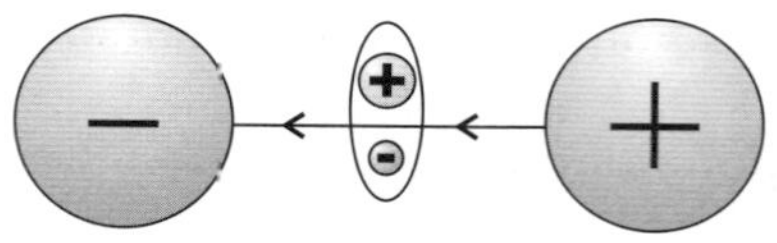

2.1 The potential difference between the spheres is increased.
State what happens to the size of the force experienced by the air particle.

....

[1]

2.2 When the potential difference is high enough, the air particle begins to break apart.
Explain why this happens.

....

....

....

[3]

[Total 4 marks]

Exam Tip

Remember to include arrows on any electric field lines you're asked to draw. The arrows on field lines should point in the direction a positively charged particle would move — towards negative charge and away from other positive charges.

Density of Materials

Warm-Up

The images below show the particles in a substance when it is in three different states of matter. Label each image to show whether the substance is a solid, a liquid or a gas.

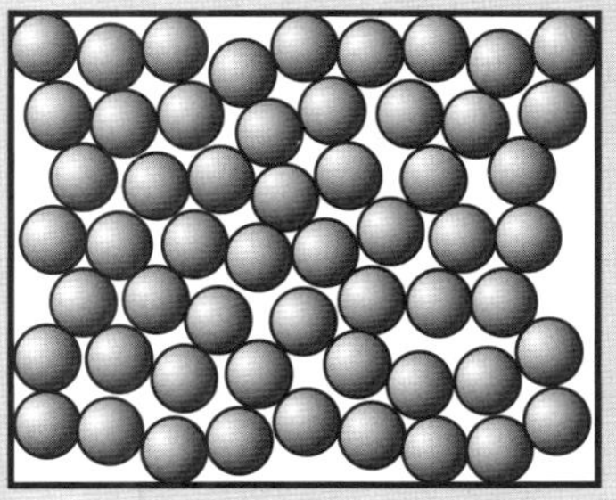

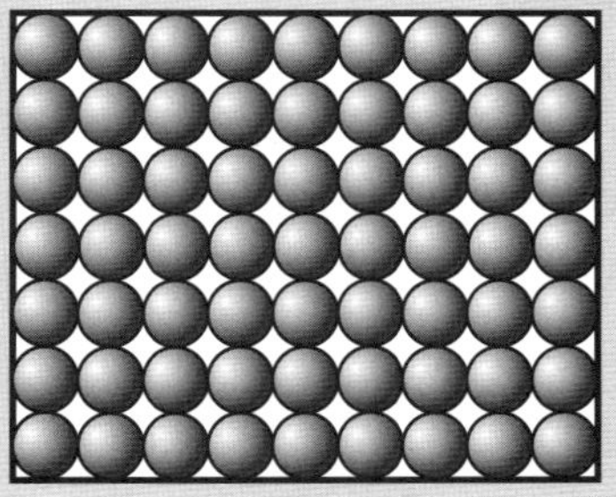

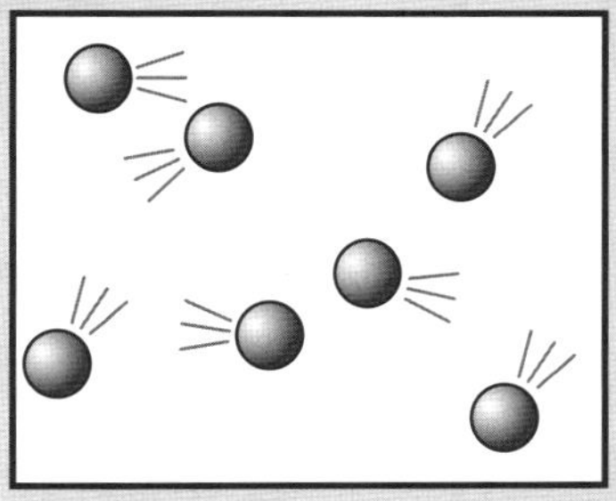

1 A 0.5 m^3 block of tungsten has a mass of 10 000 kg. Grade 4-6

1.1 Write down the equation that links density, mass and volume.

[1]

1.2 Calculate the density of tungsten.

Density = ... kg/m^3
[2]

1.3 Calculate the mass of a 0.02 m^3 sample cut from the tungsten block.

Mass = ... kg
[3]

[Total 6 marks]

2 Eric notices that ice cubes float when he puts them into a glass of water. This is because ice is less dense than liquid water. Explain what this suggests about the arrangement of the water molecules in each state. Grade 4-6

[Total 2 marks]

PRACTICAL

3 A student uses the apparatus in **Figure 1** to calculate the densities of different rings to determine what materials they are made from. Grade 6-7

Figure 1

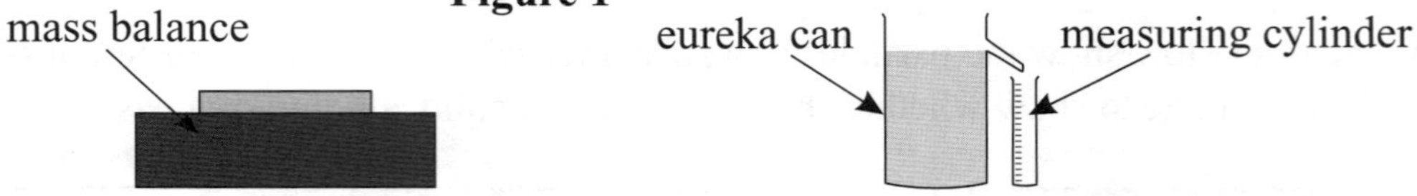

3.1* A eureka can is a beaker with a spout through which overflowing water can escape. The can is filled up to the spout so that when an object is placed in the can the displaced water flows into the measuring cylinder.
Describe the procedure for determining the density of an object using the apparatus in **Figure 1**.

....

....

....

....

....

[4]

3.2 **Table 1** shows an incomplete table of the student's results.

Table 1

Ring	Mass (g)	Water displaced (ml)	Material
A	5.7	0.30	....
B	2.7	0.60	....
C	3.0	0.30	....

Complete **Table 1** using the following information:
Density of gold = 19 g/cm^3 Density of silver = 10 g/cm^3 Density of titanium = 4.5 g/cm^3

[4]

[Total 8 marks]

PRACTICAL

4 A student investigates the density of an aluminium cola can by submerging it in a measuring cylinder of water. When completely submerged, a full can of unopened cola displaces 337 ml of water. The student then empties the can. She finds that it holds 332 ml of cola and that the mass of the empty can is 13.5 g when it is empty. Calculate the density of aluminium used to make the can. Grade 6-7

Density = ... g/cm^3

[Total 4 marks]

Exam Tip

You might be asked to explain an experiment that's used to find the density of an object. Make sure you know the different equipment you would need for finding the density of a solid or a liquid and how the results are used.

Internal Energy and Changes of State

1 Use words from the box below to complete the passage.
You can only use a word **once** and you do not need to use all the words. Grade 4-6

mass	**increases**	**temperature**	**volume**	**decreases**

When a system is heated, the internal energy of the system .... This either increases the .... of the system or causes a change of state. During a change of state the temperature and .... of the substance remain constant.

[Total 2 marks]

2 A change of state is a physical change. Grade 4-6

2.1 State the name of the following changes of state:

Gas to liquid: .... Liquid to gas: ....

[1]

2.2 State what is meant by the term 'physical change'.

....

....

[1]

[Total 2 marks]

3 Heating an object increases its internal energy. Grade 6-7

3.1 State what is meant by the term 'internal energy'.

....

[1]

3.2 Heating an object can increase its temperature.
State **two** things that the increase in a system's temperature depends on.

1. ....

2. ....

[2]

[Total 3 marks]

4 A student fills a test tube with 30 g of water. He heats the water so that it begins to boil and collects all of the water vapour produced via a tube placed into the bung of the test tube. After the test tube has cooled, he finds that the mass of the water in the test tube is now 20 g. State the mass of the water vapour the student collected. Explain your answer. Grade 6-7

....

....

....

....

[Total 2 marks]

Specific Latent Heat

1 An immersion heater is used to boil 0.50 kg of water in a sealed container. Grade 6-7

1.1 Define the term 'specific latent heat'.

....

....

[1]

1.2 The lid is removed when the water begins to boil. The immersion heater transfers 1.13 MJ of energy to evaporate all of the water. Calculate the specific latent heat of vaporisation of water. Use the equation from the Equations List.

Specific latent heat = ... MJ/kg

[3]

[Total 4 marks]

2 **Figure 1** shows a graph of temperature against time as a substance is heated. Grade 7-9

2.1 Describe what is happening during the period 3-8 minutes from the beginning of heating.

....

....

[1]

Figure 1

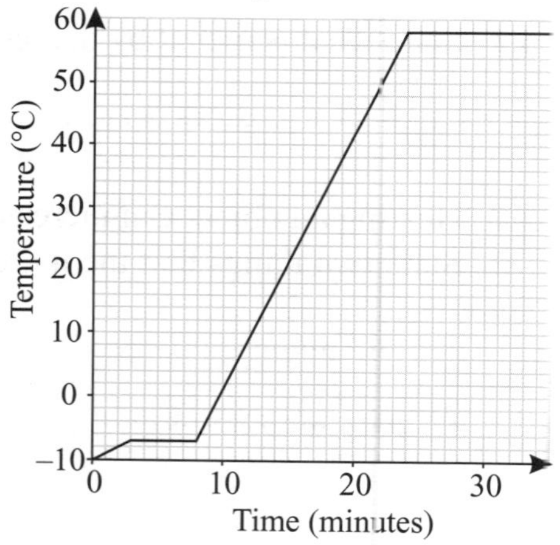

2.2 Explain, in terms of particles, why the graph is flat between 3-8 minutes even though the substance is being heated.

....

....

....

....

[3]

2.3 Give the melting and boiling points of the substance.

Melting point = ... °C

Boiling point = ... °C

[2]

[Total 6 marks]

Exam Tip

Calculation questions in the exam often contain marks for showing your working, such as rearranging equations or converting values into the correct units. This means that, even if your final answer isn't right, you might get a few marks.

Target AO3

3 A student is carrying out an experiment to determine how long it takes for ice to melt at room temperature.

Figure 2

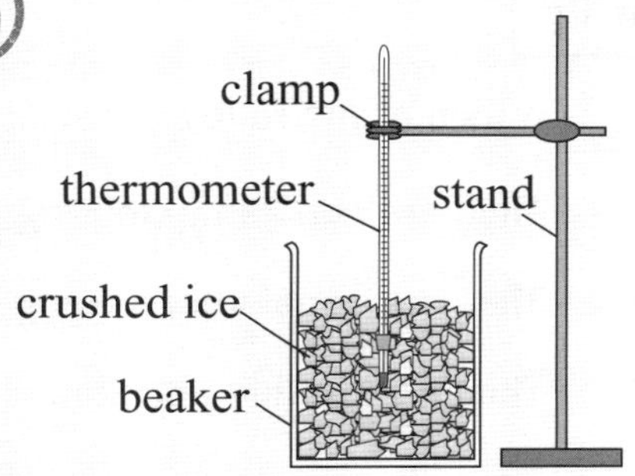

The student used the equipment shown in **Figure 2**. The beaker contains 0.05 kg of crushed ice. He recorded the temperature of the ice every minute. He stopped the experiment when he first recorded a temperature greater than 0 °C. A graph of his results is shown in **Figure 3**.

Figure 3

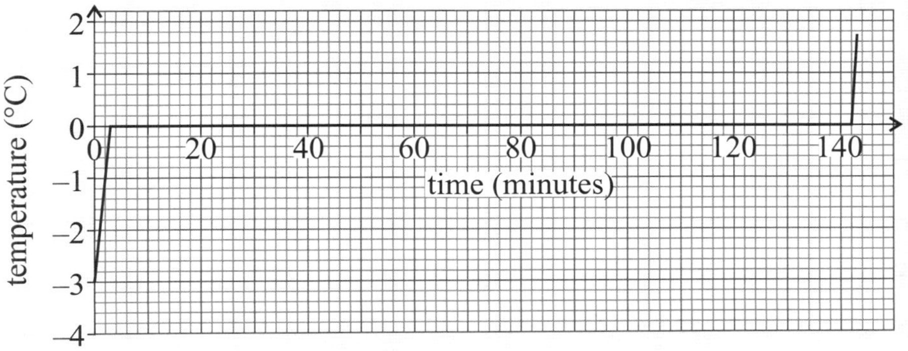

3.1 Give **two** ways the student could improve his experiment.

1. ....

....

2. ....

....

[2]

3.2 The specific latent heat of fusion of water is 334 000 J/kg. Calculate the average rate of energy transfer to the ice from the surroundings while the ice is melting. Use the correct equation from the Equations List.

rate of energy transfer = ... J/s

[4]

3.3 The student repeats the experiment with a single 0.05 kg ice cube and gets different results. He states, "This shows that my original experiment wasn't repeatable."
Is the student correct? Explain your answer.

....

....

....

[2]

[Total 8 marks]

Particle Motion in Gases

Warm-Up

Which of the following statements is true for molecules in a gas? Tick **one** box.

They are constantly moving in all directions at a constant speed. ☐

They are constantly moving in random directions at random speeds. ☐

They are fixed in position. ☐

They all move in the same direction. ☐

1 Use words from the box below to complete the passage. You can use each word **more than** once and you do not need to use all the words. Grade 4-6

potential	maximum	decreases	kinetic	increases	average

When the temperature of a gas increases, the average energy in the .... energy stores of the gas molecules increases. This .... the .... speed of the gas molecules. If the gas is kept at a constant volume, increasing the temperature .... the pressure.

[Total 3 marks]

2 A student investigates how varying the volume of a container full of a fixed mass of gas at a constant temperature affects the pressure of the gas. **Table 1** is an incomplete table of his results. Grade 6-7

Table 1

Volume (m^3)	Pressure (kPa)
8.0×10^{-4}	50
4.0×10^{-4}	100
2.5×10^{-4}	160
1.6×10^{-4}	....

Figure 1

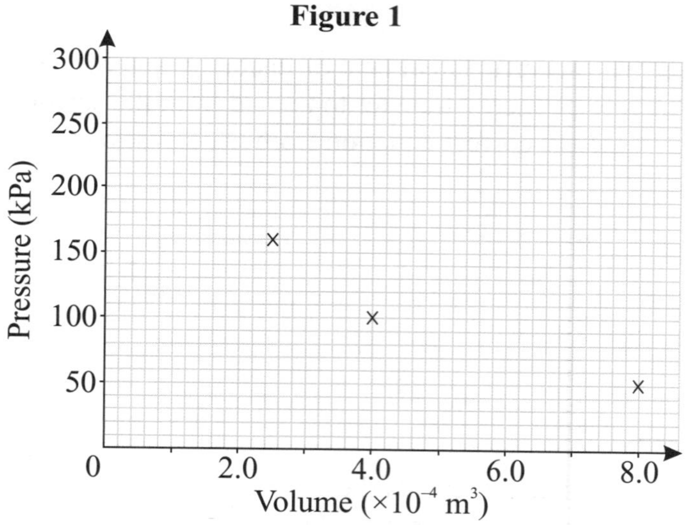

2.1 Complete **Table 1**.

[3]

2.2 Using information from **Table 1**, complete the graph in **Figure 1** by plotting the missing data and drawing a line of best fit.

[2]

[Total 5 marks]

3 **Figure 2** shows a simple piston holding a gas inside a container. The piston is air-tight. The piston is moved and the volume inside the container increases, as shown in **Figure 3**. You can assume that the temperature of the gas inside the container remains constant.

Grade 6-7

Figure 2

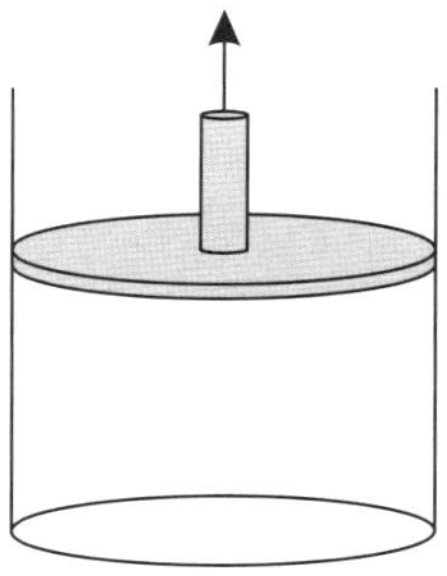

Figure 3

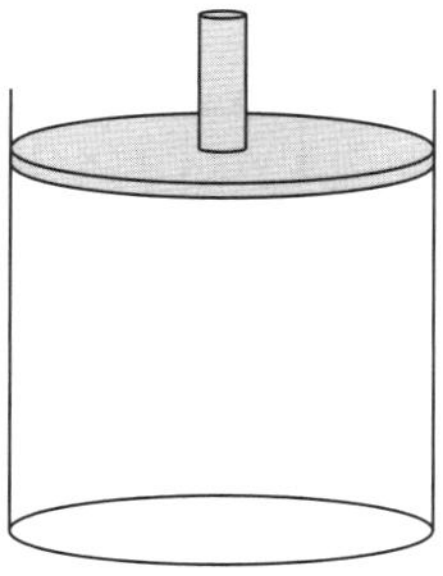

Using the particle model, define gas pressure and explain why the gas in the container in **Figure 3** is at a lower pressure than it was in **Figure 2**.

[Total 5 marks]

4* The pistons in a diesel engine work by compressing air and then spraying in droplets of diesel fuel, which then ignites. Explain how compressing the air increases its temperature until it is hot enough to ignite the diesel fuel.

Grade 7-9

[Total 6 marks]

Developing the Model of the Atom

Warm-Up

What is the typical radius of an atom?

☐ 1×10^{-10} m ☐ 1×10^{10} m ☐ 1×10^{-20} m ☐ 1×10^{-15} m

How many times smaller is the radius of a nucleus than the radius of the atom?

☐ 10 ☐ 10 000 ☐ 100 ☐ 1000

1 Our understanding of the structure of the atom has changed significantly since the early 19th century. Grade 4-6

1.1 In 1804, Dalton believed that atoms were tiny spheres which could not be broken up.
State **one** way in which this model is different to our current understanding of atomic structure.

....

[1]

1.2 The alpha particle scattering experiment provided evidence for the nuclear model of the atom.
Name and describe the model that it replaced.

....

....

[2]

1.3 What did the work of James Chadwick prove the existence of around 20 years after the atomic nucleus became an accepted scientific theory?

....

[1]

[Total 4 marks]

2 Niels Bohr discovered that electrons within an atom can only exist with defined energy levels. Grade 4-6

2.1 Describe how an electron can move between energy levels.

....

....

....

[2]

2.2 Name the type of particle created when an atom loses or gains electrons.

....

[1]

2.3 What is the charge on one of these particles if it is created by an atom losing an electron?

....

[1]

[Total 4 marks]

3* State **two** discoveries about atomic structure which arose from the alpha particle scattering experiment. In each case, state the observation that led to the discovery.

Grade 6-7

....

....

....

....

....

....

....

[Total 4 marks]

4 **Table 1** is an incomplete table showing the relative charges of the subatomic particles in an atom.

Grade 6-7

Table 1

Particle	Proton	Neutron	Electron
Relative charge	....	....	–1

4.1 Complete **Table 1**.

[2]

4.2 Describe how these subatomic particles are arranged in the atom.

....

....

....

[2]

4.3 An iron atom has 26 protons.
State the number of electrons in the atom and explain your reasoning.

....

....

....

[3]

[Total 7 marks]

Exam Tip

Remember that nothing is ever completely certain — just look at John Dalton and his ideas about atomic structure. New experiments are taking place all the time and they can completely change our models and theories. Make sure you can describe how the nuclear model has changed and how this illustrates the fact that our theories can always change.

Isotopes and Nuclear Radiation

Warm-Up

Draw a line from each form of radiation to show how ionising it is.

gamma alpha beta

moderately ionising weakly ionising strongly ionising

1 Some isotopes are unstable. They decay into more stable isotopes by emitting nuclear radiation. Grade 4-6

1.1 What is the name of this process?

....

[1]

1.2 Describe what is meant by isotopes of an element.

....

....

[2]

1.3 Some nuclear radiation is ionising. Define ionisation.

....

[1]

1.4 An unstable isotope releases a particle made up of two protons and two neutrons from its nucleus. Name this type of decay.

....

[1]

[Total 5 marks]

2 An isotope which emits alpha radiation is used in the circuit of a house's smoke detector. Ionising radiation can be damaging if the human body is exposed to it. Grade 6-7

Explain why the use of ionising radiation in the smoke detector does not pose a threat to the health of people living in the house.

....

....

....

....

[Total 2 marks]

3 One isotope of sodium is $^{23}_{11}Na$. Grade 6-7

3.1 Write down the mass number of this isotope.

....

[1]

3.2 Calculate the number of neutrons in the sodium nucleus.

Number of neutrons = ...

[1]

3.3 Which of the following is another isotope of sodium? Tick **one** box.

$^{11}_{23}Na$ ☐ $^{11}_{24}Na$ ☐ $^{23}_{12}Na$ ☐ $^{24}_{11}Na$ ☐

[1]

3.4 An isotope of neon is $^{23}_{10}Ne$. Explain whether or not the charge on the neon isotope's nucleus is different to the charge on the nucleus of the sodium isotope.

....

....

....

[2]

[Total 5 marks]

4* Ionising radiation is used to detect leaks in pipes that are buried just below the ground. An unstable isotope is introduced to one end of the pipe and, above the ground, a radiation detector is moved along the path of the pipe. Grade 7-9

Explain how this method can be used to identify the location of a leak in the pipe, and suggest what type of radiation the isotope should emit.

....

....

....

....

....

....

....

....

....

....

[Total 6 marks]

Exam Tip

If you're asked about uses of the different kinds of radiation, then think about their properties (how ionising they are, how far they travel etc.). Then just apply what you know to the situation — if you're trying to detect something from a long way away or through a thick barrier, then you want something which has a long range. Simple really...

Target AO3

5 An engineer is investigating how the thickness of paper placed between a source of beta radiation and a detector affects the amount of radiation that reaches the detector.

Grade 7-9

The engineer uses a Geiger-Muller tube to measure the amount of radiation emitted from the source that makes it through different thicknesses of paper. The results of the engineer's experiment are recorded in **Table 1**.

Table 1

thickness of paper (mm)	count-rate detected (cps)				
	Trial 1	Trial 2	Trial 3	Mean (to nearest whole number)	Uncertainty (cps)
0.2	161	157	169	162	6.0
0.3	145	150	136	144	7.0
0.4	129	122	142	131	10.0
0.5	99	122	105	109	....
0.6	93	95	98	....	2.5
0.7	85	89	81	85	4.0
0.8	67	69	74	70	3.5

5.1 Complete **Table 1** by filling in the missing values.

[2]

5.2 The engineer states that the count-rate data recorded for 0.6 mm thick paper is the most precise and the most accurate data. State and explain whether the engineer is correct.

....

....

....

[2]

5.3 Write a conclusion for the engineer's experiment based on the data in **Table 1**.

....

....

[1]

5.4 The half-life of a radioactive substance is the time taken for the count-rate from the substance to reduce to half its initial value. Explain why it is important that the source of beta radiation used in this experiment has a half-life that is much longer than the duration of the experiment.

....

....

....

[2]

[Total 7 marks]

Nuclear Equations

1 An electron is emitted from a nucleus. Grade 6-7

1.1 State the effect this has on the charge of the nucleus.

....

[1]

1.2 Explain the effect that this has on both the mass number and atomic number of the nucleus.

....

....

....

[3]

1.3 After emitting the electron, the atom is excited. It gets rid of excess energy by emitting a gamma ray. What effect does this have on the charge and mass of the nucleus?

....

[1]

[Total 5 marks]

2 A student writes down the following nuclear decay equation: $^{234}_{90}\text{Th} \longrightarrow {}^{234}_{91}\text{Pa} + {}^{0}_{0}\gamma$ Grade 7-9

2.1 Explain how you know that this equation is incorrect.

....

[1]

2.2 The student has missed out one other particle which is formed during this decay. Write down the symbol for this particle, including its atomic and mass numbers.

....

[1]

2.3 Radium (Ra) has atomic number 88. The isotope radium-226 undergoes alpha decay to form radon (Rn). Write a nuclear equation to show this decay.

....

[3]

2.4 The radon isotope then undergoes alpha decay to form an isotope of polonium (Po), which undergoes alpha decay to form an isotope of lead (Pb).
Calculate the number of neutrons in the nucleus of this lead isotope.

Number of neutrons = ...

[3]

[Total 8 marks]

Half-life

1 The graph in **Figure 1** shows how the count-rate of a radioactive sample changes over time.

Grade 4-6

1.1 Define the term 'half-life' in terms of count-rate.

....

.... *[1]*

1.2 Using **Figure 1**, determine the half-life of the sample.

Half-life = ... s *[1]*

Figure 1

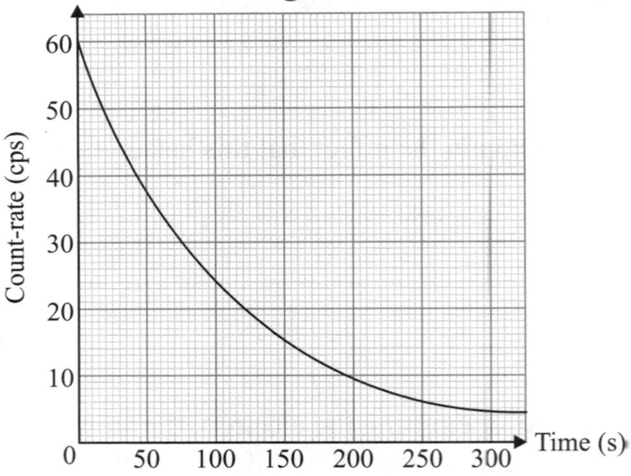

1.3 Initially, the sample contains approximately 800 undecayed nuclei. Predict how many of these nuclei will have decayed after two half-lives.

Decayed nuclei = ... *[2]*

1.4 After two half-lives, what is the ratio of the number of undecayed nuclei left to the initial number of undecayed nuclei? Tick **one** box.

1:2 ☐ 2:1 ☐ 1:4 ☐ 4:1 ☐

[1]

[Total 5 marks]

2 **Table 1** shows data about two radioactive sources.

Grade 6-7

Table 1

	Isotope 1	Isotope 2
Number of undecayed nuclei	20 000	20 000
Half-life	4 minutes	72 years

Explain which isotope will have the highest activity initially.

....

[Total 1 mark]

Exam Tip

If you come across a half-life question in the exam, and you're given a graph, it should look similar to the one in Figure 1. The numbers will change from example to example, but if you can understand that curve, you'll be halfway there.

3 The activity of a radioisotope is 8800 Bq. After 1 hour and 15 minutes, the activity has fallen to 6222 Bq. A further 1 hour and 15 minutes after that, the activity has fallen to 4400 Bq. (Grade 6-7)

3.1 Calculate the radioisotope's half-life. Give your answer in minutes.

Half-life = ... minutes
[1]

3.2 Calculate the activity of the isotope after a total time of 6 hours and 15 minutes has passed. Give your answer to 2 significant figures.

Activity = ... Bq
[2]

[Total 3 marks]

4 A radioactive sample has a 50 second half-life. The initial activity of the sample is 120 Bq. (Grade 7-9)

4.1 Complete the graph in **Figure 2** to show how the activity will change in the first 150 seconds.

Figure 2

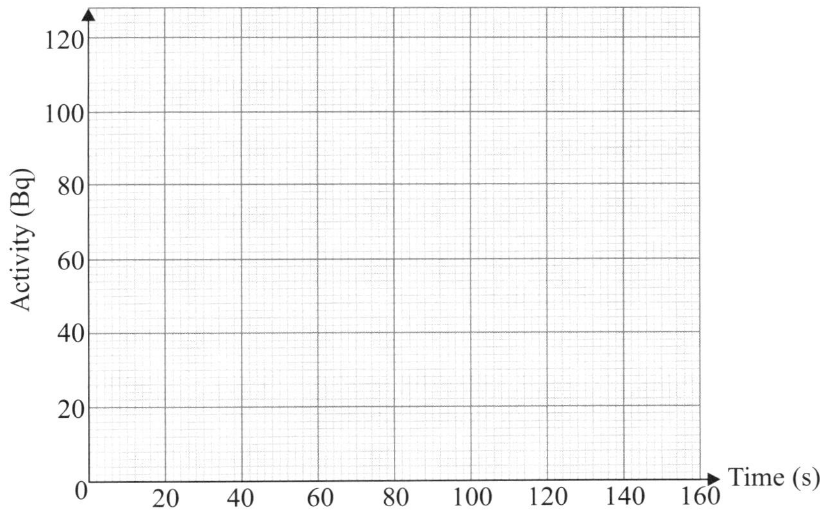

[3]

4.2 Use your graph to predict the activity of the sample after 40 seconds.

Activity = ... Bq
[1]

4.3 Calculate a prediction of the activity after 250 s.
Explain why this prediction is less likely to be correct than your prediction in 4.2.

....

....

....
[3]

[Total 7 marks]

Background Radiation and Contamination

Warm-Up

Name **one** natural source of background radiation.

....

1 Workers in a nuclear power station take many precautions to prevent unnecessary exposure to radiation. Suggest **two** methods that could be used to reduce their exposure to radiation when dealing with highly radioactive substances. Grade 4-6

1. ....

2. ....

[Total 2 marks]

2 A physicist is investigating the radioactivity of a sample. She measures the background radiation before the experiment and subtracts it from her measurements. Grade 4-6

2.1 What is meant by the term background radiation? Tick **one** box.

- The levels of alpha radiation nearby. ☐
- Radiation produced by radon gas reserves in the ground. ☐
- Low-level radiation that is around us all the time. ☐
- All radiation from man-made sources in the local area. ☐

[1]

2.2 State the type of error that the physicist is trying to avoid when she subtracts the background radiation level from her results. Explain your answer.

....

....

....

[2]

2.3 State the name given to the risk of harm to an individual due to exposure to radiation.

....

[1]

2.4 State **two** things that can affect the amount of radiation that an individual is exposed to.

1. ....

2. ....

[1]

[Total 5 marks]

3 A scientist is reviewing the safety procedures to be used in her lab. She is concerned about **contamination** and **irradiation**. Grade 6-7

3.1 Explain the difference between contamination and irradiation.

....

....

....

....

[2]

3.2 Give **one** example of how the scientist can protect herself from being irradiated by a radioactive sample with a low activity.

....

[1]

3.3 Give **two** ways in which the scientist can protect herself against contamination when handling a radioactive sample with a low activity.

1. ....

2. ....

[2]

[Total 5 marks]

4* Radium-226 is an alpha source that was used in clocks until the 1960s to make the hands and numbers glow. Explain whether a clockmaker should be more concerned about irradiation or contamination when repairing old clocks that contain radium. Grade 7-9

....

....

....

....

....

....

....

....

....

....

[Total 6 marks]

Exam Tip

It's important to remember that contamination and irradiation aren't the same thing. In the exam, you'll have to make sure you use the correct term when explaining your answers. Go back over your notes if you're unsure, then have another go at the questions on these pages. Then you can reward yourself with a cuppa and a biscuit. Smashing.

Target AO3

5 A scientist is carrying out an experiment to find the half-life of a radioactive substance. Before bringing the radioactive substance into the laboratory, the scientist needs to measure the background radiation count-rate in the laboratory.

Grade 7-9

5.1 A student was doing an experiment using a radioactive source in the same laboratory. The scientist waited for the student to finish their experiment and fully clear away their equipment before measuring the background radiation.
Explain how this will improve the accuracy of the scientist's measurements.

....

....

[1]

5.2 To measure the background radiation, the scientist measures the total counts detected by a Geiger-Muller tube and counter over 5 minutes. She repeats this measurement twice more, and records her results in **Table 1**. Use the data in **Table 1** to calculate the mean count-rate due to background radiation, in counts per second (cps).

Table 1

Trial	Total counts in 5 mins
1	598
2	641
3	624

mean count-rate = ... cps

[3]

The scientist records the count-rate from the radioactive substance every 5 minutes using the equipment in **Figure 1**.

Figure 1

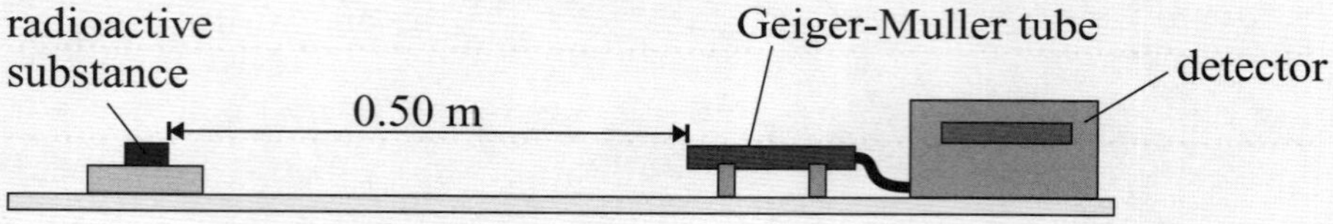

Halfway through the experiment, the Geiger-Muller tube was knocked off the bench, and needed to be put back into place.

5.3 Suggest **one** safety precaution the scientist should take when replacing the Geiger-Muller tube.

....

....

[1]

5.4 When the scientist replaces the Geiger-Muller tube, she places it 30 cm away from the source. Explain how this will affect the validity of the scientist's results.

....

....

....

[2]

[Total 7 marks]

Uses and Risk

Warm-Up

Choose some of the words on the left to fill in the blanks on the right.

mutate die survive diagnose radiation cancer sickness

Radiation can cause cells to .... or .... , which can cause cancer or radiation sickness. Radiation can also be used to treat .... and to .... illnesses.

1 Radiotherapy is used often used in the treatment of cancer. Radiation is directed towards the cancerous cells from outside of the body to kill them. Grade 6-7

1.1 What type of ionising radiation could be used in this procedure? Tick one box.

alpha ☐ beta ☐ gamma ☐ background ☐ *[1]*

1.2 The beam of radiation can be rotated around the patient, keeping the cancerous cells at the centre. Suggest how this method can minimise the risks of radiotherapy.

....

....

[2]

[Total 3 marks]

2 Sources of radiation can be used in medical imaging to explore internal organs. Iodine-123 is a radioactive isotope that is absorbed by the thyroid. Grave's disease causes an overactive thyroid, which causes the thyroid to absorb more iodine than usual. Grade 7-9

2.1 Briefly explain how iodine-123 could be used to determine if a patient has Grave's disease.

....

....

....

....

[3]

2.2 Iodine-123 emits gamma radiation.
Explain why an alpha emitter would not be used for medical imaging.

....

....

[2]

2.3 Explain why an isotope with a short half-life must be used in this type of procedure.

....

....

[1]

[Total 6 marks]

☹ ☐ 😐 ☐ ☺ ☐

Fission and Fusion

1 Below are two statements about nuclear fusion. Grade 4-6

Statement 1: During fusion, a heavier nucleus is formed by joining two lighter nuclei.
Statement 2: During fusion, some mass is converted into energy.

Which of the following is true? Tick **one** box.

Neither statement is true. ☐ Only statement 1 is true. ☐

Only statement 2 is true. ☐ Both statements are true. ☐

[Total 1 mark]

2 State **one** similarity and **one** difference between nuclear fission and nuclear fusion. Grade 4-6

Similarity: ....

....

Difference: ....

....

[Total 2 marks]

3 Fission reactors use chain reactions to produce energy. Grade 6-7

3.1* Briefly explain how the absorption of a neutron can lead to a chain reaction.

....

....

....

....

....

....

....

[4]

3.2 Chain reactions have to be controlled. This means limiting the number of neutrons causing fission. Explain what could happen if a chain reaction is uncontrolled.

....

....

[2]

[Total 6 marks]

Exam Tip

Nuclear fission and nuclear fusion may look like similar terms, but they mean very different things. Be careful to read questions with similar terms particularly carefully, or you could end up writing an answer to a very different question.

Contact and Non-Contact Forces

Warm-Up

Write each word below in the table on the right to show whether it is a scalar or vector quantity.

acceleration time temperature

mass weight force

Scalar	Vector

1 Which of the following correctly defines a vector? Tick **one** box. Grade 4-6

Vector quantities only have magnitude. ☐

Vector quantities show direction but not magnitude. ☐

Vector quantities have both magnitude and direction. ☐

Vector quantities are a push or pull on an object. ☐

[Total 1 mark]

2 A child is pulling a toy train along the floor by a piece of string. Grade 6-7
State **one** contact force and **one** non-contact force that acts on the toy.

Contact force: ....

Non-contact force: ....

[Total 2 marks]

3 **Figure 1** shows a pair of identical magnets. There is a force of repulsion between them. Grade 6-7

Figure 1

3.1 Complete the diagram in **Figure 1** by drawing another arrow representing the force that magnet B exerts on magnet A.

[2]

3.2 Magnet B is replaced by a much stronger magnet but magnet A remains the same.
Describe how you would redraw the arrows on the diagram to show this new force interaction.

....

....

[2]

[Total 4 marks]

Weight, Mass and Gravity

1 Use words from the box below to complete the passage.
You can only use a word **once** and you do not need to use all the words. Grade 4-6

weight	**kilograms**	**mass**	**directly**	**inversely**	**newtons**	**newton metres**

.... is the amount of matter in an object. .... is a force due to gravity. Mass is measured in .... whilst weight is measured in .... The weight of an object is .... proportional to its mass.

[Total 3 marks]

2 What is meant by the term 'centre of mass'? Grade 4-6

....

....

[Total 1 mark]

3 The Opportunity rover is a robot which is currently on the surface of the planet Mars.
The total mass of the Opportunity rover and its landing parachute is 350 kg. Grade 6-7

3.1 Write down the equation that links weight, mass and gravitational field strength.

....

[1]

3.2 Calculate the total weight of the Opportunity rover and its parachute when it was on the Earth.
(The gravitational field strength of the Earth = 9.8 N/kg.)

Weight = ... N

[2]

3.3 When Opportunity landed on Mars it left behind its parachute and moved away to explore.
The mass of the parachute was 209 kg. Calculate the weight of Opportunity without its parachute on Mars. (The gravitational field strength of Mars = 3.8 N/kg.)
Give your answer to 3 significant figures.

Weight = ... N

[3]

[Total 6 marks]

Exam Tip

Outside of physics, people often use the term weight when they mean mass. Make sure you get the differences straight in your head. You measure mass in kg on a set of scales, but weight is a force measured by a spring-balance (newtonmeter).

Target AO3

4 A student is doing an experiment to determine the gravitational field strength on Earth. Grade 6-7

To do this, the student intends to measure the weight of a set of iron standard masses.
Each standard mass is labelled with its mass, which is used as the value of mass in the experiment.

4.1 One of the standard masses is heavily rusted.
Suggest why this mass shouldn't be used in the experiment.

....

....

[1]

To measure the weight of a mass, the mass is placed on a small plastic tray that is hung from a newtonmeter, as shown in **Figure 1**. The force displayed on the newtonmeter is then recorded as the weight of the mass.

Figure 1

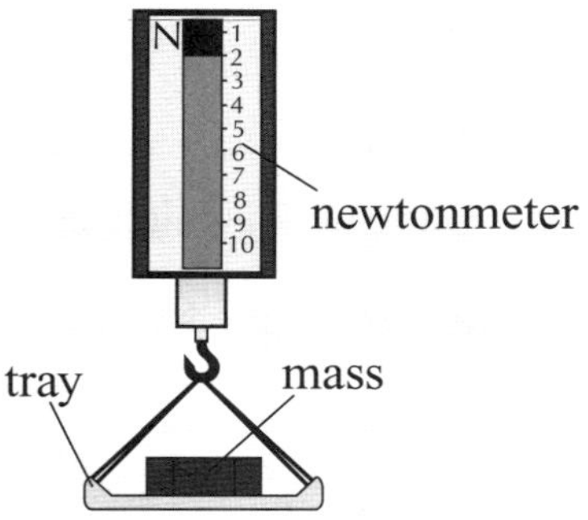

4.2 State the type of error that is introduced to the results by using this method.
Explain how this error is caused.

....

....

[2]

4.3 The student carries out the experiment, and records their results in **Table 1**.
Plot the student's results on the grid shown in **Figure 2**, and draw a line of best fit.

Table 1

Mass (kg)	Weight (N)
0.2	2.2
0.3	3.2
0.4	4.2
0.5	5.0
0.6	6.4
0.7	7.2
0.8	8.2

Figure 2

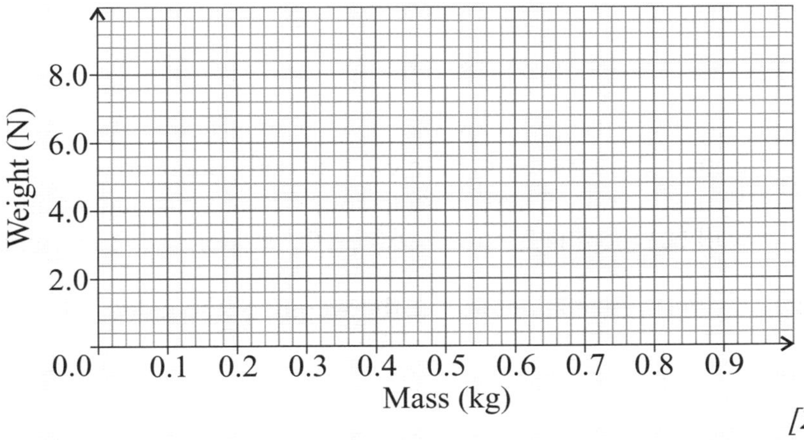

[2]

4.4 Calculate a value for the gravitational field strength using the graph in **Figure 2**.

Gravitational field strength = ... N/kg

[3]

[Total 8 marks]

Resultant Forces and Work Done

1 **Figure 1** shows four runners who are running in windy weather.
Tick the box under the runner who is experiencing the largest resultant force.

Grade 4-6

Figure 1

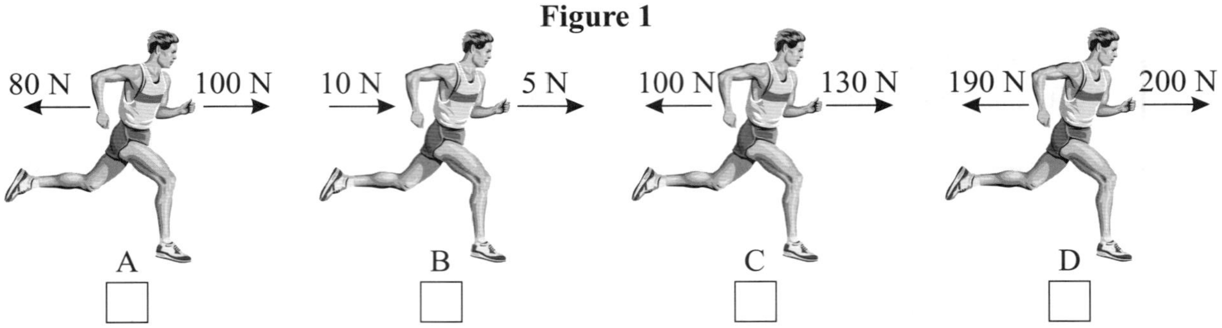

[Total 1 mark]

2 A woman pulls a 20 kg suitcase along a 15 m corridor using a horizontal force of 50 N.

Grade 6-7

2.1 Calculate the work done by the woman. Give the correct unit.

Work done = ... Unit = ...

[3]

2.2 Work has to be done against frictional forces acting on the wheels of the suitcase.
Explain the effect this has on the temperature of the suitcase.

....

....

[2]

[Total 5 marks]

3 **Figure 2** shows an incomplete free body diagram of a ladder leaning against a wall. There is no friction between the ladder and the wall but there is friction between the ladder and the ground.

Grade 7-9

3.1 Using **Figure 2**, determine the weight of the ladder, W.

Weight = ... N

[1]

3.2 Complete **Figure 2** by drawing the missing frictional force.

[2]

[Total 3 marks]

Figure 2

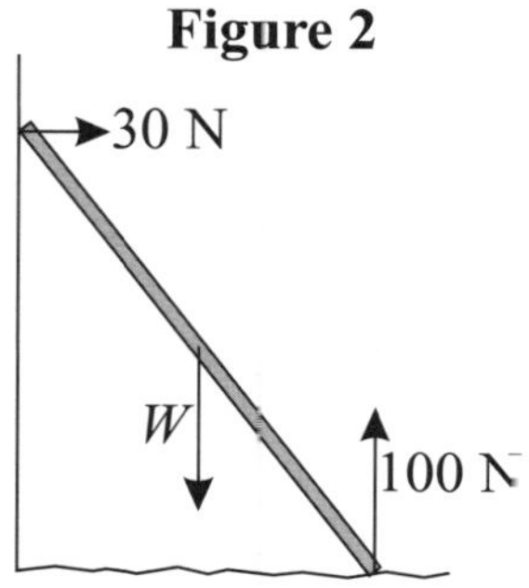

Exam Tip

Not all of the calculation questions in the exam will be nice enough to include the units as part of the answer line. It's really important to include units when you're asked for them — you won't get the full marks if you don't.

Calculating Forces

Warm-Up

Find the horizontal and vertical components of the force shown on the right. Each side of a square equals 1 N.

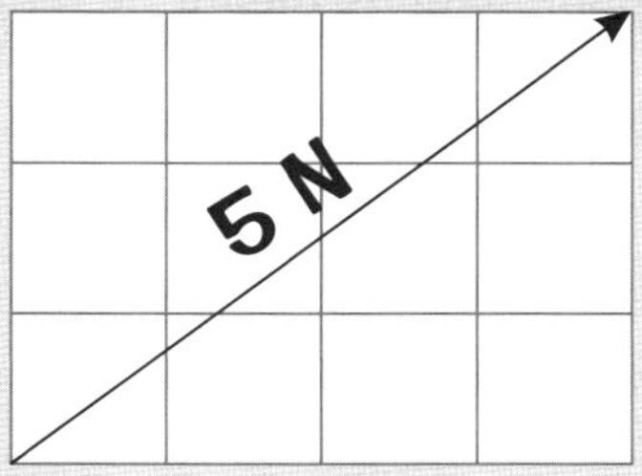

Horizontal component = ... N

Vertical component = ... N

1 **Figure 1** shows a girl on a swing. Her weight of 500 N acts vertically downwards and a tension force of 250 N acts on the ropes at an angle of 30° to the horizontal. Grade 6-7

Figure 1

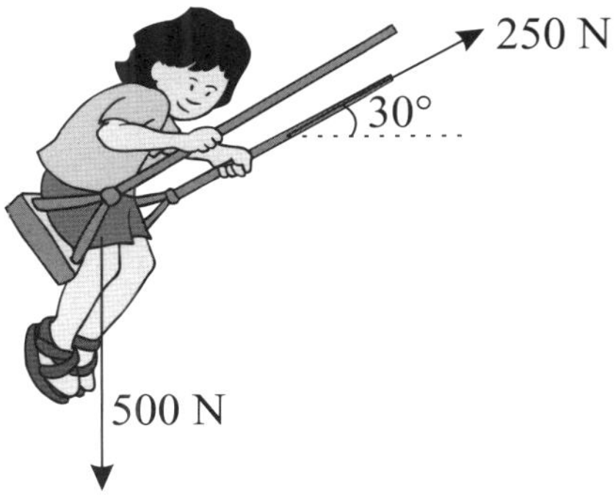

Figure 2

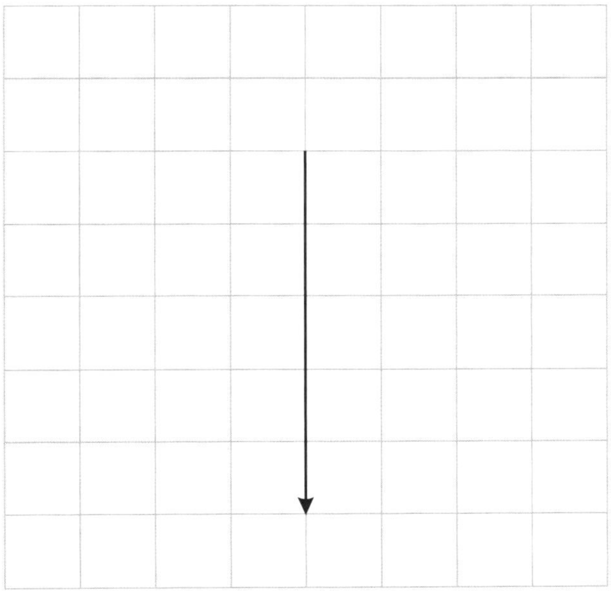

1.1 **Figure 2** shows an incomplete scale drawing for the forces acting on the girl. Only the girl's weight has been drawn so far. Calculate the scale used in the drawing.

.... cm = ... N
[1]

1.2 Complete the scale drawing in **Figure 2** to find the magnitude of the resultant force acting on the girl.

Magnitude = ... N
[2]

[Total 3 marks]

Forces and Elasticity

1 Deformations can be elastic or inelastic. Grade 4-6

1.1 Explain what is meant by the terms elastic deformation and inelastic deformation.

....

....

....

....

[2]

1.2 Stretching is one way in which forces can deform an object. State **two** other ways.

....

[1]

[Total 3 marks]

2 A student investigates the change in height of a toy horse in a playground, shown in **Figure 1**, when different people sit on it. Grade 7-9

Figure 1

2.1 When a child weighing 250 N sits on the toy horse in **Figure 1**, his feet don't touch the floor. The height of the toy horse decreases by 20 cm. Calculate the spring constant of the spring. Give the correct unit.

Spring constant = ... Unit = ...

[3]

2.2 The child gets off and the student's teacher then sits on the toy horse. Her weight is double that of the child. The student predicts that the height of the toy horse will change by 40 cm. Explain whether or not you agree with the student. State any assumptions you have made.

....

....

....

[2]

[Total 5 marks]

Investigating Springs

PRACTICAL

1 A student carried out an investigation to study the relationship between the force exerted on and the extension of a spring. He hung different numbers of 1 N weights from the bottom of the spring and measured the extension of the spring with a ruler, as shown in **Figure 1**.

Grade 6-7

Figure 1

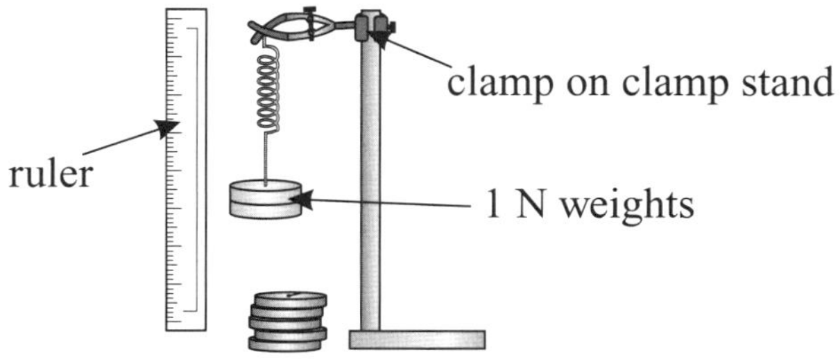

Table 1

Force (N)	Extension (cm)
0	0
1	4.0
2	8.0
3	12.0
4	15.9
5	21.6
6	30.0

Figure 2

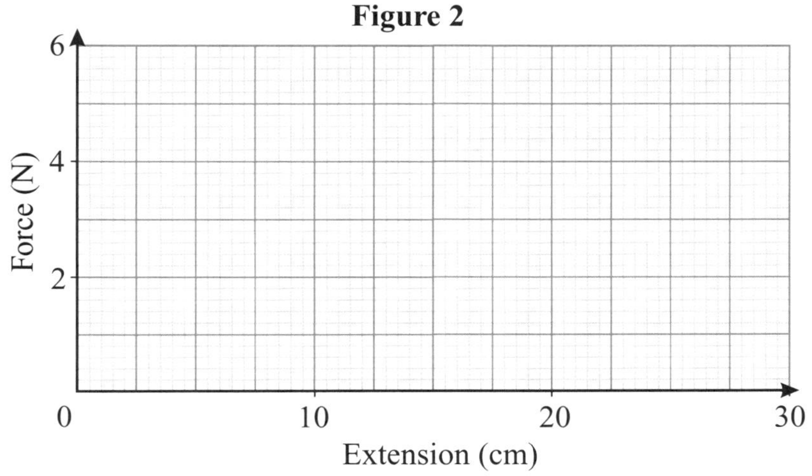

1.1 **Table 1** shows the results that the student obtained in his investigation. Draw the force-extension graph for the student's results on the axes in **Figure 2**.

[3]

1.2 Using the graph you have drawn, calculate the spring constant of the spring being tested.

Spring constant = ... N/m

[2]

[Total 5 marks]

2 Calculate the work done on a spring when it is extended elastically by 8.0 cm. The spring constant of the spring is 25 N/m.

Grade 6-7

Work done = ... J

[Total 2 marks]

Exam Tip

You need to know this practical really well — you could be asked pretty much anything about it in the exam. And make sure you draw graphs accurately with a sharp pencil. It'll really help if you need to use the graph to work something out.

Moments

1 **Figure 1** shows a box spanner used by a mechanic. He applies a force of 50 N at the end of the spanner. Calculate the size of the moment created, stating any equations you use.

Grade 4-6

Figure 1

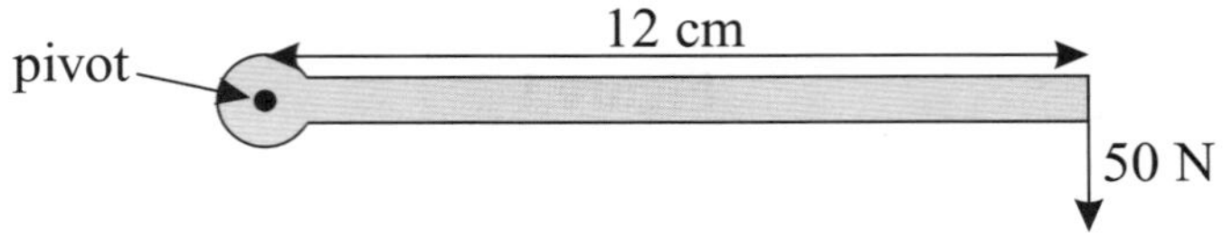

Moment = ... Nm

[Total 2 marks]

2 **Figure 2** shows a system of gears.

Grade 6-7

Figure 2

2.1 Gear A rotates anticlockwise.
In which directions do gears B and C rotate?

Gear B: ....

Gear C: ....

[2]

2.2 At what speed will gear C rotate, compared to gear A? Tick **one** box.

☐ slower than gear A ☐ at the same speed as gear A ☐ faster than gear A

[1]

[Total 3 marks]

3 **Figure 3** shows three children on a balanced seesaw.
Using the information from **Figure 3**, calculate child C's distance from the pivot.

Grade 7-9

Figure 3

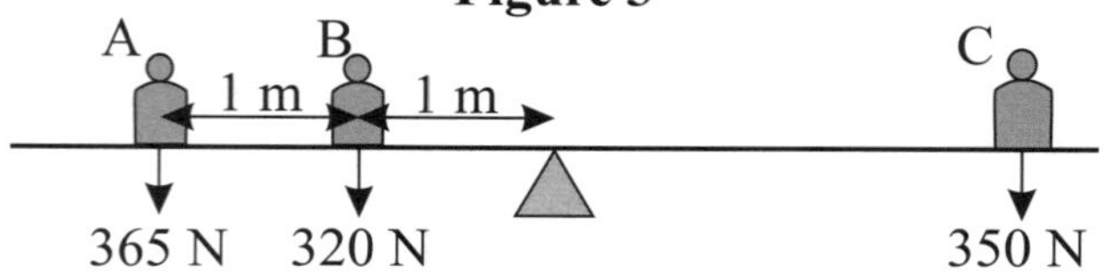

Distance = ... m

[Total 3 marks]

Exam Tip

The figures used in moments questions often feature real world examples, such as seesaws or turning gears. If you can, try to picture how the figure would move and behave in real life and apply that knowledge to your answer.

Target AO3

4 A student is carrying out an experiment to demonstrate the principle of moments. Grade 7-9

The student has the equipment shown in **Figure 4**.
Masses can be hung from holes located at fixed distances along the bar.
The bar is of uniform shape and density and the pivot is located at the bar's centre of mass.

Figure 4

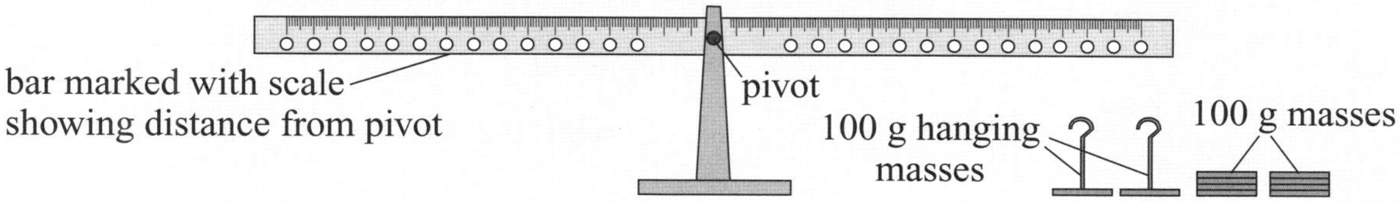

4.1* Describe an experimental method the student could carry out to demonstrate the principle of moments using the equipment in **Figure 4**.

....

....

....

....

....

....

....

....

....

....

....

....

[6]

4.2 Before carrying out the experiment, the student applies a lubricant to the pivot to reduce the friction acting on it. Explain how this will help make sure the experiment is a fair test.

....

....

....

[2]

[Total 8 marks]

Exam Tip

The key thing to remember when writing an experimental method is to make sure that it makes sense from start to finish. Have a read through after you've finished writing to check if someone could use your answer to complete the experiment.

Fluid Pressure

Warm-Up

Choose from the labels on the left to fill in the blanks on the right.
You do not need to use all of the words.

parallel gases volume solids perpendicular parsecs area pascals

Liquids and .... are both fluids.

Fluid pressure is the force exerted ....

to a surface, per unit ....

The unit of pressure is ....

1 Water in the chamber of a water pistol is squeezed out when a force is applied by the plunger. A force of 12 N is applied by a plunger with a surface area of 0.15 m^2.

Grade 4-6

1.1 Write down the equation that links pressure, force and area.

....

[1]

1.2 Calculate the pressure at the plunger.

Pressure = ... Pa

[2]

[Total 3 marks]

2 **Figure 1** shows a spouting can. A student fills the can with water and allows it to drain. Explain why water escaping from the bottom of the spouting can does so at a faster rate than water from the top.

Grade 6-7

Figure 1

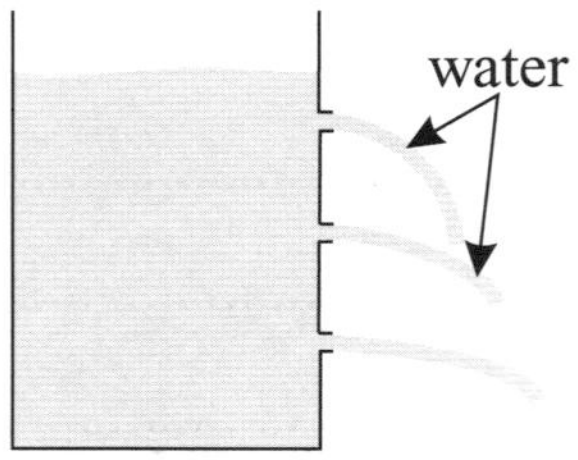

....

....

....

[Total 3 marks]

3 In a fresh water lake, a diver swimming at a depth of 5 metres below the surface will experience a pressure of approximately 151.2 kPa. At the same depth in sea water the diver would experience a pressure of 152.8 kPa. Suggest why the diver experiences different pressures in fresh water and sea water despite swimming at the same depth.

Grade 6-7

....

....

[Total 2 marks]

4 Cars use hydraulic braking systems. A hydraulic braking system like the one shown in **Figure 2** is designed to apply an equal braking force to all four wheels of the car.

Grade 6-7

Figure 2

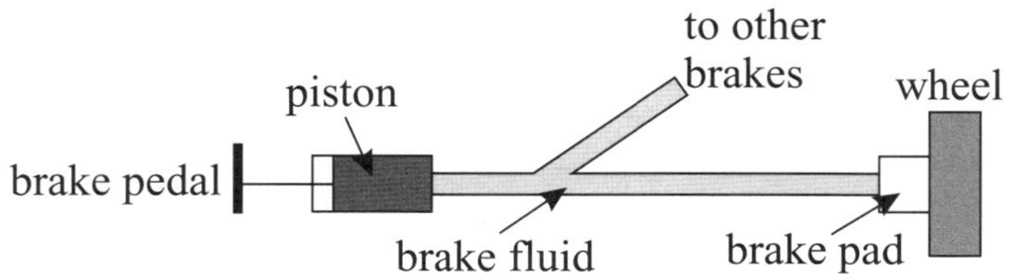

4.1 The brake pedal of a four-wheel car is connected to a piston. The head of the piston is a square, of side length 2.5 cm. Calculate the pressure transmitted throughout the hydraulic fluid when the brake is applied with a force of 100 N.

Pressure = ... Pa
[3]

4.2 The brake pad attached to one wheel has a surface area of 0.005 m^2.
Calculate the total braking force acting on the car.

Force = ... N
[3]
[Total 6 marks]

5 The bottle of lemonade shown in **Figure 3** is full to the brim.
Calculate the change in pressure in the bottle between point X and the base of the bottle. Give your answer to 2 significant figures.
Lemonade has a density of 1000 kg/m^3. Gravitational field strength = 9.8 N/kg.

Grade 7-9

Figure 3

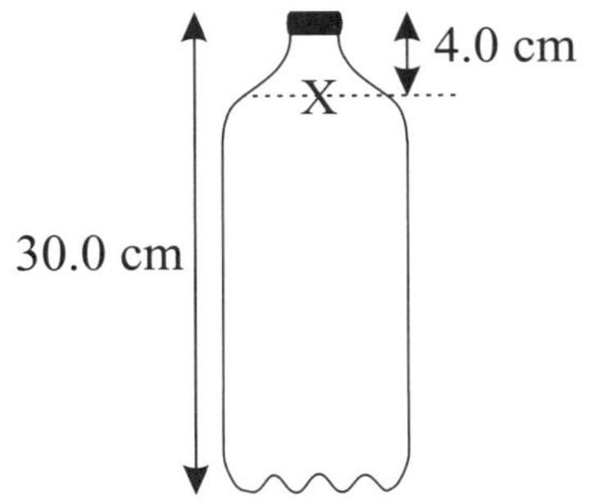

Change in pressure = ... Pa
[Total 3 marks]

Exam Tip

Don't get excited and rush straight into plugging numbers into an equation. Examiners love to sneak values in that are given in the wrong units. Take the time to spot any non-SI units, like minutes, that are hiding in the question.

Upthrust and Atmospheric Pressure

1 Use words from the box below to complete the passage.
You can only use a word **once** and you do not need to use all the words.

decreases	**thrust**	**larger**	**increases**	**upthrust**	**smaller**

In a liquid, pressure .... with depth. This means that the force acting on the bottom of a submerged object is .... than the force acting on the top of the object. This leads to a resultant force called ....

[Total 2 marks]

2 **Figure 1** shows a digital force gauge being used to measure the weight of a golf ball in air and whilst it is places in water.

Figure 1

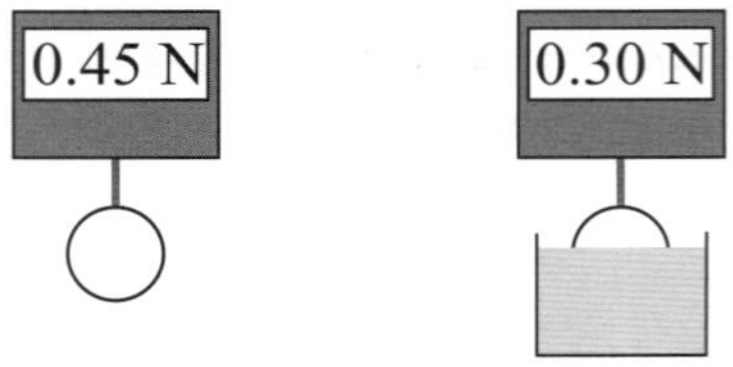

Explain why the weight of the golf ball appears to change when it is placed in the water.

....

....

[Total 3 marks]

3 A silver necklace is dropped into the ocean. Explain why the necklace sinks.
The density of silver is 10 490 kg/m^3. The density of the water is 1000 kg/m^3.

....

....

....

[Total 3 marks]

4* Explain why atmospheric pressure decreases with altitude.

....

....

....

....

....

....

....

[Total 6 marks]

Distance, Displacement, Speed and Velocity

Warm-Up

Choose from the words on the left to fill in the blanks on the right. Use each word once.

distance
velocity
vector
scalar

Displacement and .... are both .... quantities. This means they have both a size and a direction. Speed and .... are both .... quantities. They do not depend on direction.

1 **Figure 1** shows the path taken by a football kicked by a child. When it is kicked at Point A, the ball moves horizontally to the right until it hits a vertical wall at Point B. The ball then bounces back horizontally to the left and comes to rest at Point C.

Grade 4-6

Figure 1

Scale 1 cm = 1 m

1.1 What is the distance that the ball has moved through from A to B?

Distance = ... m
[1]

1.2 What is the total distance that the ball has moved through from A to C?

Distance = ... m
[1]

1.3 Draw a vector arrow on **Figure 1** to show the displacement of the ball.
[1]

1.4 What is the magnitude of the displacement of the ball after it has come to rest?

Displacement = ... m
[1]

[Total 4 marks]

2 The speed of sound varies depending upon the substance it is travelling through. State the speed of sound in air.

Grade 4-6

....

[Total 1 mark]

3 Give **three** factors that can affect a person's walking, running or cycling speed.

Grade 4-6

....

....

[Total 3 marks]

4 Explain whether a satellite orbiting the Earth at 3.07×10^3 m/s has a constant velocity. Grade 6-7

....

....

[Total 2 marks]

5 A man has just got a new job and is deciding whether to walk, cycle or take a bus to get to work. There are two routes he could take. The shorter route is along a 6 km path that only pedestrians and cyclists are allowed to use. The bus takes a longer route along a road. Grade 6-7

5.1 Write down the formula that links distance travelled, speed and time.

....

[1]

5.2 Estimate how long it would take the man to walk the pedestrian route.

Time taken = ... s

[3]

5.3 Estimate how much time would be saved if the man cycled this route instead.

Time saved = ... s

[4]

5.4 Travelling to work by bus takes 20 minutes.
The total distance covered during this time is 9.6 km.
Calculate the average speed of the bus.

Average speed = ... m/s

[3]

[Total 11 marks]

6 The speed at which an aircraft flies is often expressed in terms of its Mach number, which describes the speed in relation to the speed of sound. For example, Mach 2 is twice the speed of sound. A commercial airliner on a long-haul flight has a speed of Mach 0.8. The temperature of the air is typically –60 °C. Grade 7-9

The speed of sound is temperature dependent and can be found using:

Speed of sound in m/s = $331 + 0.6T$, where T is the temperature in °C.

Calculate the distance travelled by the jet over 5.0×10^4 s.

Distance travelled = ... km

[Total 4 marks]

Acceleration

Warm-Up

Draw one line from each scenario to the typical acceleration for that object.

A sprinter starting a race	10 m/s²
A falling object	2×10^5 m/s²
A bullet shot from a gun	1.5 m/s²

1 Briefly describe the motion of a decelerating object. Grade 4-6

....

[Total 1 mark]

2 **Table 1** shows how the speed of a car changes with time as it accelerates uniformly. Grade 6-7

Table 1

Time (s)	0	1	2	3
Speed (m/s)	0	4	8	12

2.1 Write down the formula that links acceleration, velocity and time.

....

[1]

2.2 Calculate the acceleration of the car.

Acceleration = ... m/s^2

[2]

[Total 3 marks]

3 A car accelerates uniformly at 2.5 m/s^2 from rest to a speed of 20 m/s. Calculate the time taken for the car to reach 20 m/s. Grade 6-7

Time = ... s

[Total 3 marks]

4 A train travelling at 32 m/s slows down to 18 m/s over a distance of 365 m. Calculate the deceleration of the train over this distance. Use an equation from the Equations List. Grade 7-9

Deceleration = ... m/s^2

[Total 2 marks]

Distance-Time and Velocity-Time Graphs

1 A boat is being rowed along a straight canal. Some students use a watch to time how long after setting off the boat passes marker posts spaced 100 metres apart. **Table 1** shows their results.

Table 1

Distance (m)	0	100	200	300	400	500
Time (s)	0	85	165	250	335	420

Figure 1

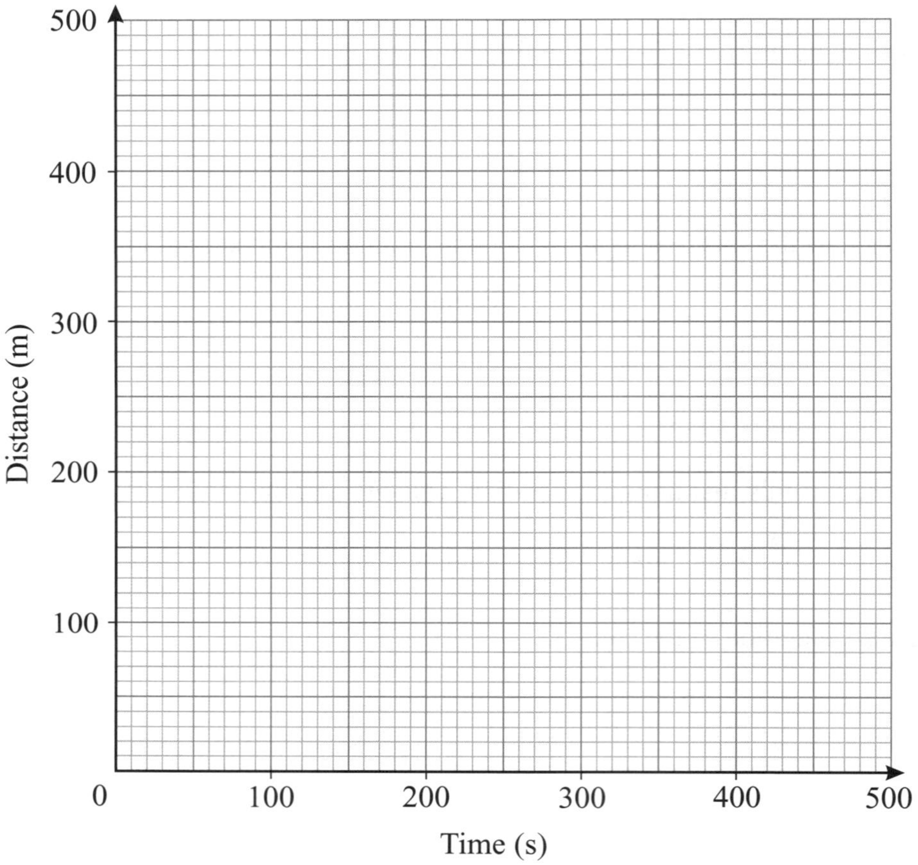

1.1 Draw the distance-time graph for the results in **Table 1** on the axes shown in **Figure 1**.

[3]

1.2 Using the graph in **Figure 1**, determine how far the boat travelled in 300 s.

Distance = ... m

[1]

1.3 Determine how long it took the boat to travel 250 m.

Time = ... s

[1]

1.4 Suggest **one** way to make the timings made by the students more accurate.

....

....

[1]

[Total 6 marks]

2 **Figure 2** shows the distance-time graph for a cyclist's bike ride.

Figure 2

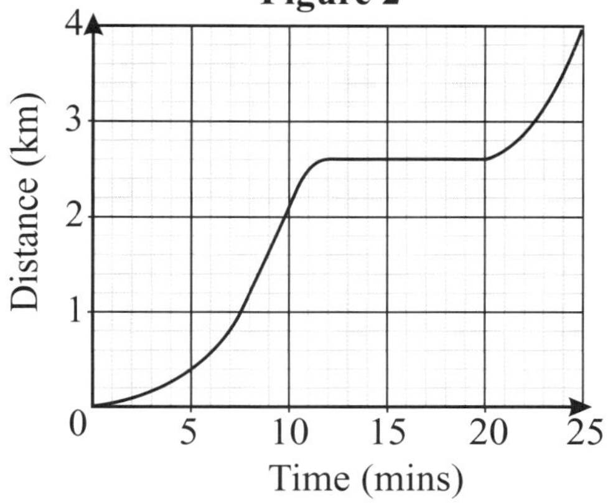

2.1 Use **Figure 2** to determine how long the cyclist rode for before stopping for a rest.

....

[1]

2.2 Describe the cyclist's motion in the first five minutes of her journey.

....

[1]

[Total 2 marks]

3 **Figure 3** shows the distance-time graph for a car's journey.

3.1 Use **Figure 3** to find the speed of the car 5 s into its journey.

Figure 3

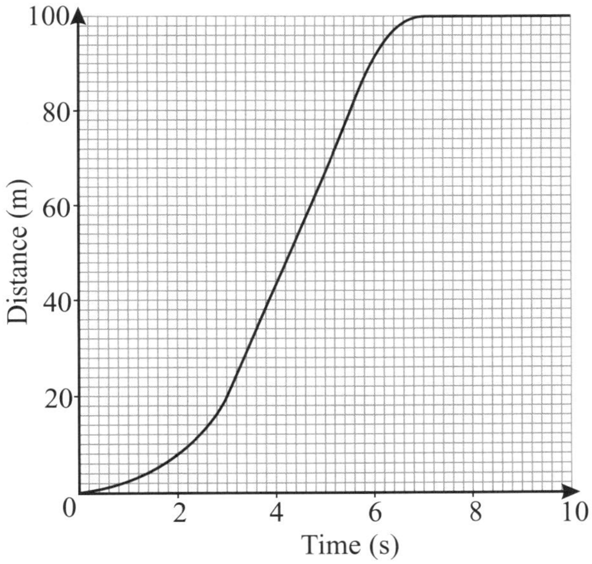

Speed = ... m/s

[3]

3.2 Use **Figure 3** to find the speed of the car 2 s into its journey.

Speed = ... m/s

[3]

[Total 6 marks]

Exam Tip

It's important to be accurate when you're asked to use a graph to find an answer. These questions do tend to include a bit of margin for error, but be careful. A small misread could cause you to end up with a significantly different answer.

4 **Figure 4** shows an incomplete velocity-time graph for a roller coaster ride. Grade 7-9

Figure 4

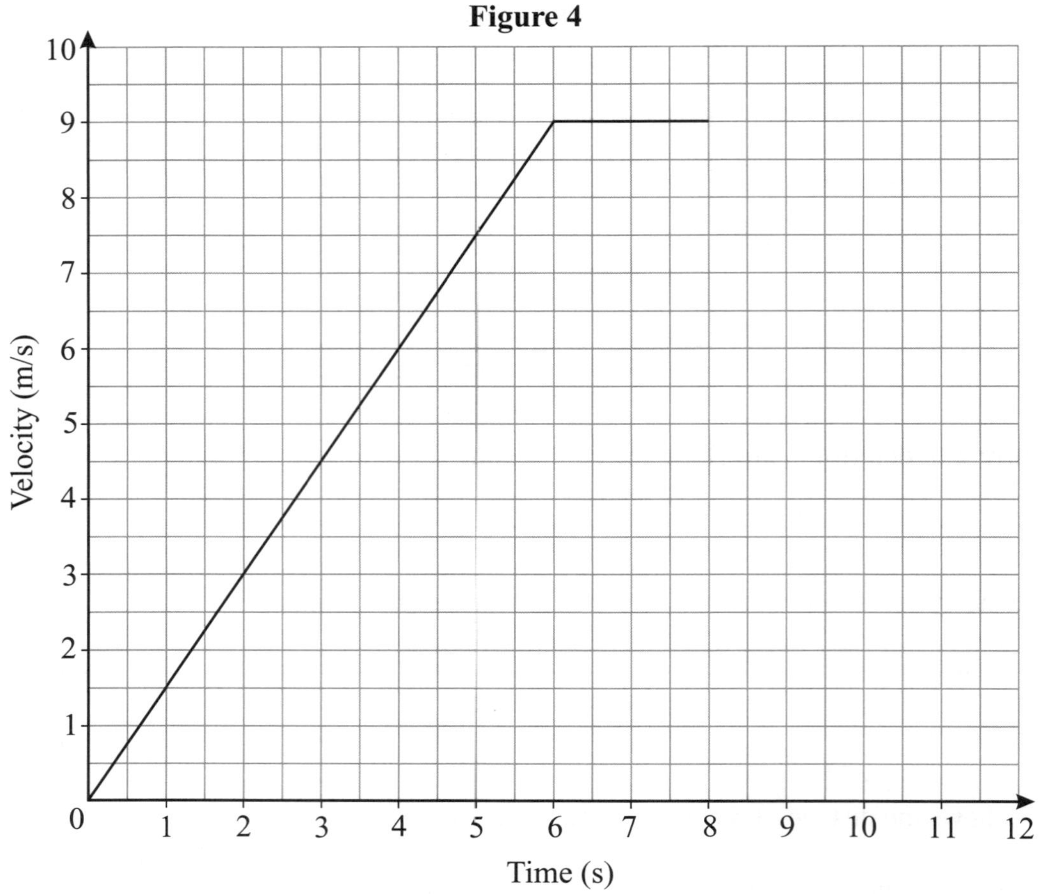

4.1 After 8 seconds, the roller coaster decelerates at an increasing rate.
It comes to rest 4 seconds after it begins decelerating.
Complete the velocity-time graph in **Figure 4** to show this.

[2]

4.2 Calculate the acceleration of the roller coaster during the first 6 seconds of the ride.

Acceleration = ... m/s^2
[2]

4.3 Calculate the distance travelled by the ride between 0 and 8 s.

Distance = ... m
[4]

4.4 Calculate the distance travelled during the entire ride to the nearest metre.

Distance = ... m
[5]

[Total 13 marks]

Target AO3

5 A teacher did an experiment to investigate the top speed of a remote-controlled car. Grade 7-9

The teacher set the car going in a straight line at full power, and measured the speed of the car with time as it travelled along a straight 120 m track. The results of his experiment are shown in the velocity-time graph in **Figure 5**.

Figure 5

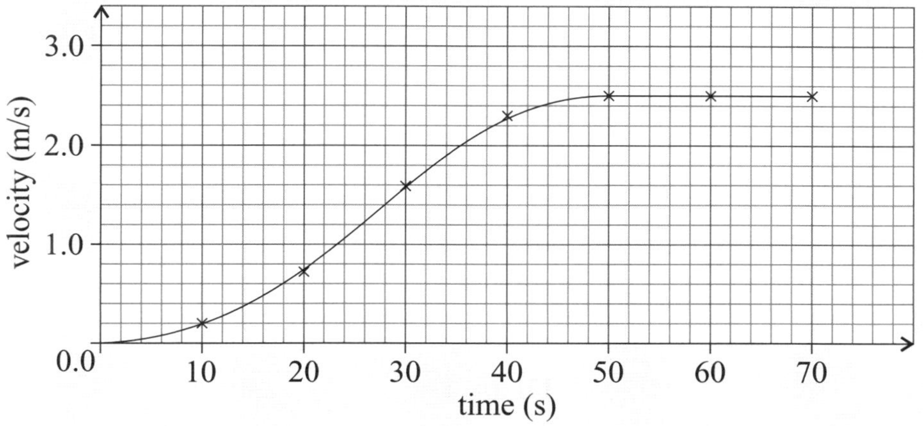

5.1 Using the graph in **Figure 5**, determine the acceleration of the car at 26 s.

Acceleration = ... m/s^2

[3]

5.2 A student wants to repeat the teacher's experiment on a smaller scale. She has a 5 m track, and a lower powered remote-controlled car. She is considering two different methods for determining the speed of the car as it travels along the track:

- Connect light gates to a data logger. Position a light gate every 50 cm along the track, and attach a 5 cm square card to the top of the car so that it is able to break the light beam of the light gates.
- Attach a ticker tape to the back of the car. The ticker tape is held in a dispenser which marks the tape at its opening every 2 s. As the car moves, it pulls the tape out of the dispenser.

Give **one** advantage and **one** disadvantage of **each** method.

....

....

....

....

....

....

....

[4]

[Total 7 marks]

Terminal Velocity

1 Any object falling (in a fluid) for long enough reaches its terminal velocity. Which statements correctly describe terminal velocity? Tick **two** boxes.

Grade 4-6

- Terminal velocity is the minimum velocity an object can fall at. ☐
- The resultant vertical force on an object falling at its terminal velocity is zero. ☐
- The resultant vertical force on an object falling at its terminal velocity equals its weight. ☐
- Terminal velocity is the maximum velocity an object can fall at. ☐

[Total 1 mark]

2 A ball is dropped and falls for 6 seconds before reaching its terminal velocity of 30 m/s. After 15 seconds the ball hits the ground. Draw a velocity-time graph for the first ten seconds of the ball's motion on the axes shown in **Figure 1**.

Grade 6-7

Figure 1

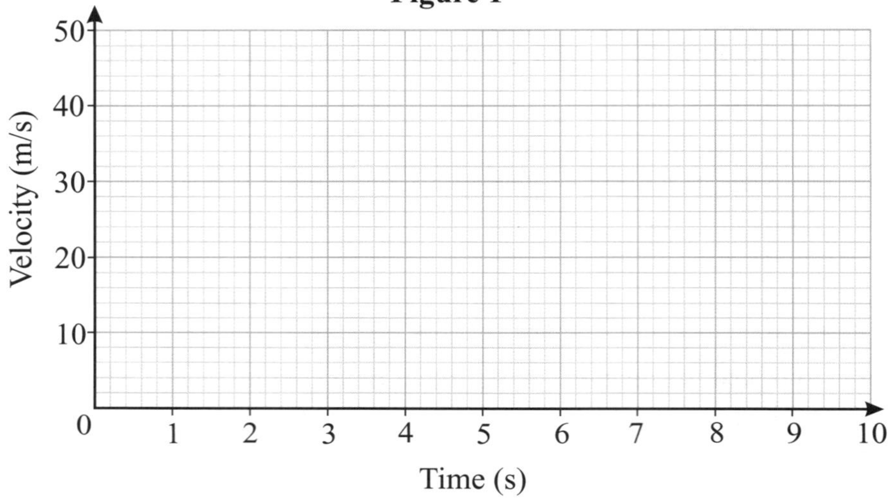

[Total 2 marks]

3 A student drops a large book and a cricket ball that both have the same weight from a tall building. Explain why both objects eventually fall at a constant velocity and why the terminal velocity of the book is lower than the terminal velocity of the ball.

Grade 7-9

....

....

....

....

....

....

[Total 5 marks]

Exam Tip

Remember that the acceleration of a falling object is continuously decreasing due to air resistance until it reaches zero. That means you won't be able to use any of those fancy equations for uniform acceleration that you're used to.

Newton's First and Second Laws

1 State Newton's First Law for a stationary object. Grade 4-6

....

....

[Total 1 mark]

2 Use words from the box below to complete the passage. You can only use a word **once** and you do not need to use all of the words. Grade 4-6

area	mass	inversely	directly	resistive	resultant

Newton's Second Law states that the acceleration of an object is ....

proportional to the .... force acting on the object and

.... proportional to the .... of the object.

[Total 3 marks]

3 **Figure 1** shows the horizontal forces acting on a motorbike travelling at a constant velocity. Grade 6-7

Figure 1

3.1 There are two resistive forces acting on the bike. Suggest what these forces may be.

....

....

[2]

3.2 The engine provides a driving force of 5.0 kN. One of the resistive forces has a magnitude of 3.85 kN. Calculate the size of the second resistive force.

Force = ... N

[1]

[Total 3 marks]

4 A 5.0 kg vase is knocked from a shelf. Grade 6-7

4.1 Write down the formula that links force, mass and acceleration.

....

[1]

4.2 Calculate the resultant force acting on the vase as it begins to fall.
Acceleration due to gravity, $g = 9.8$ m/s^2.

Force = ... N

[2]

[Total 3 marks]

5 A 1450 kg car accelerates uniformly from rest. It reaches 24 m/s in 9.2 s.
Calculate the force needed to cause this acceleration. Grade 6-7

Force = ... N

[Total 4 marks]

6 **Figure 2** shows a 7520 kg lorry. The driver spots a hazard ahead and applies the brakes. The lorry decelerates uniformly and comes to a stop 50 m after the brakes are applied. Estimate the braking force needed to stop the lorry. Grade 7-9

Figure 2

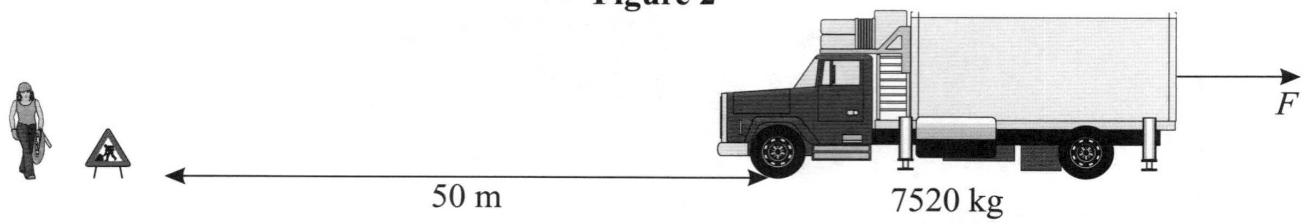

Force = ... N

[Total 5 marks]

Exam Tip

Watch out for questions talking about constant or uniform acceleration over a distance. They can be tricky and require a lot of steps. If you're struggling, read the question carefully, pick out the key bits of information and write them all down. Then look on the equation sheet to see if there are any equations you can use to find the values the question is asking for.

Inertia and Newton's Third Law

Warm-Up

Which of the following is Newton's Third Law? Tick **one** box.

- A non-zero resultant force is needed to cause a change in speed or direction. ☐
- A resultant force is inversely proportional to the mass of an object. ☐
- When two objects interact, they exert equal and opposite forces on each other. ☐
- A resultant force of zero leads to an equilibrium situation. ☐

1 **Figure 1** shows the forces acting on a gymnast in equilibrium balancing on two beams. Grade 4-6

1.1 State the force exerted by each of the gymnast's hands on the balance beams.

Figure 1

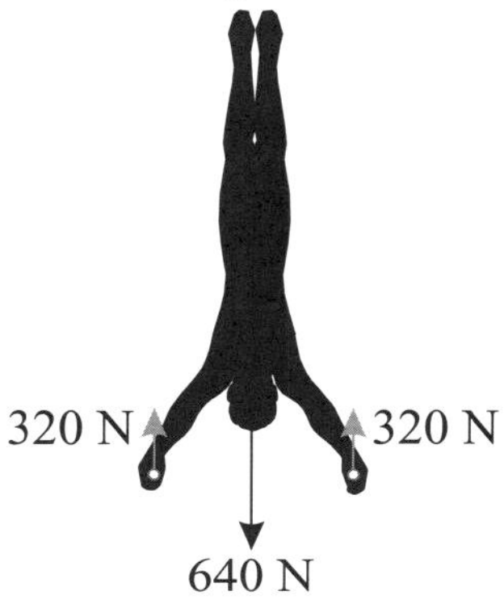

Force = ... N
[1]

1.2 State the name of this force.

....
[1]

1.3 State the size of the attractive force exerted on the Earth by the gymnast.

Force = ... N
[1]
[Total 3 marks]

2 Define the following terms: Grade 6-7

2.1 Inertia

....
[1]

2.2 Inertial mass

....
[1]
[Total 2 marks]

Exam Tip

Learning definitions isn't a fun part of revising (if there even are any), but knowing them is an easy way to pick up a few marks. When it comes to the exam, remember to include any necessary key terms as part of your definition answers.

PRACTICAL

Investigating Motion

1 **Figure 1** shows the apparatus used by a student to investigate the effect of varying force on the acceleration of a trolley. The trolley is on a frictionless, flat surface.

Grade 6-7

Figure 1

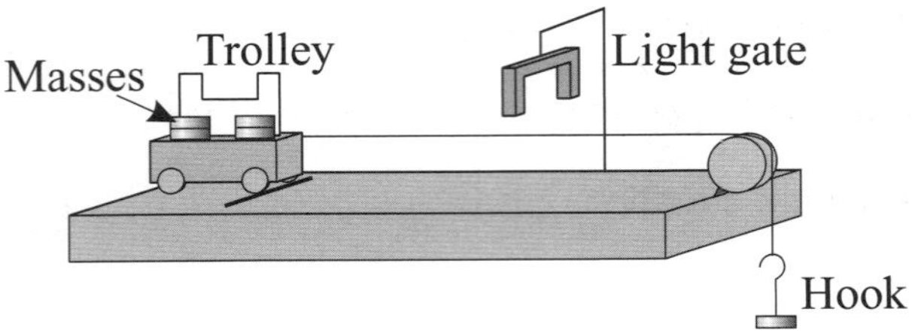

Figure 2

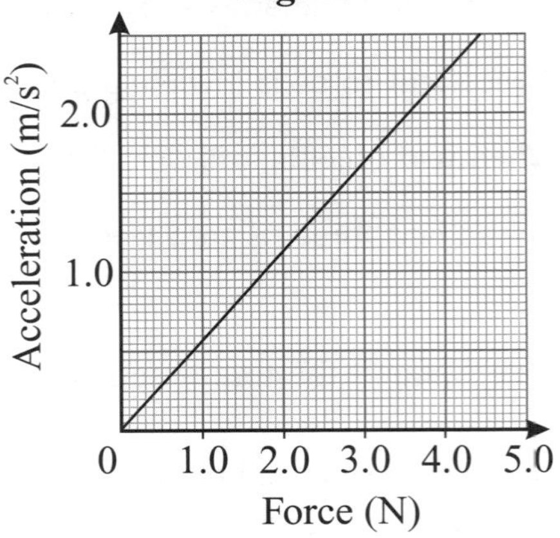

When the hook is allowed to fall, the trolley accelerates. The force acting on, and the acceleration of, the trolley are recorded. The student repeats this process, each time moving a mass from the trolley to the hook. The weight of each mass is calculated to be 1.0 N. **Figure 2** is a graph of acceleration against force for the trolley.

1.1 Give **one** conclusion that can be made from **Figure 2**.

....

[1]

1.2 Write down the formula that links force, mass and acceleration.

....

[1]

1.3 Calculate the mass of the system from **Figure 2**.

Mass = ... kg

[3]

[Total 5 marks]

2 A second student investigates how the mass of a trolley affects its motion down a fixed ramp. The accelerating force on the trolley is the component of the trolley's weight that acts along the ramp. The student adds masses to the trolley and each time measures its final speed at the bottom of the ramp to calculate its acceleration. Explain why this experiment will not correctly show the relationship between the mass and acceleration of the trolley.

Grade 7-9

....

....

....

....

....

[Total 2 marks]

Stopping Distances

1 Define the following terms: Grade 4-6

1.1 Thinking distance

....

[1]

1.2 Braking distance

....

[1]

[Total 2 marks]

2 The thinking distance for a driver in a car travelling at 40 mph is 12 m. The braking distance is 24 m. Calculate the car's stopping distance when it is travelling at 40 mph. Grade 4-6

Stopping Distance = ... m

[Total 1 mark]

3 When a vehicle's brakes are applied, energy is transferred away from the kinetic energy stores of the wheels. State what causes this and describe the effect it has on the brakes. Grade 6-7

....

....

....

....

[Total 2 marks]

4* Explain the importance of a car having brakes and tyres that are in good condition and the effect this will have on stopping distance and safety. Grade 6-7

....

....

....

....

....

....

....

....

....

[Total 6 marks]

Reaction Times

1 What is the typical reaction time for a person? Grade 4-6

☐ 1.3 – 1.8 s ☐ 0.2 – 0.9 s ☐ 0.01 – 0.02 s ☐ 2.0 – 3.0 s

[Total 1 mark]

2 Give **three** things that could affect a person's reaction time. Grade 4-6

1. ....

2. ....

3. ....

[Total 3 marks]

3 A teacher tests the reaction times of two of her students by measuring how far a ruler falls vertically before the student catches it. Grade 4-6

3.1 Describe **one** other method that can be used to test people's reaction times.

....

[1]

3.2 **Table 1** shows the results. The values in the table show the distance the ruler falls in cm during each attempt. Complete the table by working out the average distance fallen by the ruler for each student.

Table 1

	Attempt 1	Attempt 2	Attempt 3	Average
Student A	7.0	7.1	6.9	....
Student B	8.4	8.2	8.3	....

[2]

3.3 Which student has the fastest average reaction time? Give a reason for your answer.

....

[1]

3.4 Suggest **two** ways the teacher could make the experiment a fair test.

....

....

[2]

3.5 The teacher then repeats the experiment. This time, she has a third student talk to the student being tested. Predict how this will affect the reaction times of both students A and B.

....

[1]

[Total 7 marks]

4 Describe the steps involved when using the ruler drop experiment to investigate reaction times. Grade 6-7

....

....

....

....

....

....

....

[Total 5 marks]

5* A man is driving home late at night. He listens to loud music as he drives to keep himself alert. He is impatient to get home so drives quickly. Explain the safety implications of the man's actions. Grade 6-7

....

....

....

....

....

....

....

[Total 4 marks]

6 A student tests his reaction time with a metre ruler using a ruler drop experiment. He catches the metre ruler after it has fallen 45.0 cm. Calculate his reaction time. Grade 7-9

The acceleration due to gravity is 9.8 m/s^2.

Reaction time = ... s

[Total 4 marks]

Exam Tip

For long explanation answers make sure you cover every point mentioned in the question. You won't get all of the marks if you miss out part of what they're asking for, no matter how much you write for the rest of your points.

More on Stopping Distances

1 **Table 1** shows how the stopping distance of a car varies with speed. Grade 6-7

Table 1

Speed (mph)	0	10	20	30	40	50	60	70
Stopping distance (m)	0	5	12	23	36	53	73	96

Figure 1

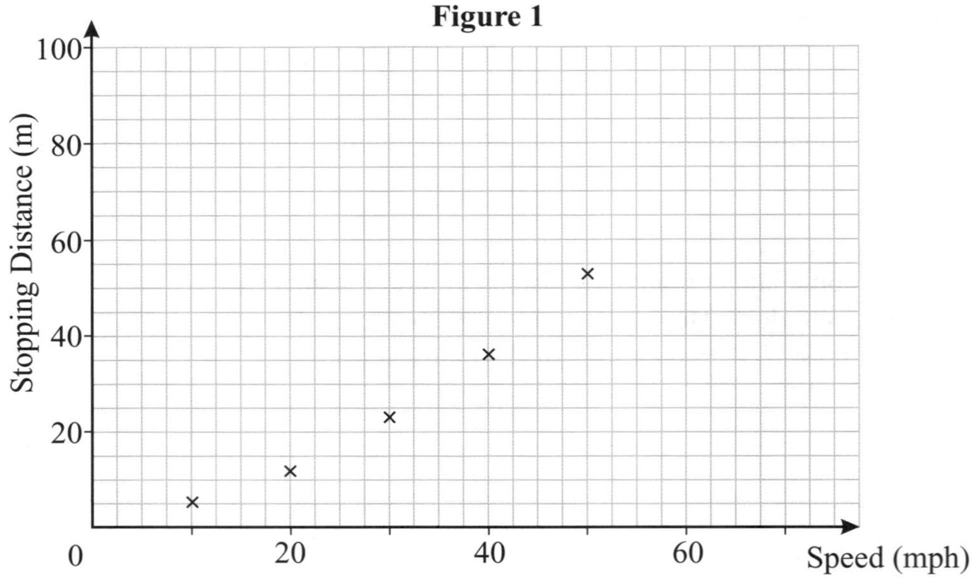

1.1 Using the data in **Table 1**, complete the graph shown in Figure 1, including a line of best fit.

[3]

1.2 Using **Figure 1**, find the stopping distance for a car travelling at 35 mph.

Stopping distance = ... m

[1]

1.3 Calculate how much further the car would travel before stopping if it was travelling at 65 mph.

Distance = ... m

[2]

[Total 6 marks]

2 The stopping distance for a truck travelling at 18 m/s is 45 m. The truck driver has a reaction time of 0.50 s. Estimate the stopping distance for the truck if it were to travel at 36 m/s. Grade 7-9

Stopping distance = ... m

[Total 5 marks]

Momentum

Warm-Up

The snippets below show the parts of a description of momentum.
Number each snippet 1 to 5 to show the correct order. The first one has been done for you.

☐ ...vector quantity and is equal to...

1 Momentum is a property of...

☐ ...moving objects.

☐ ...mass × velocity.

☐ It is a...

1 A motorbike is travelling at 25 m/s and has 5500 kg m/s of momentum. (Grade 4-6)

1.1 Write down the equation that links momentum, mass and velocity.

....

[1]

1.2 Calculate the mass of the motorbike.

Mass = ... kg

[3]

[Total 4 marks]

2 **Figure 1** and **Figure 2** show a Newton's cradle. All of the balls on the cradle have the same mass. (Grade 6-7)

When a ball is lifted and allowed to hit the others as shown in **Figure 1**, it causes the last ball in the line to move outwards, as shown in **Figure 2**. The balls in between appear to remain stationary. The velocity of the first ball when it hits the second ball is equal to the velocity of the final ball when it starts to move. Using conservation of momentum, explain this behaviour.

Figure 1 **Figure 2**

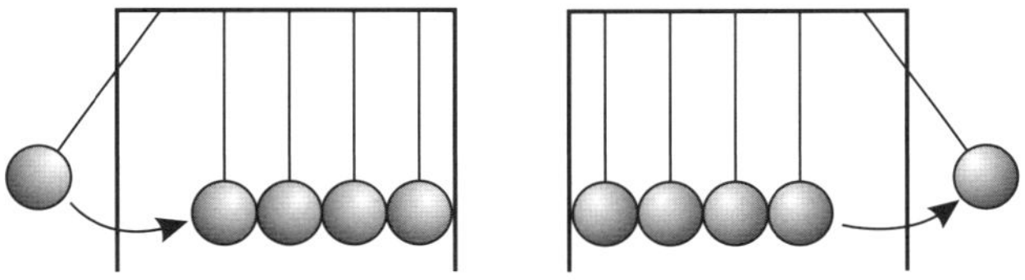

....

....

....

....

....

....

[Total 4 marks]

Exam Tip

Like a lot of topics in Forces, remembering how momentum is calculated can help you to describe and explain it.

Target AO3

3 A student is doing an investigation into the conservation of momentum using an air track. Grade 7-9

The student's experimental set-up is shown in **Figure 3**. Vehicles A and B have equal mass.

Figure 3

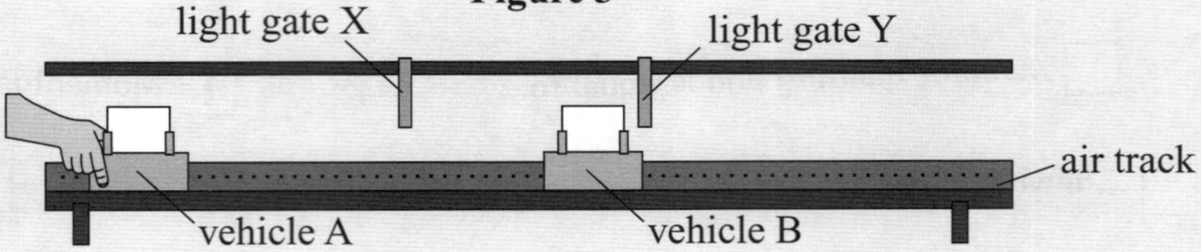

The vehicles that travel along the air track experience negligible friction, as they are lifted just above the track by jets of air. The student pushes vehicle A with their hand to start it moving towards vehicle B, which is at rest. The speed of vehicle A immediately before it collides with vehicle B is measured by light gate X. The speeds of vehicles A and B immediately after the collision are measured by light gate Y. The student's results are shown **Table 1**.

Table 1

Trial number	1	2	3	4	5	6	7	8
Speed of A before collision (m/s)	0.15	0.19	0.26	0.30	0.34	0.41	0.47	0.52
Speed of A after collision (m/s)	0.04	0.07	0.11	0.10	0.12	0.20	0.19	0.22
Speed of B after collision (m/s)	0.10	0.12	0.15	0.19	0.21	0.20	0.27	0.30

3.1 In one of the trials, the vehicles stuck together. Identify this trial.

....

[1]

3.2 The student wants to take repeat measurements of the speeds of vehicles A and B for each initial speed of vehicle A. Suggest why this might not be possible with the current experimental set-up.

....

....

[1]

3.3 The student plans to repeat the experiment multiple times, while varying the mass of vehicle B. They intend to change the mass of vehicle B by attaching strips of modelling clay along each side of the vehicle. Suggest why the results of the student's experiment are likely to be less accurate as they increase the mass of vehicle B.

....

....

....

[2]

[Total 4 marks]

Exam Tip

For some of the harder AO3 questions, you might be presented with a lot of data. Don't get overwhelmed though. The trick is to pick out the pieces of information that you'll need in order to answer the question and then move on.

Changes in Momentum

1 State what the rate of change of an object's momentum is equal to. (Grade 4-6)

....

[Total 1 mark]

2 A ball has its momentum changed by 10 kg m/s in 0.1 s.
Calculate the force acting on the ball. (Grade 6-7)

Force = ... N

[Total 2 marks]

3 During a collision, an air bag is activated in a car. Explain how the air bag reduces the risk of the driver being injured during the collision. (Grade 6-7)

....

....

....

....

[Total 4 marks]

4 **Figure 1** shows two American football players running towards each other. They collide and cling together in the tackle.
Calculate the velocity that they move together with after the tackle. (Grade 7-9)

Figure 1

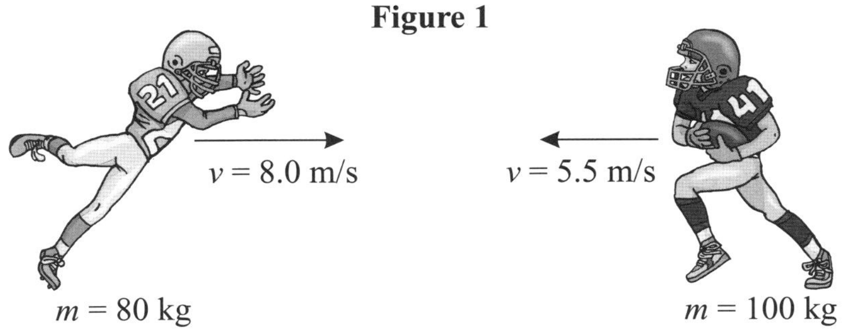

Magnitude of velocity = ... m/s

Direction = ...

[Total 5 marks]

Transverse and Longitudinal Waves

1 A student produces two types of waves on a spring, A and B, as shown in **Figure 1.** Grade 4-6

Figure 1

A 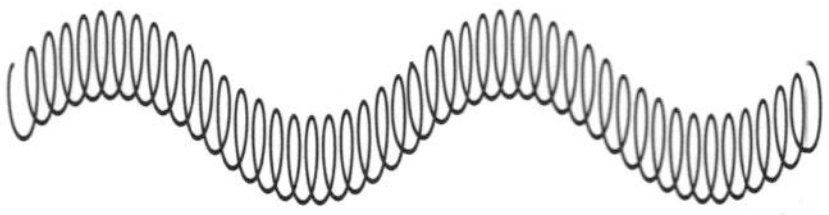 B 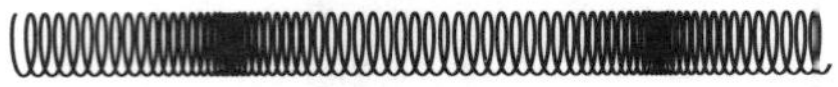

1.1 State whether each spring shows a transverse or a longitudinal wave.

Wave A: .... Wave B: ....

[1]

1.2 Label the wavelength of wave A on **Figure 1**.

[1]

1.3 Define the term 'amplitude'.

....

[1]

1.4 Give **one** example of a transverse wave.

....

[1]

[Total 4 marks]

2 **Figure 2** shows a loudspeaker. It produces a sound wave with a frequency of 200 Hz. Grade 6-7

Figure 2

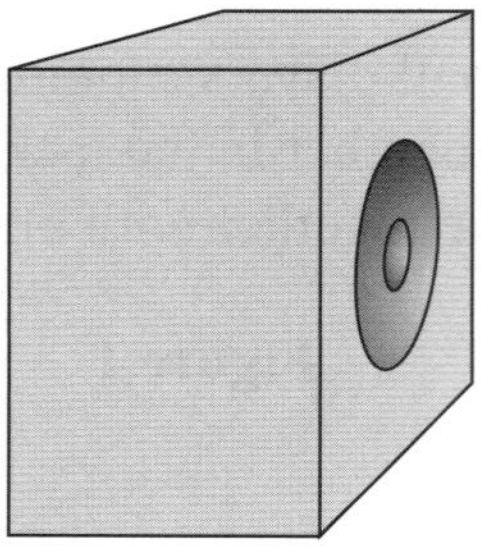

2.1 Draw an arrow on **Figure 2** to show the direction in which the sound wave transfers energy.

[1]

2.2 Calculate the period of the sound wave.

Period = ... s

[2]

2.3 Describe the difference between a longitudinal wave and a transverse wave.

....

....

....

[2]

[Total 5 marks]

Experiments with Waves

PRACTICAL

1 **Figure 1** shows ripples on the surface of some water in a ripple tank. The signal generator producing the ripples is set to a frequency of 12 Hz. A student measures the distance between the first and last visible ripple as 18 cm, as shown in **Figure 1**.

Grade 6-7

Figure 1

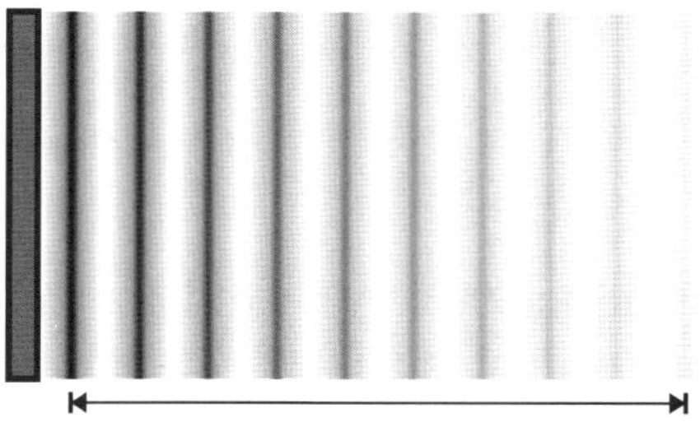

1.1 The student finds it difficult to measure the distance because the ripples are moving. Suggest and explain what the student could do to make the measurement easier.

....

....

....

[2]

1.2 Calculate the speed of the ripples in the water.

Speed = ... m/s

[3]

[Total 5 marks]

2* Describe a method to measure the speed of waves on a string.

Grade 7-9

....

....

....

....

....

....

....

....

....

[Total 6 marks]

Reflection

Warm-Up

At the boundary with a new material, a wave can be reflected, absorbed or transmitted. Draw a line to match each option to the correct definition.

wave is reflected	it passes through the material
wave is absorbed	it bounces back off the material
wave is transmitted	it transfers all energy to the material

1 **Figure 1** shows two mirrors that meet at 90°. A ray of light hits one of the mirrors. Complete the diagram to show the path of the light ray as it reflects off both mirrors. You should draw normal lines to help you construct your diagram. Grade 6-7

Figure 1

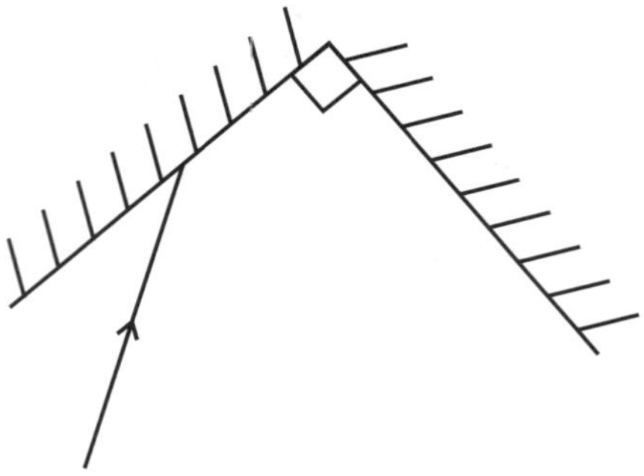

[Total 2 marks]

2 A man is wearing mirrored sunglasses. Anyone looking at him can see their reflection in the glasses but cannot see his eyes. The man can still see through the glasses. Grade 6-7

2.1 Describe what happens to the light as it passes from the surroundings to the mirrored sunglasses.

....

....

[2]

2.2 One of the lenses of the sunglasses has been damaged, and has become covered in tiny scratches. Describe how the reflective properties of the damaged and undamaged lenses are different. State what effect this will have on any reflected images formed by the lenses.

....

....

....

[3]

[Total 5 marks]

Exam Tip

Remember that the angles of incidence and reflection are both measured from the normal — a line perpendicular to the surface at the point of reflection. Get into the habit of drawing the normal whenever a ray reaches a surface to make sure you're getting your ray diagrams right. Draw them as dotted lines so that they're not confused with rays.

Target AO3

PRACTICAL

Grade 6-7

3 A student is investigating the law of reflection. In a dimly lit room, the student shines a beam of light at a fixed point on a plane mirror from different angles. Each time, they measure the light beam's angle of incidence and angle of reflection from a line drawn at a normal to the point of incidence. They use the equipment shown in **Figure 2**.

Figure 2

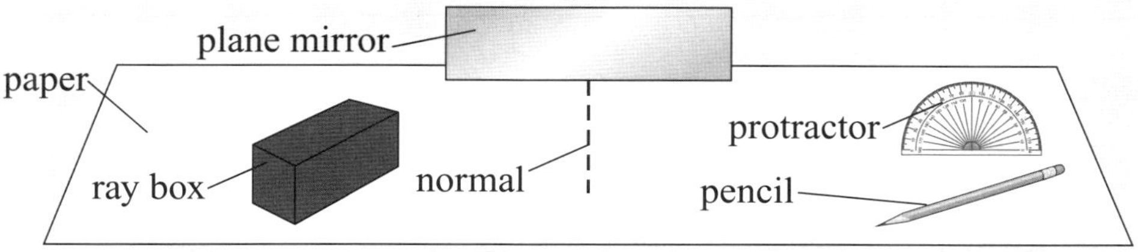

3.1 The smallest angle the protractor can measure is 1°. The 1° increments marked on the edge of the protractor are approximately 0.9 mm apart. The student sets up the ray box so that the beam of light it produces is less than 0.9 mm wide. Explain how this will improve the student's results.

....

....

....

....

[3]

3.2 The student's results are shown in **Table 1**. Plot the results on the grid in **Figure 3**, and draw a line of best fit.

Table 1

Angle of incidence (°)	Angle of reflection (°)
10	14
15	19
20	24
25	28
30	34
35	39
40	45
45	49
50	53

Figure 3

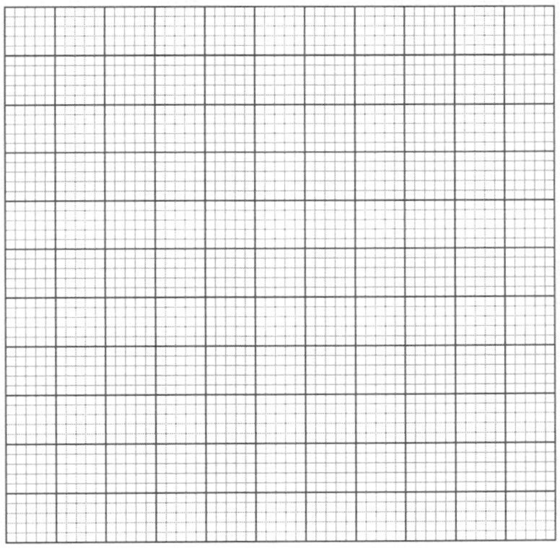

[3]

3.3 The student's results don't agree with the law of reflection.
Explain how this is shown by the graph, and suggest what may have caused this error.

....

....

....

....

[2]

[Total 8 marks]

Electromagnetic Waves and Refraction

1 Electromagnetic waves form a continuous spectrum. Grade 4-6

1.1 Use words from the box below to complete the following sentences.

a vacuum	**glass**	**sound**	**longitudinal**	**transverse**	**water**

All waves in the electromagnetic spectrum are ....

All electromagnetic waves travel at the same speed in ....

[2]

1.2 **Figure 1** shows a graph of intensity against wavelength for two objects at different temperatures.
Name the part of the electromagnetic spectrum that the peak wavelength of object B lies in.

....

[1]

Figure 1

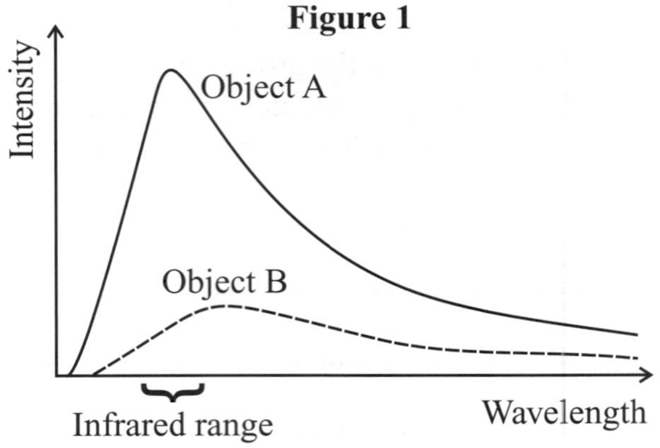

1.3 The peak wavelength for object A lies within the infrared range of the electromagnetic spectrum. Describe an example of infrared radiation transferring energy from a source to an absorber.

....

....

[2]

[Total 5 marks]

2 **Figure 2** shows wave fronts of light passing from air into glass. As the wave fronts enter the glass they slow down. Grade 6-7

Figure 2

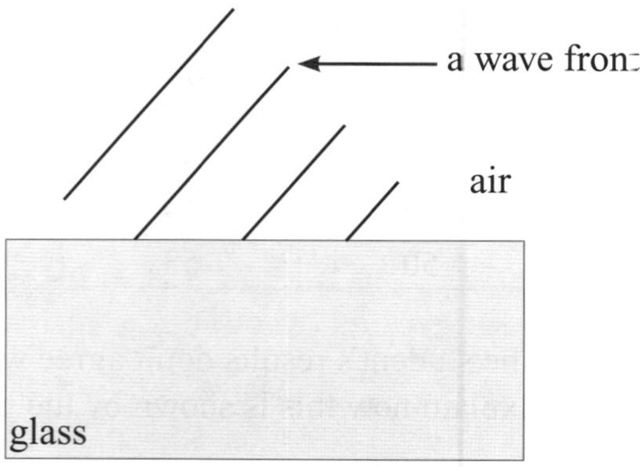

2.1 Complete the diagram in **Figure 2** by completing the wave fronts inside the glass.

[2]

2.2 Draw a ray on **Figure 2** to show how a light ray is refracted as it passes from air into glass. On your diagram, label the incident ray, refracted ray, and normal line.

[3]

[Total 5 marks]

Exam Tip

As well as making sure that you draw your diagrams clearly and with a sharp pencil, make sure that every part is well labelled. Draw a single, clear arrow to what you want to label and give yourself enough room to write it out.

Investigating Light

PRACTICAL

1 A student was investigating the reflection of light by different types of surface. She set up a ray box, a mirror and a piece of white card as shown in **Figure 1**.

Grade 6-7

Figure 1

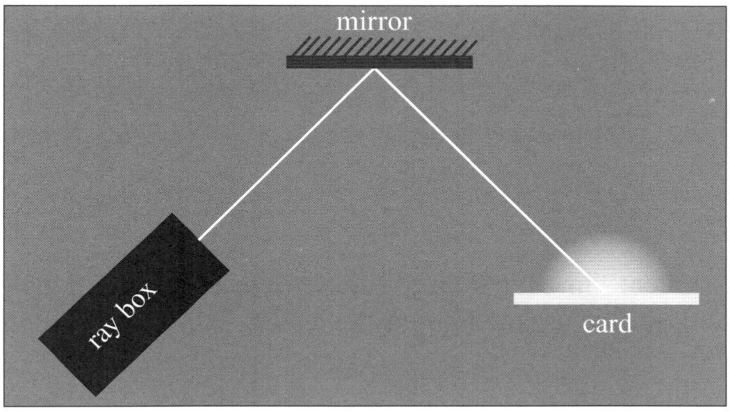

1.1 The student measured the angle of incidence and angle of reflection at the mirror. State what she would notice about these measurements.

....

[1]

1.2 Name the type of reflection which is observed at the mirror and at the card.

At the mirror: ....

At the card: ....

[2]

1.3 The student concluded that the surface of the white card was rough, rather than smooth. Explain how light is reflected from a rough surface and how this led to the behaviour observed at the card.

....

....

....

[2]

1.4 Explain why a ray-box was used for this experiment. Suggest another piece of apparatus which the student could have used to achieve the same effect.

....

....

....

[3]

[Total 8 marks]

2 A student is investigating refraction through different materials. The student uses a ray box to shine a ray of light into blocks of materials at a fixed angle, *I*. He traces the path of the ray entering and leaving the block on a sheet of paper.

Grade 6-7

Figure 2

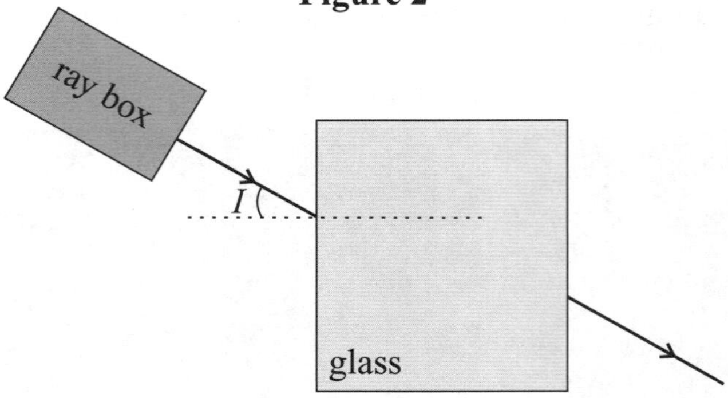

2.1 **Figure 2** shows the student's investigation for light refracted through a glass block. Complete the diagram by drawing the light ray as it passes through the glass block.

[1]

2.2 The student measures the angle of refraction, *R*, of the light ray as it enters the block. **Table 1** shows the results for a range of materials. Measure the angle of refraction for the light ray entering the glass block in **Figure 2**, and hence complete **Table 1**.

[1]

Table 1

Material	*I*	*R*
Cooking Oil	30°	20°
Water	30°	22°
Plastic	30°	20°
Glass	30°	....

2.3 State how the speed of the light ray changes as it passes from air into the glass block. Explain how the result in **Table 1** shows this is the case.

....

....

[2]

2.4 Name the material which changed the speed of the light ray the least. Explain your answer.

....

....

....

[3]

2.5 Cooking oil and water are both liquids, so need to be placed within transparent solid containers to be used in this experiment. Explain why the student should ensure that the containers he uses have thin walls.

....

....

[2]

[Total 9 marks]

Exam Tip

Being aware of certain facts, like how glass refracts light, is a useful way to check that your answers make sense in the exam.

Radio Waves

Warm-Up

Tick the appropriate boxes to sort the radio-wave facts from the fiction.

	True	False
Long-wave radio can be transmitted across long distances.	☐	☐
Long-wave radio uses diffraction to follow the curve of the Earth's surface.	☐	☐
Short-wave radio can only be used over short distances.	☐	☐
Radio waves with very short wavelengths do not travel well through obstacles.	☐	☐

1* Describe how an electrical signal generates a radio wave in a TV signal transmitter. Explain how this radio wave can generate an electrical signal in a distant TV aerial. Grade 6-7

....

....

....

....

....

....

....

[Total 4 marks]

2* A family from northern England are on holiday in France. Explain why they are unable to listen to their local FM radio station from back home, but are still able to listen to the same long-wave radio broadcasts as they do at home. Grade 7-9

....

....

....

....

....

....

....

....

....

....

....

[Total 6 marks]

EM Waves and Their Uses

1 A student uses a microwave oven to cook a jacket potato on a glass plate. Grade 6-7

1.1 Describe how microwaves cook the potato in the microwave oven.

....

....

....

[3]

1.2 The student cooks the potato on the glass plate for 10 minutes. She removes them from the microwave oven and measures the temperature of the potato and the edge of the glass plate. Her results are shown in **Table 1**.

Table 1

Object	Temperature / °C
Potato	78
Glass plate	30

Explain why there is a temperature difference between the potato and the edge of the glass plate.

....

....

....

[2]

1.3 State the other type of electromagnetic radiation which is commonly used to cook food.

....

[1]

[Total 6 marks]

2 A police helicopter has an infrared camera attached to its base. The camera can be used to detect people trying to hide in the dark. Explain the advantages of using an infrared camera rather than a normal camera for this purpose. Grade 7-9

....

....

....

....

[Total 3 marks]

Exam Tip

Describe questions can be worth quite a few marks, so it's important to know how to tackle them in the right way. Be careful to include all of the key points in your description, otherwise you could throw away crucial marks.

More Uses of EM Waves

Warm-Up

Sort the EM uses below into the table. Some of the uses may appear in more than one column.

Uses of EM waves

A artificial suntanning

B fibre optic data transmission

C energy efficient light bulbs

D revealing invisible ink

E medical imaging of bones

F cancer treatment

UV Rays	Visible Light	X-rays	Gamma Rays

1 X-rays and gamma rays can both be used in medical imaging. Grade 6-7

1.1 Briefly describe how a medical tracer can be used to create an internal body image.

....

....

....

[2]

1.2 Explain why gamma rays are suitable for medical imaging.

....

....

[1]

1.3 Explain how X-rays are used to form images of a patient's skeleton.

....

....

....

....

[3]

1.4 Exposure to both X-rays and gamma rays can be dangerous to humans. Suggest **one** precaution taken by medical workers who use X-rays or gamma rays when imaging patients.

....

[1]

[Total 7 marks]

Exam Tip

You may be asked to explain why a given electromagnetic wave is suited to a particular use. So make sure you understand the properties of the different electromagnetic wave types, and know some of their most common uses.

Dangers of Electromagnetic Waves

1 Some types of electromagnetic wave can be harmful to people. Grade 6-7

1.1 Describe how X-rays and gamma rays can cause cancer.

....

....
[2]

1.2 Another type of harmful electromagnetic radiation is ultraviolet radiation.
Give **two** damaging effects of ultraviolet light.

....

....
[2]

[Total 4 marks]

2 **Table 1** lists the radiation doses for some common medical procedures. Grade 7-9

Table 1

Procedure	**Typical effective dose (mSv)**	**Lifetime additional risk of fatal cancer per examination**
X-ray image of skull	0.07	1 in 300 000
X-ray image of lower spine	1.3	1 in 15 000
CT scan of head	2	1 in 10 000

2.1 The lifetime additional risk of fatal cancer from a CT scan of the chest is 1 in 2500.
Use **Table 1** to estimate the typical effective dose of a CT scan of the chest.

Typical effective dose = ... mSv
[2]

2.2* Nuclear medicine scans use gamma rays to create images of internal organs, but have a high effective radiation dosage. Discuss the risks involved in performing this type of scan, and why the procedure might go ahead despite the risks.

....

....

....

....

....

....

....

....
[6]

[Total 8 marks]

Lenses

1 **Figure 1** shows a lens being used to focus light. The diagram is to scale. Grade 4-6

Figure 1

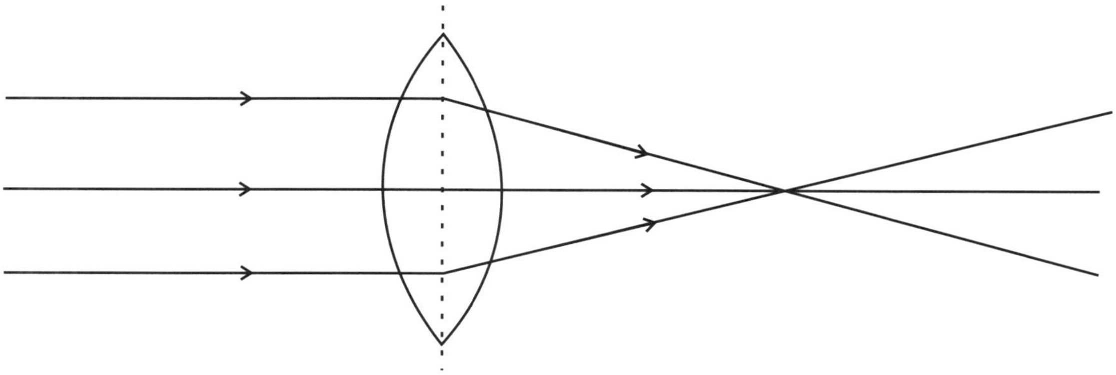

1.1 Label the following parts on **Figure 1**: parallel rays convex lens principal focus

[3]

1.2 Measure the focal length of the lens in **Figure 1**.

Focal length = ... cm
[1]

1.3 How do lenses focus light? Tick **one** box.

By refracting light. ☐
By reflecting light. ☐
By dispersing light. ☐
By absorbing light. ☐

[1]
[Total 5 marks]

2 **Figure 2** shows a concave lens. Draw four rays entering the lens parallel to the lens axis. Continue these rays as they pass through the lens to show how their paths change. Grade 6-7

Figure 2

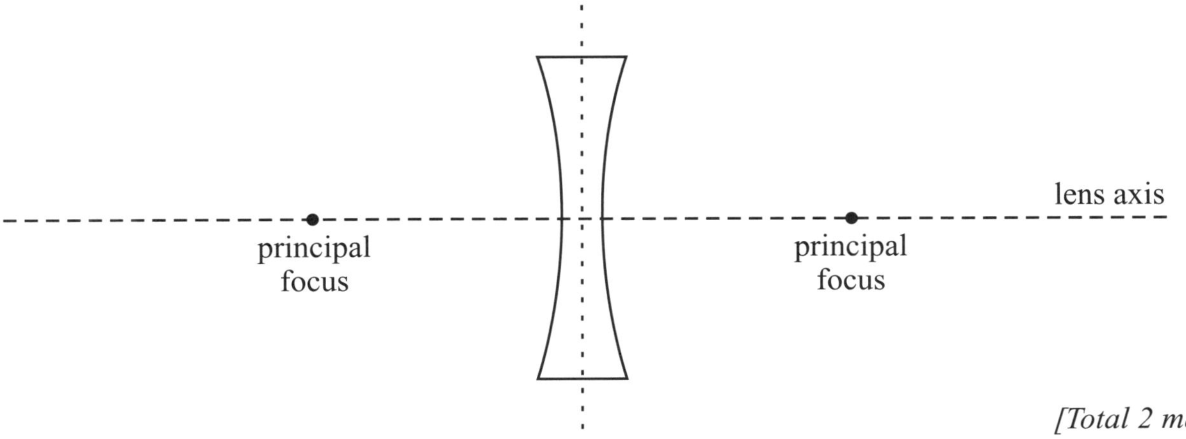

[Total 2 marks]

Exam Tip

When drawing ray diagrams with lenses, always make sure you draw the ray which goes through the centre of the lens. This ray will always hit the lens perpendicular to the surface, so it won't be refracted. It can be a useful guide for the rest of the diagram — especially when you're drawing diagrams of images, which you'll encounter on the next page.

Images and Ray Diagrams

1 Ray diagrams are used to visualise how lenses produce images. Grade 4-6

1.1 Complete the ray diagram in **Figure 1** below. Draw the image formed.

Figure 1

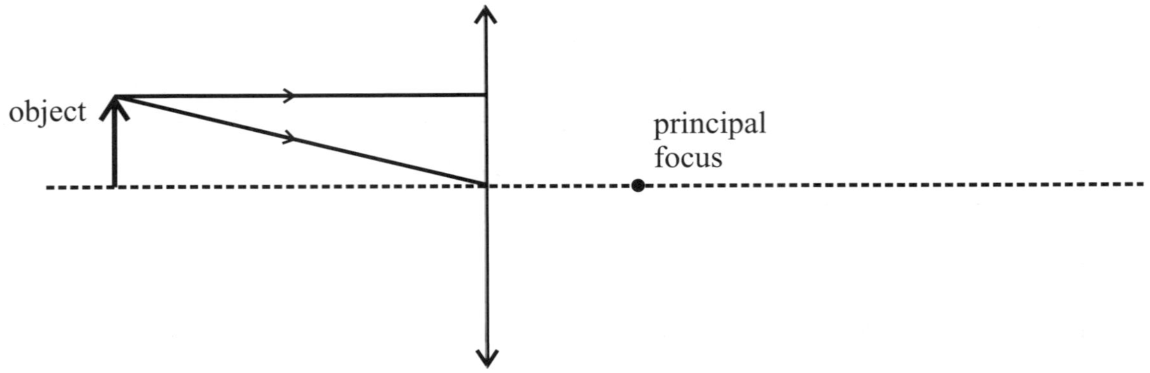

[3]

1.2 Is the image real, or virtual? Explain your answer.

....

....

[2]

[Total 5 marks]

2 An object is placed to the left of a convex lens.
The distance between the object and the lens is **less** than the focal length. Grade 6-7

Figure 2

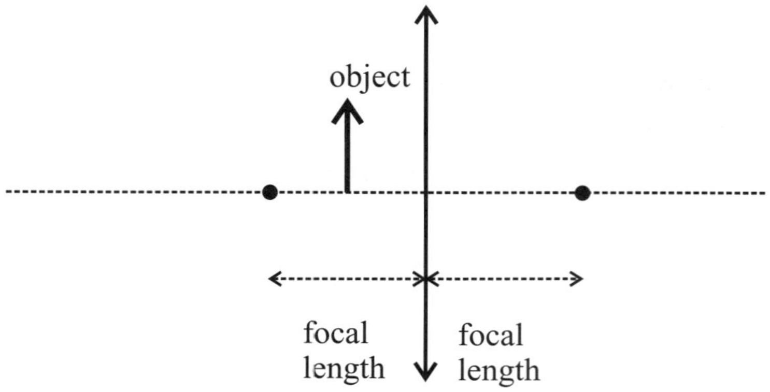

2.1 Complete the ray diagram in **Figure 2** to show the image that is formed.
Label the image as real or virtual.

[4]

2.2 The lens is moved so that the distance between the object and the lens is equal to twice the focal length. Give **two** differences between the new image and the image created in **Figure 2**.

....

....

[2]

[Total 6 marks]

Concave Lenses and Magnification

1 **Figure 1** shows some concave lenses. Grade 4-6

1.1 Tick the boxes below the **two** diagrams which correctly show how concave lenses refract light.

Figure 1

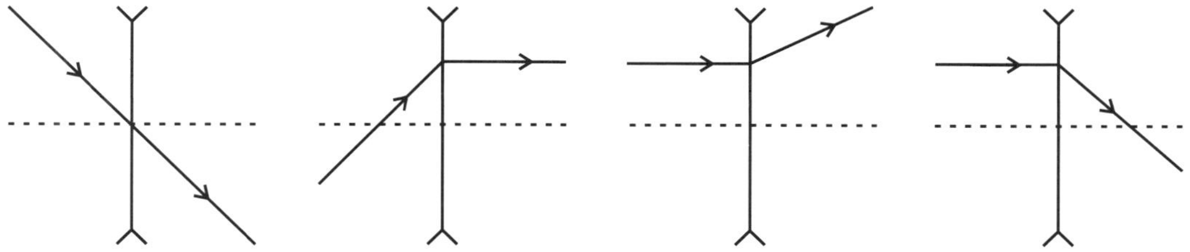

A ☐ B ☐ C ☐ D ☐

[2]

1.2 Complete the ray diagram in **Figure 2** to show the image of the object formed by the concave lens.

Figure 2

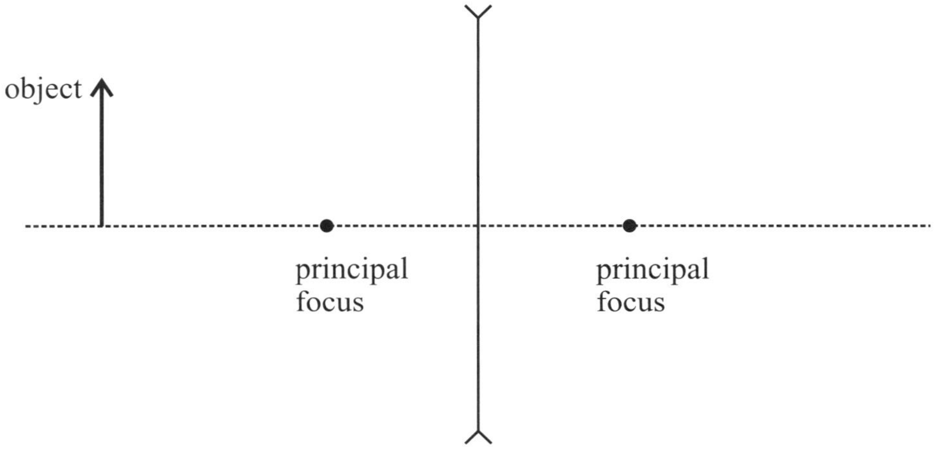

[3]

[Total 5 marks]

2 **Figure 3** shows a convex lens. Complete the ray diagram and calculate the magnification of the lens. The height of the object is 20 mm. Grade 7-9

Figure 3

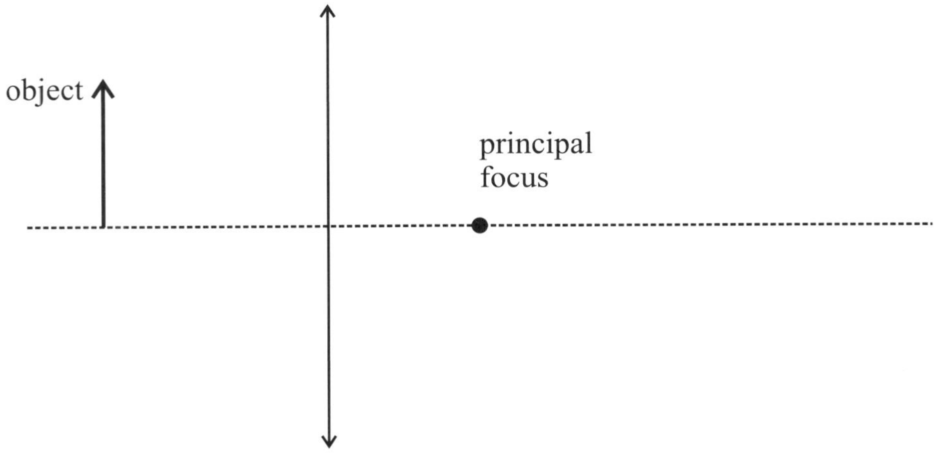

Magnification = ...

[Total 5 marks]

Visible Light

Warm-Up

Here's a diagram of a transparent green cube.
Continue the appropriate rays to show which colours of light are transmitted by the cube.

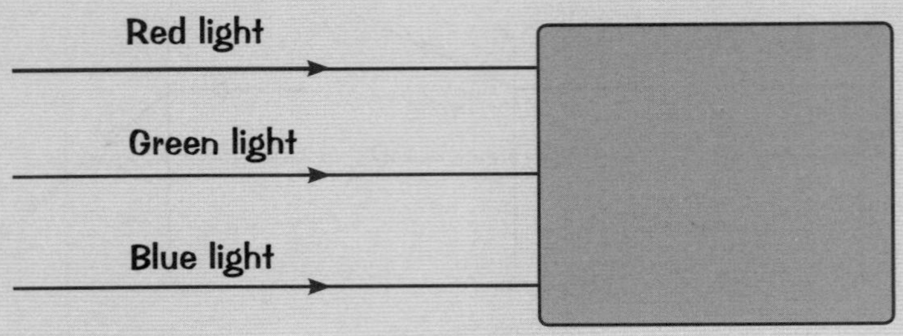

1 A student is investigating colour by looking at two footballs.
One football is red, the other is white.

Grade 4-6

1.1 Both of the footballs are opaque. Describe what is meant by the term opaque.

....

....

[1]

1.2 Describe how the footballs interact with the light waves to make one football look red and the other football appear white.

....

....

....

[2]

1.3 The student looks at the footballs through a red filter. Both footballs now look red.
Explain why this happens.

....

....

[2]

1.4 The student now looks at the footballs through a green filter.
State and explain what colour each football appears.

....

....

....

....

[3]

[Total 8 marks]

2 **Table 1** shows some wavelengths of light from the visible light spectrum and their corresponding colours. Grade 6-7

Table 1

Colour	Wavelength (nm)
blue	470
green	540
red	680

Figure 1

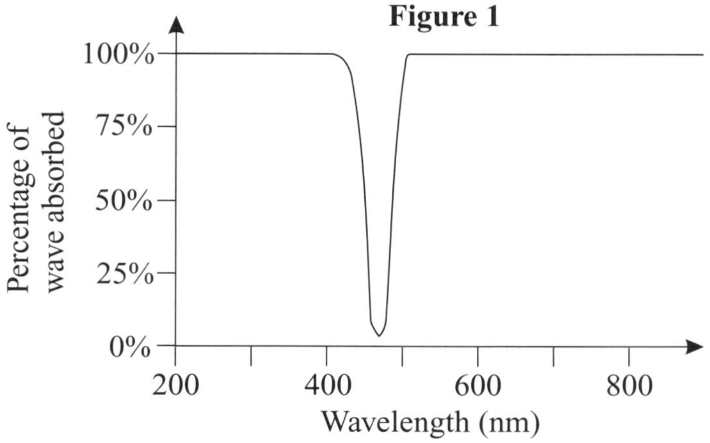

2.1 **Figure 1** shows the percentage of light of different wavelengths absorbed by an object. State whether the object is opaque or transparent.

....

[1]

2.2 What colour is the object?

....

[1]

2.3 Draw the absorption graph on the axes below for a perfectly black object.

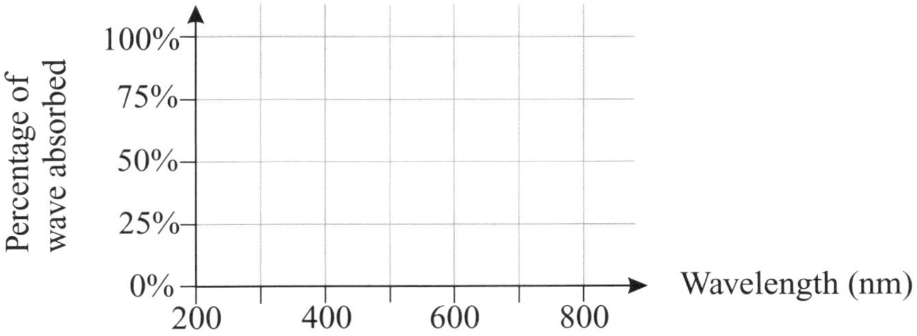

[1]

2.4 A purple colour can be produced from a mixture of red and blue light. On the axes below, sketch the absorption graph for an opaque purple object that reflects only red and blue light.

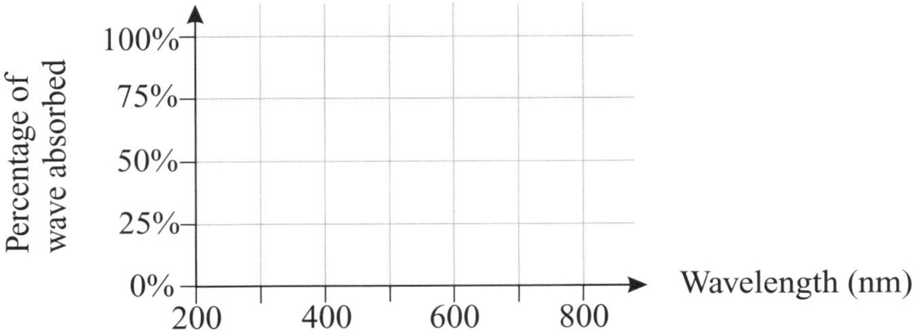

[3]

[Total 6 marks]

Infrared Radiation and Temperature

1 All bodies emit and absorb radiation. Grade 4-6

1.1 Which of the following statements is true? Tick **one** box.

Only objects that are hotter than 100 °C emit infrared radiation. ☐

Only objects that are cooler than 0 °C absorb infrared radiation. ☐

All objects emit and absorb infrared radiation. ☐

No object can absorb infrared radiation. ☐

[1]

1.2 An object is absorbing the same amount of radiation as it emits.
State what is happening to the temperature of this object.

....

[1]

1.3 State what would happen to the temperature of the object if it were to emit more radiation than it absorbed.

....

[1]

[Total 3 marks]

PRACTICAL

2 A student uses a Leslie cube, shown in **Figure 1**, to investigate how different materials radiate energy.
A Leslie cube is a hollow cube whose faces are made out of different materials. Grade 6-7

Figure 1

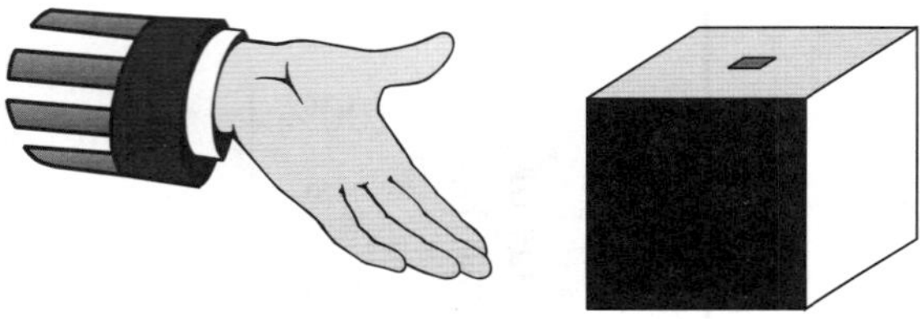

The student fills the cube with hot water and places his hand near to each surface.
He records how warm his hand feels in front of each surface.
The four sides of the cube are matte black, shiny black, matte white and shiny white.

2.1 Predict which side the student's hand would feel warmest in front of.

....

[1]

2.2 Predict which side the student's hand would feel coolest in front of.

....

[1]

2.3 Suggest **one** way to improve the student's experiment.

....

[1]

[Total 3 marks]

Exam Tip

Take the time to read the question intros carefully before diving into writing your answer. You'll have to write your answer differently depending on the command word used in the question. You could miss these if you just skim over the question.

Target AO3

PRACTICAL

Grade 7-9

3 A student is investigating the rate of cooling due to the emission of infrared radiation.

He is investigating 3 different steel cans, A, B and C, of equal size and shape. Can A is painted with matt navy blue paint. Can B is painted with glossy navy blue paint. Can C is painted in glossy white paint. For each can, the student uses the equipment shown in **Figure 2**. The student fills each can with 500 g of hot water. Once the water in the can reaches 50 °C, the student records the temperature of the water. He then records the temperature of the water every 30 seconds, for 4 minutes.

Figure 2

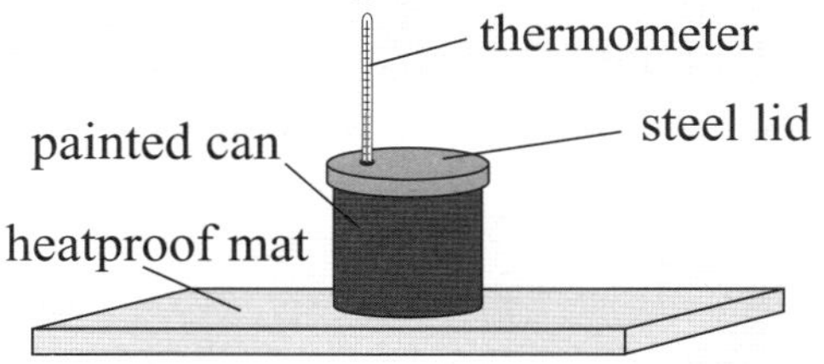

3.1 Identify **three** ways that the student has made sure that the results of the experiment will be valid.

1. ....

....

2. ....

....

3. ....

....

[3]

3.2 Predict the can in which the water will cool fastest. Justify your prediction.

....

....

....

[2]

3.3 The student's results for one can are shown in **Table 1**. His results for the other cans are shown in the graph in **Figure 3**. Plot the results in **Table 1** on **Figure 3**, and draw a curve of best fit.

Table 1

Time (s)	Temperature of water in can (°C)
0	50.0
30	47.0
60	44.5
90	42.5
120	40.5
150	39.5
180	39.0
210	38.5
240	38.0

Figure 3

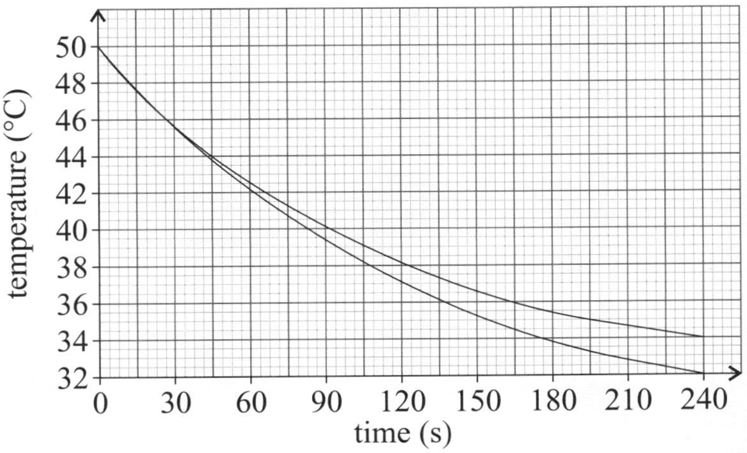

[2]

[Total 7 marks]

Black Body Radiation

1 Perfect black bodies are the best possible emitters of radiation. Grade 4-6

1.1 Define a perfect black body.

[1]

1.2 A white star expands and its surface appears redder in colour.
Describe how the surface temperature of the star has changed.

[1]

1.3 Which of the following is true for the radiation emitted by any object? Tick **one** box.

The radiation emitted covers a narrow range of wavelengths. ☐

The intensity of radiation emitted is the same for all wavelengths. ☐

The radiation emitted covers a large range of wavelengths. ☐

The intensity of radiation emitted is independent of the object's temperature. ☐

[2]

[Total 4 marks]

2* Electromagnetic radiation from the Sun affects the temperature of the Earth. Explain, with respect to the radiation emitted by the Sun and the Earth, how the temperature of the Earth remains approximately constant. Grade 7-9

[Total 6 marks]

Exam Tip

Remember — the intensity of radiation is just how much energy is being transmitted by the radiation in a certain amount of time. So the more infrared radiation given out by an object, the higher the intensity of infrared radiation.

Sound Waves

1 The human ear is specialised to detect sound waves. (Grade 4-6)

1.1 Give the frequency range of normal human hearing.

[1]

1.2 Describe the function of the ear drum in the ear.

[2]

[Total 3 marks]

2 Two children have made a toy telephone out of plastic pots and a piece of string. The string is tied to the bases of the pots and is pulled tight. A child speaking into one plastic pot can be heard by the child at the other end. (Grade 6-7)

2.1 Describe how the toy telephone transmits sounds between the two children. Your answer should refer to the movement of particles as the sound wave is transmitted.

[5]

2.2 State what usually happens to the wavelength and frequency of a sound wave as it passes from air to a solid material.

[2]

[Total 7 marks]

Exam Tip

Remember that sound waves come from vibrating objects. They're transmitted through a medium as longitudinal waves.

Ultrasound

1 Ultrasound is frequently used in medicine.

1.1 Define ultrasound.

....

.... *[1]*

1.2 Tick the boxes next to the frequencies which would produce ultrasound.

☐ 30 mHz ☐ 30 kHz ☐ 30 Hz ☐ 30 MHz

[2]

[Total 3 marks]

2 Describe how ultrasound can be used to create an image of a foetus.

....

....

....

....

[Total 3 marks]

3 A submarine uses echo-location to work out how far it is above the ocean floor. It sends a pulse of ultrasound and measures the reflection, as shown in **Figure 1**. A trace of the original and reflected pulses is shown in **Figure 2**.

Figure 1

Figure 2

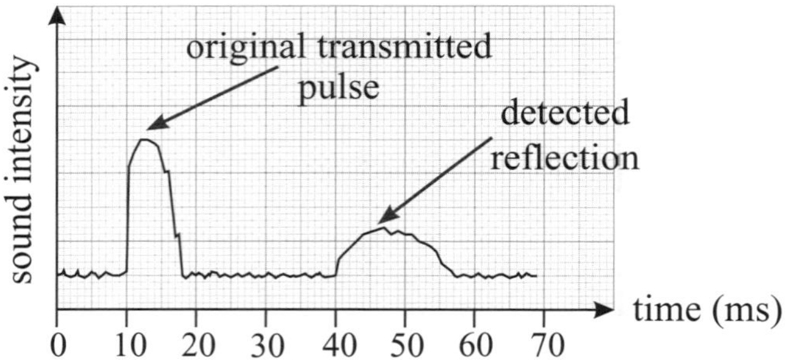

3.1 What is the time interval between the start of the original pulse and the start of the reflected pulse, as shown in **Figure 2**?

.... ms *[1]*

3.2 The sound waves travelled at a speed of 1500 m/s. Calculate the distance between the submarine and the ocean floor.

.... *[3]*

[Total 4 marks]

Exploring Structures Using Waves

Warm-Up

Complete the table shown by stating whether each property describes an S-wave, a P-wave, or both. The first has been done for you.

Property of the wave	Type of wave
Can transfer energy through the Earth	Both
Is a transverse wave	
Can pass through a liquid	
Can pass through a solid	

1 **Figure 1** shows a picture of the Earth. Seismic waves are being produced at point A. Two seismometers are detecting the waves at positions B and C. At B, both S and P waves are detected, but the detector at C is only detecting P waves. Grade 6-7

Figure 1

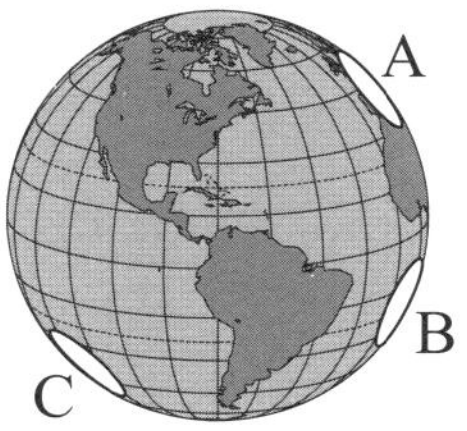

1.1 Explain how this indicates that part of the Earth's core is made from liquid.

....

....

....

[2]

1.2 **Figure 2** shows how the velocity of a P-wave changes as it travels through the Earth.

Explain why the velocity of the wave suddenly changes at depth X and Y.

....

....

....

....

....

[2]

[Total 6 marks]

Figure 2

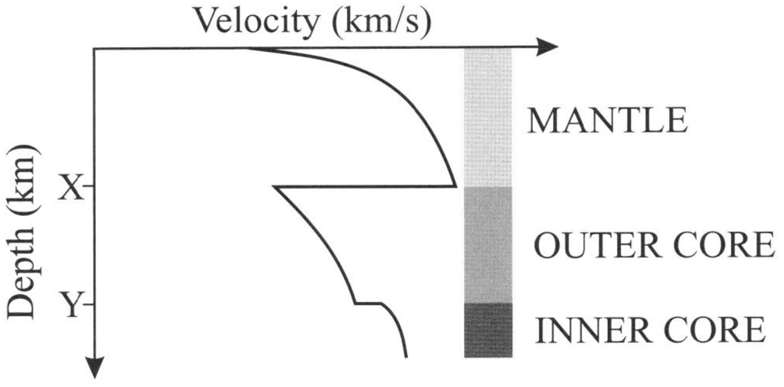

Exam Tip

Exams are all about time management. If you're struggling to remember the information you need to answer a question, don't panic, and just move on to another question. It's better to move on than struggle with the same question for ages. You can always come back to any questions that you skipped later on, if you have time, and have another go at them.

Permanent and Induced Magnets

Warm-Up

Complete the sentence using one of the words below.

non-contact contact nuclear

Magnetic force is an example of a .... force.

1 Magnets have magnetic fields. Grade 4-6

1.1 Define the term magnetic field.

....

....

[1]

1.2 Name **two** magnetic materials.

1. ....

2. ....

[2]

1.3 **Figure 1** shows a bar magnet. Draw the magnetic field lines onto the diagram in **Figure 1**.

Figure 1

[2]

1.4 Which of the following statements are correct for magnets? Tick **two** boxes.

Like poles attract each other. ☐

The magnetic field at the north pole of a magnet is always stronger than at the south pole. ☐

The closer together the magnetic field lines, the stronger the magnetic field. ☐

Magnetic field lines point from the north pole to the south pole of a magnet. ☐

The force between a magnet and a magnetic material can be attractive or repulsive. ☐

[2]

[Total 7 marks]

2 A block of cobalt is held in place near to a bar magnet, as shown in **Figure 2**. Grade 6-7

Figure 2

2.1 A steel paperclip is placed against the block of cobalt at point P, shown on **Figure 2**.
The paperclip sticks to the block of cobalt. State why this is the case.

[2]

2.2 The bar magnet is removed. Explain what happens to the paperclip.

[2]

[Total 4 marks]

3 A student wants to investigate the magnetic field of a horseshoe magnet, shown in **Figure 3**. Grade 6-7

Figure 3

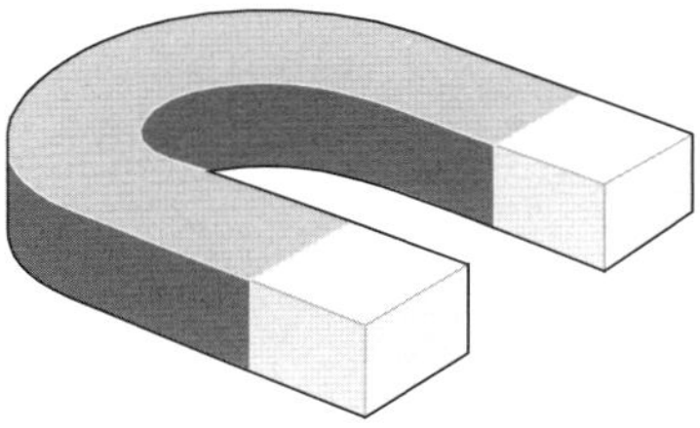

3.1* Explain how a compass could be used to determine the magnetic field of the magnet.

[4]

3.2 State what would happen to the compass if you were to move it far away from any magnets.
Explain why this would happen.

[2]

[Total 6 marks]

Exam Tip

If you're asked to sketch out a diagram, don't be afraid to use all the space that's given to you. It's far, far better to draw a diagram that looks weirdly gigantic than one that's tiny and tricky for the examiner to read properly.

Electromagnetism

1 **Figure 1** shows a wire which has a current flowing through it.
The arrow show the direction of the current.

Grade 4-6

Figure 1

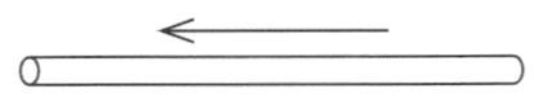

1.1 The flow of charge creates a magnetic field around the wire.
On **Figure 1**, draw field lines showing the direction of the magnetic field created.

[2]

1.2 The direction of the current is reversed. State the effect this will have on the magnetic field.

....

[1]

1.3 State **one** way in which the magnetic field strength around the wire could be increased.

....

[1]

[Total 4 marks]

2 A solenoid with an iron core is an electromagnet.

Grade 4-6

2.1 State one difference between permanent magnets and electromagnets.

....

....

[1]

2.2 Describe the magnetic field inside the centre of a solenoid.

....

....

[2]

2.3 Which of the following statements about a current-carrying solenoid is true? Tick **one** box.

- There will be no magnetic field if the wire of the solenoid is stretched out straight. ☐
- It is not possible to change the strength of the magnetic field around the solenoid. ☐
- If the current is stopped, there will no longer be a magnetic field around the solenoid. ☐
- The direction of the magnetic field does not depend on the direction of the current. ☐

[1]

[Total 4 marks]

3 A current-carrying solenoid has a magnetic field outside it similar to a bar magnet.

3.1 State **one** way in which the magnetic field strength of a solenoid can be increased.

....

[1]

3.2 The north pole of a magnet is brought near to the current-carrying solenoid as shown in **Figure 2**. State whether the north pole is **attracted** or **repelled** by the solenoid. Explain why.

Figure 2

....

....

....

[3]

[Total 4 marks]

4* **Figure 3** shows a circuit for an electric bell.

Figure 3

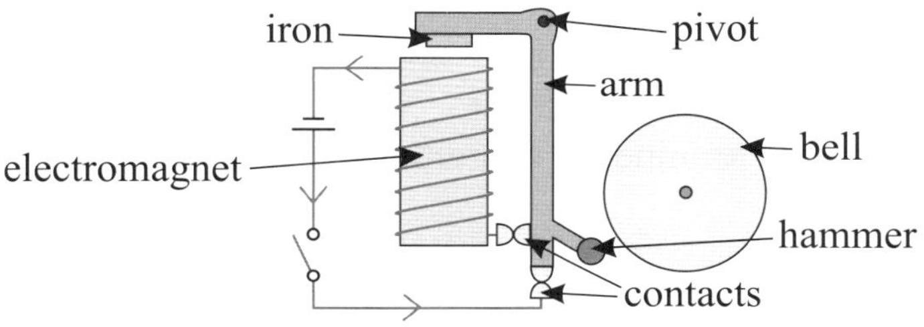

Explain how the circuit uses electromagnetism to sound the bell.

....

....

....

....

....

....

....

....

[Total 6 marks]

Exam Tip

A current carrying-wire will always produce a magnetic field around it. No matter what position the wire is in, or what shape it's been bent into, the magnetic field around it will always depend on the direction of the current.

The Motor Effect

1 A wire is placed between two magnets, as shown in **Figure 1**. A current is flowing through the wire, in the direction shown.

Figure 1

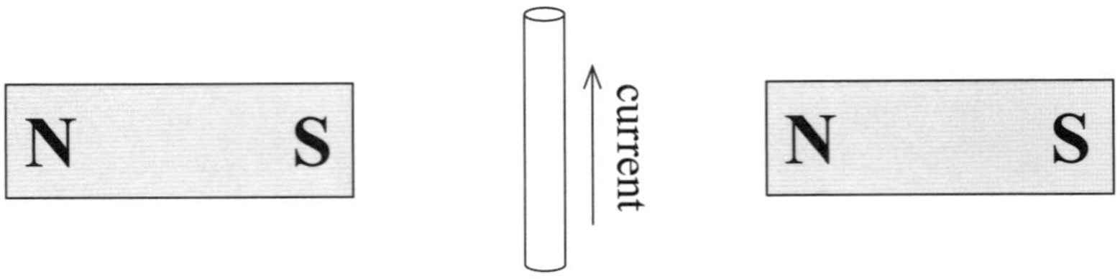

1.1 What will happen to the wire? Tick **one** box.

It will move to the left. ☐

It will move away from you, into the paper. ☐

It will move towards you, out of the paper. ☐

It will remain stationary. ☐

[1]

1.2 State the name of this effect and explain what causes it.

....

....

[2]

1.3 State **three** factors which determine the magnitude of the force acting on the wire.

1. ....

2. ....

3. ....

[3]

[Total 6 marks]

2 A 0.75 m section of wire, carrying a current of 0.4 A, is placed into a magnetic field. When the wire is perpendicular to the field, it experiences a force of 1.2 N. Calculate the magnetic flux density of the field. Give the correct unit in your answer.

Magnetic flux density = ...

Unit = ...

[Total 4 marks]

Exam Tip

If you're struggling to remember Fleming's left-hand rule, think thuMb, First finger and seCond finger.

Electric Motors and Loudspeakers

1 The loudspeaker in a pair of headphones uses an alternating current to produce sound. Use words from the box to complete the description of how loudspeakers work.

Grade 4-6

moment	**coil**	**permanent magnet**	**force**	**pressure**
paper cone	**current**	**wire**	**electromagnet**	**wave**

An alternating current is passed through a coil of wire. The coil is surrounded by a

.... and attached to the base of a paper cone. When the coil carries

a current, it experiences a ...., so the paper cone moves.

This allows variations in .... to be converted into variations

in .... in sound waves.

[Total 3 marks]

2 **Figure 1** shows part of a basic dc motor. A coil of wire is positioned between two magnetic poles and allowed to rotate.

Grade 6-7

Figure 1

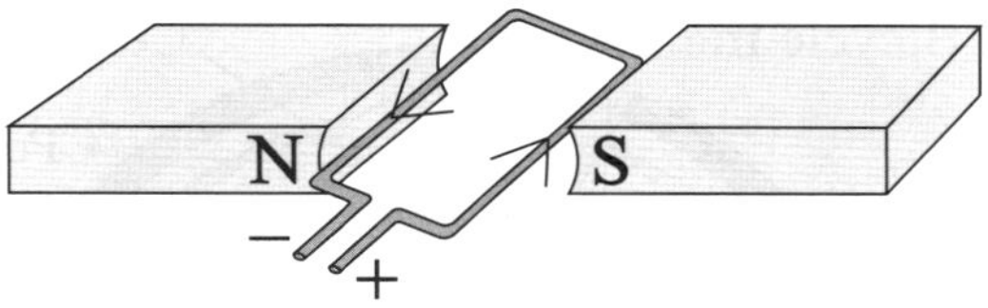

2.1 State the direction in which the coil will turn (**anticlockwise** or **clockwise**).

....

[1]

2.2 Explain why the coil turns.

....

....

....

[2]

2.3 Explain how a dc current can be used to make the coil in **Figure 1** continue to rotate in the same direction.

....

....

....

....

[2]

[Total 5 marks]

The Generator Effect

1 This question is about statements A and B, shown below. Grade 6-7

A A potential difference is induced when an electrical conductor moves relative to a magnetic field.

B A potential difference is induced when there is a change in the magnetic field around an electrical conductor.

Which of the following is correct? Tick **one** box.

Only statement **A** is true. ☐

Only statement **B** is true. ☐

Both statements **A** and **B** are true. ☐

Neither statement **A** nor **B** is true. ☐

[Total 1 mark]

2 **Figure 1** shows a device fixed to the frame of a bicycle. When the bicycle wheel turns, it causes the generator wheel to turn. This then generates electricity to power the bicycle's lamp. Grade 7-9

Figure 1

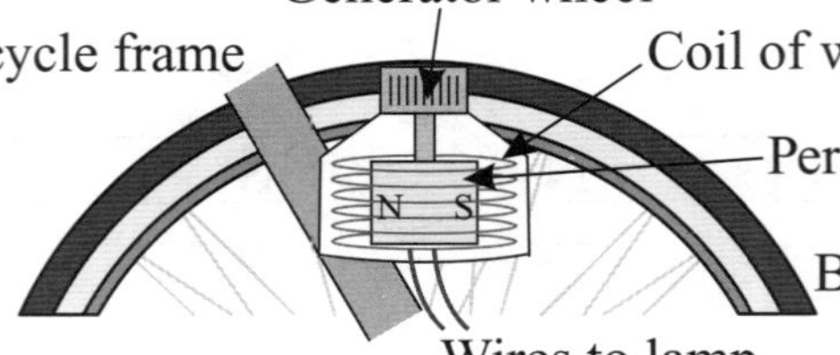

2.1 Describe how the device uses the generator effect to power the bicycle's lamp.

....

....

....

....

[3]

2.2 A cyclist is riding a bicycle with the device fitted. She wants to increase the lamp's brightness. State **one** way in which she can do this.

....

[1]

2.3 The current that the device generates creates its own magnetic field. Describe the direction that the magnetic field will be created in.

....

....

[1]

[Total 5 marks]

Generators and Microphones

Warm-Up

Draw lines between the boxes to describe each type of generator.

Alternators...	...use a split-ring commutator...	...and generate dc.
Dynamos...	...use slip rings and brushes...	...and generate ac.

1 **Figure 1** shows part of the inside of a microphone. Grade 6-7

Figure 1

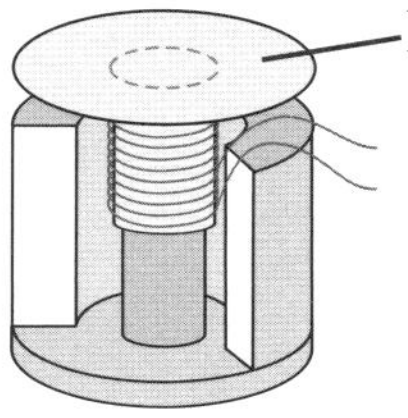

A sound wave hits the diaphragm. Describe how this is converted into an electrical signal.

....

....

....

....

....

[Total 3 marks]

2 **Figure 2** shows a basic alternator. **Figure 3** shows the alternator's output potential difference (pd) trace when the wire is rotated. The frequency of rotation of the wire is doubled. On **Figure 3**, sketch the new output pd trace. Grade 7-9

Figure 2

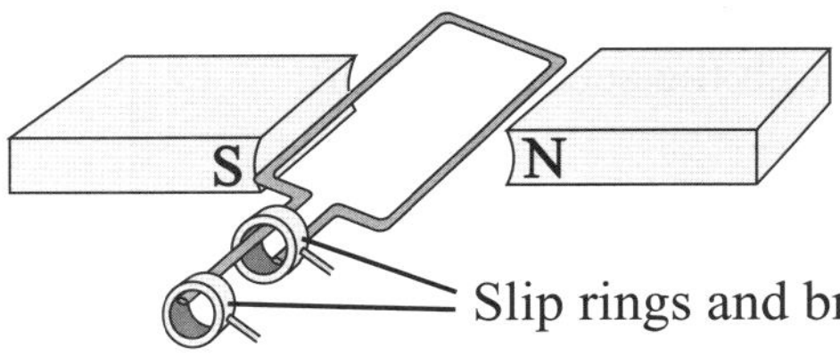

Figure 3

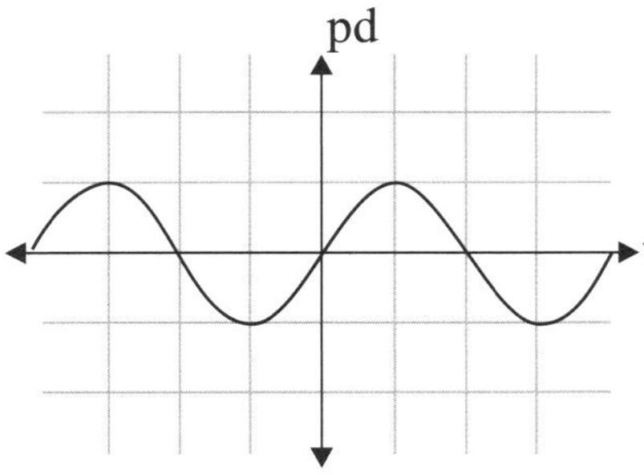

[Total 2 marks]

Exam Tip

It's useful to remember that a generator is a bit like a motor in reverse (and so a microphone is a loudspeaker in reverse). It's easy to get them mixed up though, so think about the purpose of a particular device — is movement being converted into an electrical signal (e.g. a microphone), or is the electrical signal being converted into movement (e.g. a loudspeaker)?

Transformers

1 Put these statements in the correct order to describe how current flows in a transformer. Grade 4-6

A This causes a changing magnetic field in the iron core.

B If the secondary coil is part of a complete circuit, this causes a current to be induced.

C This changing magnetic field induces an alternating pd in the secondary coil.

D An alternating current is applied across the primary coil.

Correct order: ....

[Total 1 mark]

2 A transformer has 12 turns in the primary coil. An input potential difference of 240 V is converted to an output potential difference of 80 V. Grade 6-7

2.1 Calculate the number of turns on the secondary coil.

Number of turns = ...

[3]

2.2 State the type of transformer described above.

....

[1]

[Total 4 marks]

3 A transformer has 30 turns on the primary coil and 40 turns on the secondary coil. The potential difference across the primary coil is 12 V. You can assume that the transformer is 100% efficient. Grade 6-7

3.1 Calculate the output potential difference.

Output pd = ... V

[3]

3.2 The current and potential difference for the transformer is altered. The current through the primary coil is now 20 A and the potential difference is 30 V. The potential difference across the secondary coil is 40 V. Calculate the current through the secondary coil.

Output current = ... A

[3]

3.3 Suggest **one** reason why the change in 3.2 might be made.

....

[1]

[Total 7 marks]

Target AO3

4 A student is doing an investigation into the properties of a transformer. They want to determine how the output potential difference, V_o, is related to the ratio of the number of turns on the secondary coil, N_s, to the number of turns on the primary coil, N_p.

Grade 6-7

The student constructs a basic transformer from a square iron core and two lengths of insulated wire. They then connect each coil to a circuit, as shown in **Figure 1**. The input potential difference, V_i, of 1.2 V is provided by an alternating power supply.

Figure 1

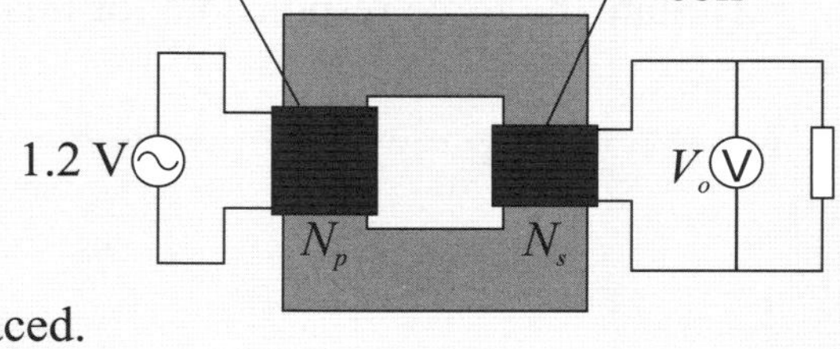

Before starting the experiment, the student notices that the insulation on the secondary coil has been worn through, and so she replaces the wire with an undamaged one.

4.1 Give **two** reasons why it is important that the wire is replaced.

....

....

....

[2]

The student carries out her experiment, and plots her results on a graph of V_o against the ratio $\frac{N_s}{N_p}$, as shown in **Figure 2**.

Figure 2

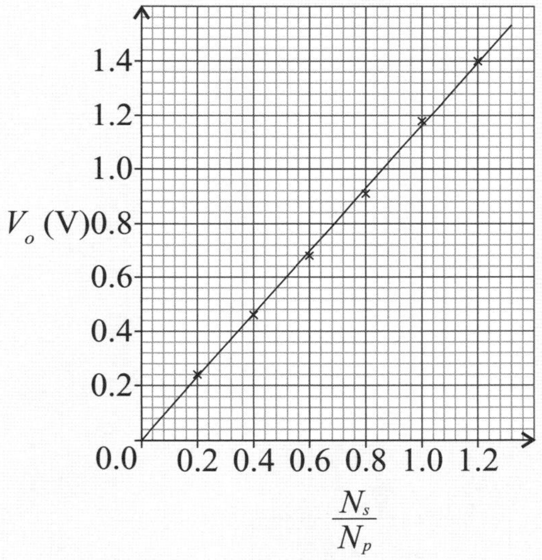

4.2 Calculate the gradient of the graph in **Figure 2**.

gradient = ... V

[2]

4.3 State whether the results in **Figure 2** agree with the relationship $\frac{V_o}{V_i} = \frac{N_s}{N_p}$. Justify your answer.

....

....

....

....

....

[3]

[Total 7 marks]

Exam Tip

When working out the gradient of a line, start off by drawing a right-angled triangle with your line as the longest side. Your triangle should cover more than half the length of the line. Next, write down the coordinates of the points on your line that are also the corners of the triangle. You can then use these coordinates to work out the gradient of the line.

The Life Cycle of Stars

1 A star begins to form when a nebula is pulled together and compressed. Grade 4-6

1.1 What is meant by the term 'nebula'?

....

[1]

1.2 State the force responsible for this 'pulling together'.

....

[1]

[Total 2 marks]

2 The basic life cycle of a star with the same mass as the Sun is shown below.
Fill in the gaps to complete the life cycle of a star of 25 times the mass of the Sun. Grade 4-6

Mass of the Sun **25 × Mass of the Sun**

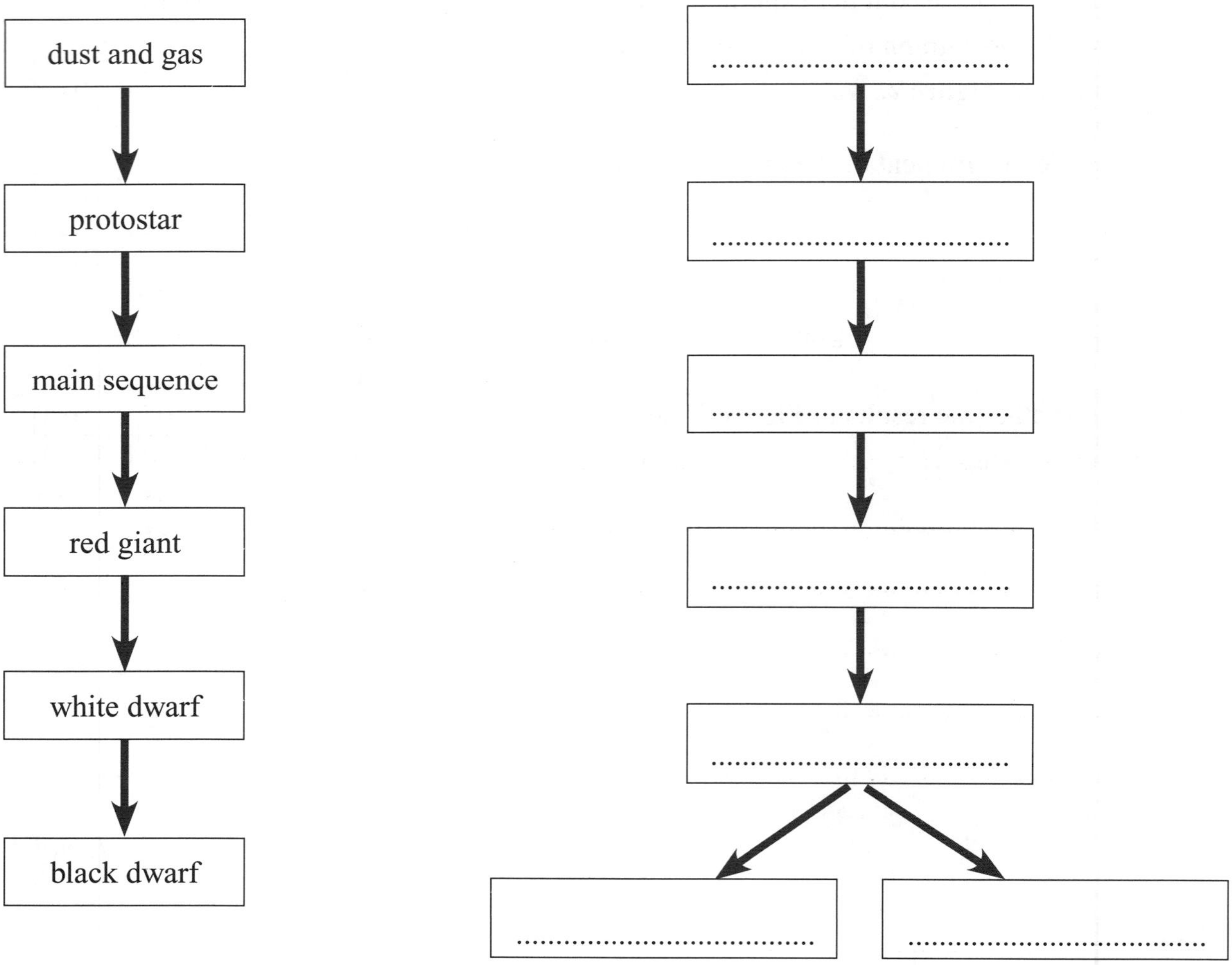

[Total 5 marks]

3 Stars are fuelled by a process known as nuclear fusion. Grade 6-7

3.1 Use the correct words from the box to complete the following passage on nuclear fusion in stars.

density	**temperature**	**hydrogen**	**nebula**
bond	**helium**	**collide**	**iron**

As a protostar ages, its .... and .... increase.

This causes particles to .... with each other more often. When the temperature gets hot enough, ... nuclei fuse together and create .... nuclei.

This process is known as nuclear fusion.

[3]

3.2 When a star reaches the 'main sequence' stage of its lifetime, it is stable.
Explain how nuclear fusion keeps a star stable.

....

....

....

[2]

3.3 State the effect fusion has on the main sequence star's size, and the temperature of its core.

....

....

[2]

[Total 7 marks]

4 Our Sun is currently in the main sequence phase of its life cycle. When the Sun runs out of fuel, it will eject its outer layers to form a planetary nebula, leaving behind a white dwarf, which will gradually cool and fade away. Describe the final life cycle stages of a star with a mass much greater than our Sun, once it has stopped being a red supergiant. Grade 6-7

....

....

....

....

....

....

[Total 3 marks]

Exam Tip

This is one of those bits of physics where there's just a lot of words and facts you need to learn. You need to remember the names of all of the different stages of the life cycles of stars of different sizes, as well as what's going on in each stage.

The Solar System and Orbits

Warm-Up

Put the objects listed below into the table so that they're sorted into the correct groups.

The Moon
Pluto
Earth
Hubble Space Telescope
Neptune
Communications satellite
Venus

Planet	Dwarf Planet	Natural Satellite	Artificial Satellite

1 Galaxies contain multiple stars and their planetary systems. Grade 4-6

1.1 Name the star in our solar system.

....

[1]

1.2 Name the galaxy that our solar system is in.

....

[1]

[Total 2 marks]

2 Different objects in our solar system have different orbits. Grade 4-6

2.1 Complete **Table 1** to show what each type of object orbits around.

Table 1

Object	Orbits around...
dwarf planet	....
moon	....

[2]

2.2 Name the force that causes a moon's orbit.

....

[1]

2.3 Planets are another type of object in our solar system. State **one** similarity and **one** difference between the orbits of a planet and a moon in our solar system.

....

....

[2]

[Total 5 marks]

3 The planets all move in circular orbits around the Sun. They each experience a constant acceleration.

Grade 7-9

3.1 On **Figure 1**, draw arrows indicating the direction of the planet's acceleration, and the direction of the planet's instantaneous velocity.

Figure 1

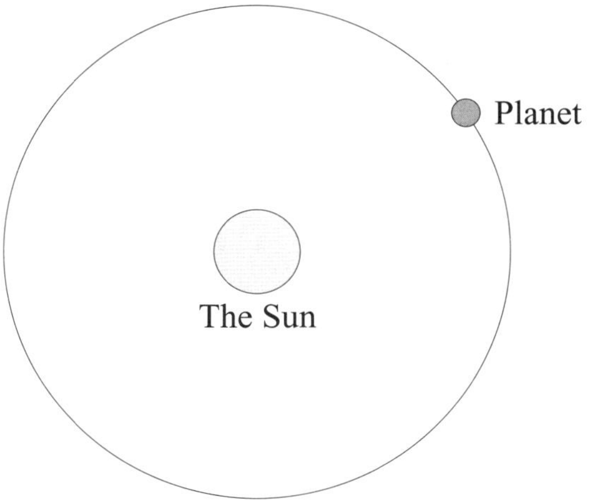

[2]

3.2* Explain why this acceleration changes the planet's velocity but not its speed.

....

....

....

....

....

....

....

[6]

[Total 8 marks]

4 Satellite A and satellite B are two identical artificial satellites in stable orbits around the Earth. Satellite A is orbiting closer to Earth in comparison to satellite B. State the difference in their velocities. Explain your answer.

Grade 7-9

....

....

....

....

....

[Total 4 marks]

Exam Tip

To answer some of these questions, you need to know the definitions of different terms like speed, velocity, artificial/natural satellites... If you want the best chance of getting those marks in the exam, you'll need to learn them — so get cracking!

Red-shift and the Big Bang

1 The Big Bang theory is the currently-accepted theory of how the universe was formed. Grade 4-6

1.1 Which **two** of the following statements form the basis of the Big Bang theory?
Put ticks in the appropriate boxes to indicate your answers.

- [ ] The universe will one day collapse.
- [ ] The universe started off hot and dense.
- [ ] The universe is expanding.
- [ ] The universe has existed forever.

[2]

1.2 Many things about the universe are still not understood.
Name **one** feature of the universe that is still unexplained.

....

[1]

[Total 3 marks]

2 Many theories of the universe suggest it is expanding. Grade 6-7

2.1 Give **two** observations that support the idea that the universe is expanding.

....

....

....

[2]

2.2 Explain why galaxies are not pulled apart by the expansion of the universe.

....

[1]

2.3 Use the correct words from the box to complete the following passage about the universe.

stabilising	**accelerating**	**decelerating**
decreased	**increased**	**stabilised**

Recent observations of distant supernovae indicate that the speed at which distant galaxies are receding has ....

This suggests that the expansion of the universe is ....

[2]

[Total 5 marks]

3 **Table 1** shows a list of galaxies and their distance from Earth in light years. Grade 6-7

Table 1

Galaxy	Distance From Earth (light years)
Cigar Galaxy	12 million
Black Eye Galaxy	24 million
Sunflower Galaxy	37 million
Tadpole Galaxy	420 million

3.1 Light from distant galaxies is observed to undergo red-shift.
Explain what is meant by the term 'red-shift'.

....

....

[1]

3.2 Suggest which of the galaxies in **Table 1** will have the greatest observed red-shift.
Explain your answer.

....

....

....

[3]

3.3 State how you would expect the observed red-shift of light from the Black Eye Galaxy to have changed in 2000 years' time compared to its current red-shift. Explain your answer.

....

....

....

[3]

3.4 A new galaxy is discovered. Light from this galaxy is red-shifted more than that of the Cigar Galaxy, but less than that of the Sunflower Galaxy.
Suggest a possible distance of this new galaxy from the Earth.

....

[1]

[Total 8 marks]

Exam Tip

The Big Bang theory is the leading theory of the creation of the universe — but it wasn't always. In the exam, you might be asked to describe why theories can be changed over time. So be prepared to think about why this theory has become so widely accepted, and what would cause a new theory to replace it as the favoured explanation.

Mixed Questions

1 A student uses a compass to investigate magnetic field patterns. Grade 4-6

1.1 The compass contains a permanent bar magnet.
Describe the difference between a permanent magnet and an induced magnet.

....

....

[2]

1.2 The student moves the compass around the current-carrying solenoid shown in **Figure 1**.
The student uses the compass to plot the magnetic field produced by the solenoid.
Sketch the magnetic field produced by the solenoid on **Figure 1**.

Figure 1

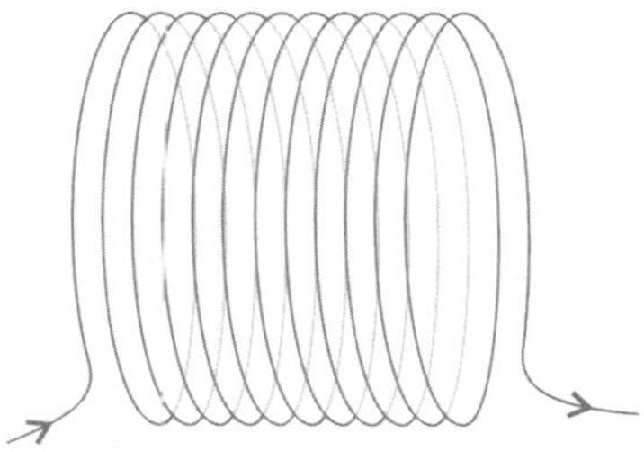

[3]

[Total 5 marks]

2 Background radiation is around us all the time. Grade 4-6

2.1 Give **one** man-made source of background radiation.

....

[1]

2.2 Use words from the box below to complete the passage about radioactive decay.
You can only use a word once and you do not need to use all of the words.

can	**stable**	**cannot**	**unstable**	**forced**	**random**

Radioactive decay is where a nucleus releases radiation to become more ....

It is a .... process, which means you .... predict which individual nucleus in a sample will decay next.

[2]

2.3 The term 'activity' can be used when describing a radioactive source.
Define activity and state the unit it is measured in.

....

[2]

2.4 The term 'half-life' can also be used when describing a source of radiation.
Define half-life in terms of activity.

....

[1]

[Total 6 marks]

3 **Figure 2** shows an electric fan. Grade 4-6

Figure 2

3.1 The fan is connected to the mains with a cable that contains three wires.
What is the name of this type of cable? Tick **one** box.

☐ three-colour cable ☐ two-core cable ☐ three-core cable ☐ triple cable

[1]

3.2 Complete **Table 1** to show the properties of each wire in the cable.

Table 1

Name of wire	Colour of insulation	Potential difference (V)
Live	....	....
....	blue	....
....	....	0

[3]

3.3 The fan works by transferring energy. Use phrases from the box below to complete the passage.
You can only use a phrase once and you do not need to use all of the phrases.

electrically	**thermal**	**by heating**	**kinetic**	**mechanically**	**elastic potential**

Energy is transferred .... from the mains supply to the

.... energy store of the fan's blades.

[2]

3.4 The fan has a power of 30 W. Calculate the energy transferred by the fan in 30 minutes.

Energy transferred = ... J

[2]

[Total 8 marks]

4 A student tests the relationship between potential difference and current for a filament bulb. Grade 4-6

4.1 **Figure 3** shows four *I*-*V* characteristics.
Tick the box under the *I*-*V* characteristic for a filament bulb.

Figure 3

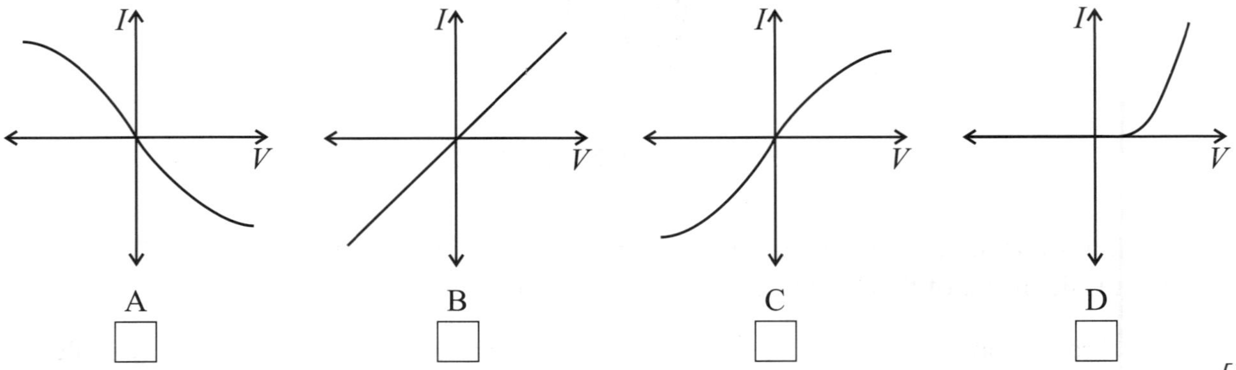

[1]

At a potential difference of 240 V the current through the bulb is 1.2 A.

4.2 Write down the equation that links potential difference, current and resistance.

....

[1]

4.3 Calculate the resistance of the bulb.

Resistance = ... Ω

[3]

[Total 5 marks]

5 Waves on a string are an example of a transverse wave. Grade 4-6

5.1 Which of the following are examples of longitudinal waves? Tick **two** boxes.

☐ sound waves ☐ S-waves ☐ P-waves ☐ gamma rays

[1]

A wave on a string has a wavelength of 60 cm and a frequency of 40 Hz.

5.2 Calculate the period of the wave. Give your answer in milliseconds.

Period = ... ms

[3]

5.3 Write down the equation that links wave speed, frequency and wavelength.

....

[1]

5.4 Calculate the speed of the wave.

Speed = ... m/s

[2]

[Total 7 marks]

6 A child is playing with a remote-controlled toy car. Grade 6-7

Figure 4

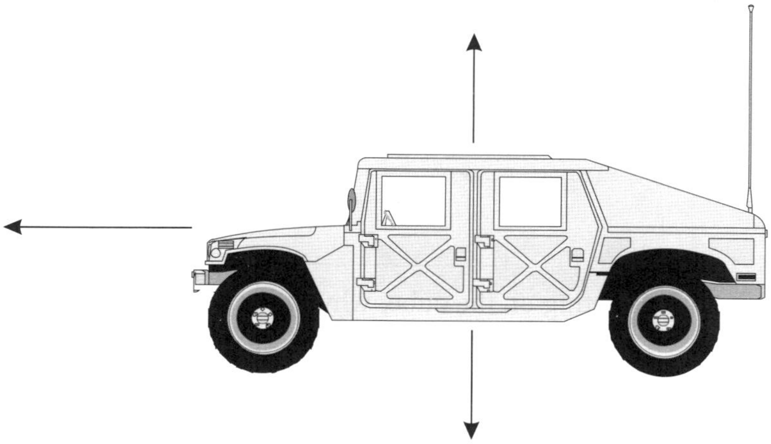

6.1 **Figure 4** shows an incomplete force diagram for the toy. Complete the force diagram to show the resultant resistive force acting on the car as it travels at a steady speed.

[2]

6.2 Write down the equation that links distance travelled, speed and time.

....

[1]

6.3 Calculate the distance the car travels in 30 seconds at a steady speed of 5.0 m/s.

Distance travelled = ... m

[2]

6.4 The car has a mass of 0.50 kg.
Calculate the energy in the kinetic energy store of the car as it travels at 5.0 m/s.

Energy = ... J

[2]

The car is powered by an electric motor. The efficiency of the motor is 65%.
During a short journey, 1200 J of energy was transferred to the motor.

6.5 Write down the equation that links efficiency, the useful output energy transfer and the useful input energy transfer.

....

[1]

6.6 Calculate the useful output energy transferred by the motor during the journey.

Output energy = ... J

[2]

[Total 10 marks]

7 A 10 cm × 10 cm × 10 cm block of material A is placed in a beaker of water. It floats when 7 cm of the cube is submerged in the water, as shown in **Figure 6**. Material A is less dense than water.

Grade 6-7

Figure 5

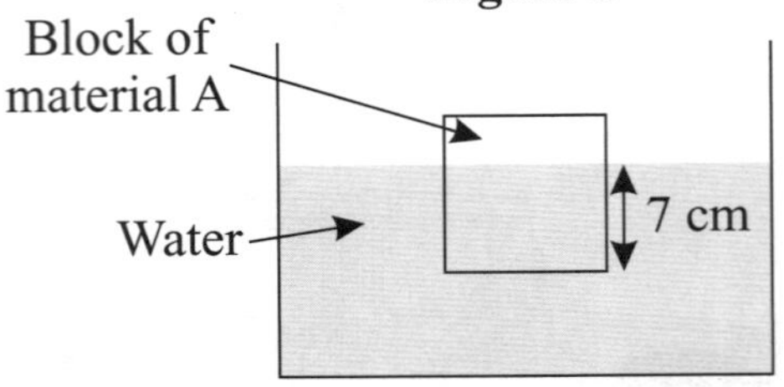

7.1 Explain, in terms of the forces acting on the cube, why the cube floats in water.

....

....

....

....

....

[4]

7.2 Write down the equation that links density, mass and volume.

....

[1]

7.3 Water has a density of 1000 kg/m^3. Calculate the mass of the water displaced by the cube.

Mass = ... kg

[4]

[Total 9 marks]

8 1.2 kg of water, initially at 10.0 °C, is heated in a saucepan until it boils. The saucepan is left until all of the water evaporates. Calculate how much energy has been transferred to the water during this process. Give your answer in kJ and to 2 significant figures. The specific heat capacity of water is 4.2 kJ/kg. The specific latent heat of vaporisation is 2300 kJ/kg.

Grade 6-7

Energy transferred = ... kJ

[Total 5 marks]

9 **Figure 6** shows a velocity-time graph for a cyclist's journey. Grade 6-7

Figure 6

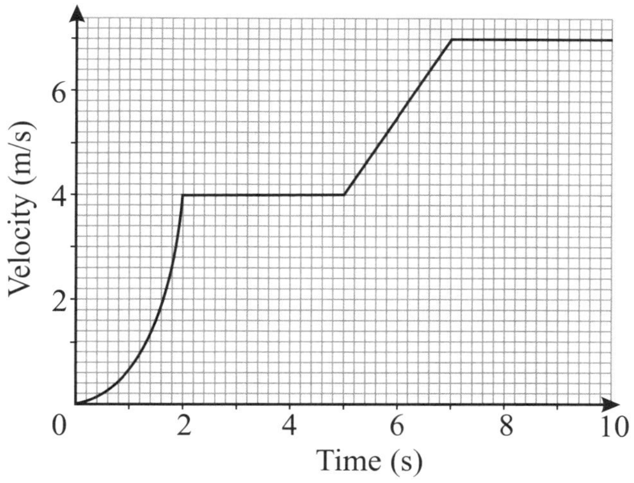

9.1 Describe the motion of the cyclist:

During the first two seconds of the journey: ....

At four seconds from the start of the journey: ....

Between 5-7 s from the start of the journey: ....

[3]

9.2 Calculate the acceleration of the cyclist 6 seconds from the start of his bike ride.

Acceleration = ... m/s^2

[3]

9.3 Ten seconds after the beginning of the cyclist's bike ride, a car turns out of a junction 12 m in front of him. The cyclist is alert and quickly applies the bike's brakes, which provide a constant braking force of 440 N. The combined mass of the man and the bicycle is 83 kg. Calculate the deceleration of the bicycle.

Deceleration = ... m/s^2

[3]

9.4 Use your answer from 9.3 to determine whether or not the cyclist will hit the car. Write down any assumptions you make about the cyclist's reaction time.

....

[5]

[Total 14 marks]

Exam Tip

If you're given a graph about motion (or asked to draw one) it could be a velocity-time graph or a distance-time graph. You'll need to check which one it is so you can get the details straight, like what a straight line or the gradient represents.

10 A student is investigating the pressures of different liquids. She fills three identical containers with a different liquid, then places a pressure sensor in each one. The sensor is held at the same depth in each case, as shown in **Figure 7**. **Table 2** shows her results.

Grade 7-9

Figure 7

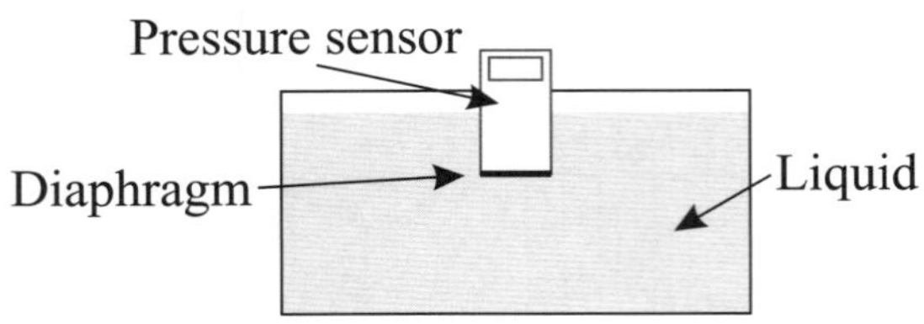

Table 2

Liquid	Density (kg/m^3)	Pressure due to column of liquid (Pa)
Brine	1200	1800
Olive oil	800	1200
Water	1000	1500

10.1 Write down the equation that links pressure, force and area.

....

[1]

10.2 The pressure sensor diaphragm has an area of 5.0×10^{-3} m^2.
Calculate the force exerted on the diaphragm by olive oil in the experiment shown in **Figure 11**.

Force = ... N

[3]

10.3 At a depth of 15 cm, the pressure caused by a fourth liquid is 2850 Pa.
Calculate the density of the new liquid. Use an equation from the Equations List.

Density = ... kg/m^3

[3]

10.4* Using the particle model, explain why, at a given depth, the pressure caused by a column of the new liquid is larger than the pressure caused by a column of water.

....

....

....

....

....

....

....

[4]

[Total 11 marks]

PRACTICAL

11 A student is investigating the properties of visible light. She uses the set-up in **Figure 8** to test how different materials refract light. Grade 7-9

She begins by shining a thin ray of white light into one block of material and marking where the light ray emerges from the block. She then places a block of a different material next to the first block, leaving no air gap. She repeats this for a range of transparent and translucent materials.

Figure 8

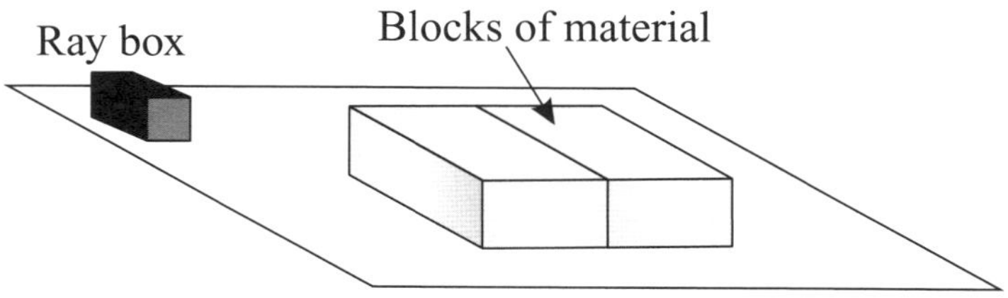

Figure 9

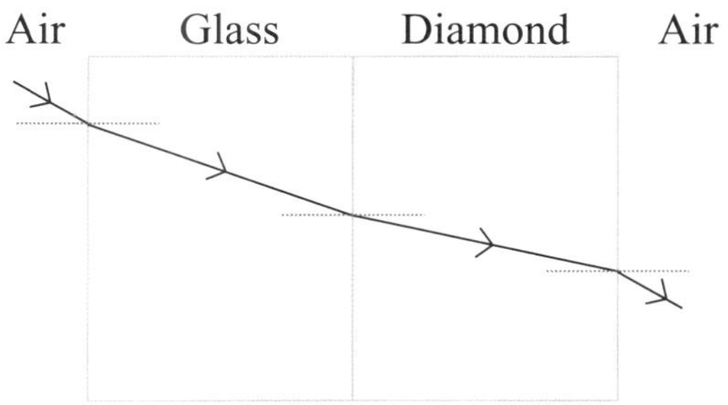

Figure 10

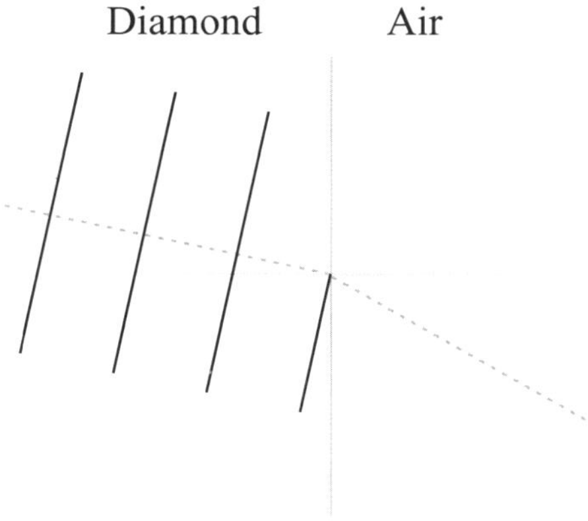

11.1 Complete the wave front diagram in **Figure 10** for the light ray crossing the boundary between diamond and air.

[2]

11.2* Explain why the light ray refracts when it crosses the boundary between diamond and air. Your answer should refer to the wave fronts drawn in **Figure 10**.

....

....

....

....

....

....

....

....

....

....

[6]

[Total 8 marks]

12 A student is designing a basic electronic toy. He wants the toy to be able to light up and spin around. He creates a basic circuit of a battery connected to a motor. He connects two filament bulbs and a fixed resistor in parallel to the motor. The two bulbs and the resistor are all in series with each other. The bulbs and the motor can be switched on and off separately.

Grade 7-9

12.1 Draw the circuit diagram for the circuit created by the student.

[5]

12.2 The student turns on the motor alone. The potential difference across the motor is 6.0 V and a current of 70.0 mA flows through the motor. After 15 minutes, the student switches off the motor and measures the temperature of the motor's casing.
He finds that it has increased by 6.0 °C.

The motor's casing has a mass of 25.0 g.
The material it is made from has a specific heat capacity of 120 J/kg °C.
Calculate the amount of energy that is usefully transferred by the motor in 15 minutes.
You can assume that all energy not transferred to thermal energy store of the motor's casing is usefully transferred.

Energy usefully transferred = ... J

[5]

12.3 Explain **one** modification that the student could make to the toy to make it more efficient.

....

....

....

[2]

[Total 12 marks]

Exam Tip

Sometimes you'll be given a lot of values in one question — make sure you pay attention to the units of each value, especially when there are loads to keep track of. You may need to convert some before plugging them into your equations.

13 **Figure 11** shows a basic model of how the national grid uses step-up and step-down transformers to vary the potential difference and current of the electricity it transmits.

Grade 7-9

Figure 11

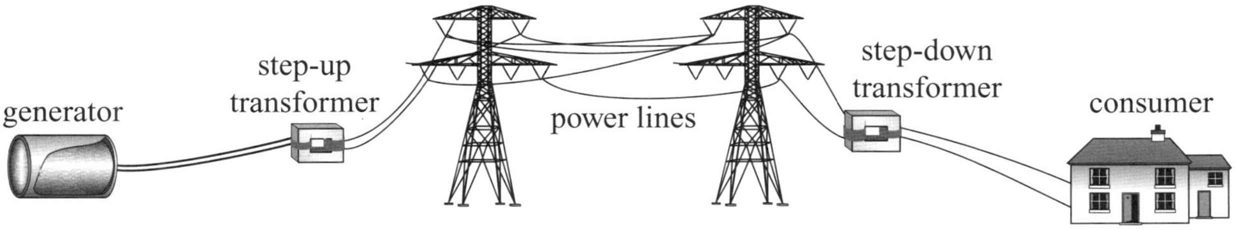

13.1 A power station's generator produces electricity at a potential difference of 25 kV and a current of 4100 A. It is connected to the national grid by a step-up transformer that has 1400 turns on its primary coil and 21 000 turns on its secondary coil. You can assume that the transformer is 100% efficient. Calculate the current of the electricity transmitted by the national grid. Use equations from the Equations List.

Current = ... A

[4]

13.2 Each minute, 34.92 GJ of energy is transferred to the generator. Calculate the efficiency of the generator, assuming its power output is constant.

Efficiency = ... %

[5]

13.3 Describe the unwanted energy transfers that occur whilst electricity is being transmitted by the national grid. Explain the causes of these transfers and why transmitting electricity at a lower current reduces these unwanted energy transfers.

....

....

....

....

....

....

....

[5]

[Total 14 marks]

14 Nuclear power stations generate electricity from nuclear fission. (Grade 7-9)

14.1* Describe the steps involved in producing a forced nuclear fission reaction in a power station. Explain how control rods, which absorb neutrons, can be used to control the plant's output power.

....

....

....

....

....

....

....

....

....

....

....

[6]

14.2* Nuclear fission produces nuclear waste. One radioactive isotope in nuclear waste is caesium-137. Caesium-137 has a half-life of 30 years. It produces beta and gamma radiation as it decays. Explain the safety implications of storing the nuclear waste produced by the plant and the precautions needed to reduce the risks posed by storing nuclear waste.

....

....

....

....

....

....

....

....

....

....

....

[6]

[Total 12 marks]

Exam Tip

Remember to look out for questions like these, where you get marks for how well you write your answer. You could write some short bullet points as a quick plan to help you organise what you want to talk about before writing your full answer.

Answers

Topic 1 — Energy

Page 1 — Energy Stores and Systems

1.1 An object or a group of objects. ***[1 mark]***

1.2 Energy is transferred from: apple's gravitational potential energy store / apple's kinetic energy store ***[1 mark]***
Energy is transferred to: apple's kinetic energy store / thermal energy store of the apple and surroundings (as the apple hits the ground) ***[1 mark]***

1.3 E.g. work being done by the current in the circuit ***[1 mark]***.

2 Level 0: There is no relevant information. ***[No marks]***
Level 1: There is a brief explanation of one of the energy transfers, with no mention of the forces doing the work. ***[1 to 2 marks]***
Level 2: There is a clear description of the energy transfers that take place, as well as the forces that are doing the work. ***[3 to 4 marks]***
Here are some points your answer may include:
Gravitational force does work on the bike.
This causes energy to be transferred from the gravitational potential energy store of the bicycle to its kinetic energy store.
Friction force does work between the brake pads and the wheels.
This causes energy to be transferred from the bicycle's kinetic energy store to the thermal energy store of the brake pads.

Page 2 — Kinetic and Potential Energy Stores

1 $E_e = \frac{1}{2}ke^2 = \frac{1}{2} \times 20 \times 0.01^2$ ***[1 mark]*** $=$ **0.001 J** ***[1 mark]***

2 Energy lost from the g.p.e. store = energy gained in the kinetic energy store ***[1 mark]***
$E_p = mgh = 0.1 \times 9.8 \times 0.45 = 0.441$ J ***[1 mark]***
$E_k = \frac{1}{2}mv^2$
So $v = \sqrt{(2 \times E) \div m}$
$= \sqrt{(2 \times 0.441) \div 0.1}$ ***[1 mark]***
$= 2.969...$ ***[1 mark]*** = **3 m/s (to 1 s.f.)** ***[1 mark]***

3.1 $E_e = \frac{1}{2}ke^2 = \frac{1}{2} \times 144 \times 0.10^2$ ***[1 mark]*** $= 0.72$ J
It is assumed that all of the energy stored in the elastic potential energy store of the elastic band is transferred to the kinetic energy store of the ball bearing ($E_e = E_k$)
so energy = **0.72 J** ***[1 mark]***

3.2 Speed of child A's ball bearing:
$E_k = \frac{1}{2}mv^2 = 0.72$ J
so $v^2 = (2 \times 0.72) \div 0.0100 = 144$ ***[1 mark]***
$v = 12$ m/s so child B's ball bearing speed is:
2×12 m/s $= 24$ m/s ***[1 mark]***
$E_k = \frac{1}{2}mv^2 = \frac{1}{2} \times 0.0100 \times 24^2 = 2.88$ J ***[1 mark]***
$E_e = \frac{1}{2}ke^2 = 2.88$ J
so $k = (2 \times 2.88) \div 0.10^2$ ***[1 mark]***
$= 576 =$ **580 N/m (to 2 s.f.)** ***[1 mark]***

Pages 3-4 — Specific Heat Capacity

Warm-up
The energy needed to raise 1 kg of a substance by 1 °C.

1.1 $\Delta E = mc\Delta\theta$ so $c = \Delta E \div m\Delta\theta$ ***[1 mark]***
$= 15\,000 \div (0.3 \times 25)$ ***[1 mark]***
Specific heat capacity = **2000** ***[1 mark]***

1.2 The current flowing through the immersion heater does work ***[1 mark]***, transferring energy electrically ***[1 mark]*** to the thermal energy store of the immersion heater ***[1 mark]***. It is then transferred from the thermal energy store of the immersion heater to the thermal energy store of the liquid ***[1 mark]***.

2.1 Yes, he is correct. The foam will serve as insulation, which will reduce the transfer of energy away from the block while it is being heated ***[1 mark]***. This means the student's energy measurements will more accurately reflect the amount of energy that is transferred to the block and causes an increase in temperature ***[1 mark]***.

2.2 Material C has the highest specific heat capacity ***[1 mark]***. E.g. The higher the specific heat capacity of a material, the more energy is required to increase the temperature of 1 kg of the material by 1 °C ***[1 mark]***. Material C had the smallest increase in temperature when the same amount of energy was transferred to the same mass of each material, so it must have the highest specific heat capacity ***[1 mark]***.

You could also have answered this question using the specific heat capacity equation. $Q = mc\Delta T$, so the gradient of the graph is equal to $\frac{1}{mc}$. Since m is the same for all of the materials, this means the line with the shallowest gradient shows the highest specific heat capacity.

2.3 Valid results are repeatable and reproducible. To confirm that his results are repeatable, the student should repeat the experiment with the same method, and check that he gets very similar results ***[1 mark]***. To confirm his results are reproducible, he should repeat the experiment using different equipment and/or a different experimental method, and check that he gets very similar results ***[1 mark]***.

Pages 5-6 — Conservation of Energy and Power

Warm-up
Power is the **rate of** energy transfer or **work done**.
It is measured in **watts**.

1 E.g. energy transferred to a less useful energy store ***[1 mark]***.

2.1 Energy can be created.
Energy can be destroyed.
[1 mark for both correct answers, otherwise no marks if more than two boxes have been ticked]

2.2 Useful energy store: e.g. kinetic energy store (of shaver) ***[1 mark]***
Wasted energy store: e.g. thermal energy store (of shaver or surroundings) ***[1 mark]***

2.3 E.g. it would reduce the battery life of the battery / it would make the battery go flat quicker / it would mean the battery must be recharged more often ***[1 mark]***.

3.1 $P = W \div t$ ***[1 mark]***

3.2 $W = Pt = 35 \times 600$ ***[1 mark]*** = **21 000 J** ***[1 mark]***

3.3 $P = E \div t$
so $t = E \div P = 16\,800 \div 35$ ***[1 mark]*** = **480 s** ***[1 mark]***

4.1 It will decrease the time ***[1 mark]*** because more energy is being transferred to the kinetic energy store of the car per second ***[1 mark]*** so the car speeds up more quickly ***[1 mark]***.

4.2 The same amount of energy is needed to accelerate the car with both engines. The energy transferred by the old engine:
$P = E \div t$, so $E = P \times t = 32\,000 \times 9.0$ ***[1 mark]***
$= 288\,000$ J ***[1 mark]***
The time taken for the new engine to transfer the same amount of energy is:
$P = E \div t$, so $t = E \div P = 288\,000 \div 62\,000$ ***[1 mark]***
$= 4.645...$
= **4.6 s (to 2 s.f.)** ***[1 mark]***

Page 7 — Conduction and Convection

1 Convection occurs in **liquids** and **gases**. It is where a change in **density** causes particles to move from **hotter** to **cooler** regions.
[3 marks for all correct, otherwise 2 marks for 3-4 correct, 1 mark for 1-2 correct]

2.1 E.g. make sure all of the blocks are the same thickness / make sure the blocks are identical shapes/sizes / measure the time taken for a larger change in temperature / take repeat measurements to calculate an average ***[1 mark]***.

2.2 Energy is transferred by heating to the kinetic energy stores of the particles at the bottom of the block ***[1 mark]***. These particles collide with other particles in the block, and transfer energy mechanically to the kinetic energy stores of other particles ***[1 mark]***. This continues, transferring energy through the whole block ***[1 mark]***.

2.3 It has a higher thermal conductivity than the other blocks ***[1 mark]***.

Pages 8-9 — Reducing Unwanted Energy Transfers

Warm-up

Wearing a more streamlined helmet

1 Thicker walls decrease the rate of energy lost from a house. Bricks with a higher thermal conductivity transfer energy at a faster rate.
[1 mark for both correct, no marks if more than two boxes have been ticked]

2.1 through the roof ***[1 mark]***

2.2 E.g. install loft insulation (to reduce convection) ***[1 mark]***

2.3 E.g. use draught excluders (to reduce convection) / install double glazing (to reduce conduction) / hang thick curtains (to reduce convection) / reduce the temperature difference between inside and outside the home
[1 mark for each sensible suggestion]

3 Doing work against friction causes energy to be dissipated/ wasted (usually to thermal energy stores) ***[1 mark]***. After lubricating the axle, the frictional forces acting on it were reduced ***[1 mark]***. This means that less energy is dissipated as the handle (and axle) is turned and so more energy is transferred to the kinetic energy store of the handle (and axle) and the bucket ***[1 mark]***.

4 Best: C Second best: B Worst: A ***[1 mark]***
The thicker a sample is, the slower the rate of energy transfer through it ***[1 mark]*** so sample B will be a better insulator than sample A ***[1 mark]***. Air has a lower thermal conductivity than glass (so it transfers energy at a slower rate than glass does) ***[1 mark]*** so even though samples B and C are the same thickness, sample C is a better insulator than sample B ***[1 mark]***.

Pages 10-11 — Efficiency

1.1 Efficiency = Useful output energy transfer ÷ Total input energy transfer ***[1 mark]***

1.2 Efficiency = 16 000 ÷ 20 000 ***[1 mark]***
= **0.8** ***[1 mark]***

You'd also get the mark for giving the efficiency as a percentage (80%).

2 Efficiency = 75% = 0.75
Efficiency = Useful power output ÷ Total power input
So Total power input = Useful power output ÷ Efficiency ***[1 mark]***
= 57 ÷ 0.75 ***[1 mark]*** = **76 W** ***[1 mark]***

3.1 Useful output power of the air blower:
Efficiency = Useful power output ÷ Total power input
so Useful power output = Efficiency × Total power input
= 0.62 × 533 ***[1 mark]***
= 330.46 W ***[1 mark]***
Useful power output of the turbine:
Efficiency = 13% = 0.13
Total power input = Useful power of air blower
Useful power output = Efficiency × Total power input
= 0.13 × 330.46 ***[1 mark]***
= 42.9598
= **43 W (to 2 s.f.)** ***[1 mark]***

3.2 E.g. adding more sails (so there is a larger surface area for the air to hit) / increasing the size of the sails (so there is a larger surface area for the air to hit) / adding a lubricant to the moving parts of the turbine (to reduce friction) / changing the angle of the sails so they get hit by more wind ***[2 marks — 1 mark for each sensible suggestion]***

4.1 E.g. the student could measure the temperature of the water in the kettle, so that they can be sure they measure the energy transferred to increase the water's temperature to 100 °C (not any more or less) ***[1 mark]***.

4.2 The student will record an inaccurate value of energy transferred to the kettle for this reading ***[1 mark]***. This is because some of the residual energy in the kettle's thermal energy store from the previous trial will be transferred to the water and begin to increase its temperature, so less energy will need to be transferred from the power supply to boil the water ***[1 mark]***.

4.3 The results are not consistent with the prediction.
By calculating the efficiencies at different volumes from the data in Table 1, using efficiency = $\frac{\text{useful energy output}}{\text{total energy input}}$ ***[1 mark]***, it can be seen that:
E.g. for 660 cm^3 of water, efficiency = 0.168 ÷ 0.212
= 0.792... ***[1 mark]***,
while for 2000 cm^3 of water, efficiency = 0.504 ÷ 0.547
= 0.921... ***[1 mark]***.
Therefore, the efficiency of the kettle was greater for a larger volume of water than a smaller volume (the opposite of the student's prediction) ***[1 mark]***.

You don't have to have done the exact same calculations we have here. As long as you've come to the right conclusion and have done some calculations to show that efficiency is larger for a bigger volume than a smaller volume,. you'll get the marks.

Pages 12-13 — Energy Resources and Their Uses

Warm-up

Renewable — bio-fuel, solar, tidal, geothermal, wave power, hydroelectricity, wind

Non-renewable — oil, coal, gas, nuclear fuel

1 E.g. a non-renewable energy resource will one day run out ***[1 mark]*** but a renewable energy resource can be replenished as it is used ***[1 mark]***.

2.1 coal, oil, (natural) gas ***[1 mark]***

2.2 E.g. generating electricity / burning coal on fires / using gas central heating / using a gas fire / coal in steam trains
[2 marks — 1 for each correct answer]

2.3 Bio-fuels are solids, liquids or gases that are produced from plant products or from animal waste ***[1 mark]***.

2.4 E.g. because fossil fuels will eventually run out / because fossil fuels harm the environment
[1 mark for any correct answer].

3 E.g. during winter, there are fewer hours of daylight, but the weather is usually more windy ***[1 mark]***, so wind turbines will be able to generate more electricity during winter ***[1 mark]***. However, during the summer, there will be more daylight hours and the weather will be less windy ***[1 mark]***, so solar panels will be more favourable ***[1 mark]***. By installing both, the university will have a more reliable electricity supply throughout the year ***[1 mark]***.

4.1 How to grade your answer:
Level 0: There is no relevant information. ***[No marks]***
Level 1: There is a brief description of the reliability or environmental impact of one of the energy resources. ***[1 to 2 marks]***
Level 2: There is a clear and detailed description of the reliability and environmental impacts of both energy resources, as well as some similarities between them. ***[3 to 4 marks]***

Here are some points your answer may include:
Both energy resources are reliable.
Tides come in and out at known times.
Except in times of drought, there is always water available for a hydroelectric power plant to work.
Hydroelectric power plants require the flooding of valleys, which causes a loss of habitat for any animals living there.
The plants in the valley die during the flood and rot, which releases gases that contribute to global warming.
Using tides to generate electricity creates no pollution, but tidal barrages do alter the habitat of nearby animals.

4.2 How to grade your answer:
Level 0: There is no relevant information. ***[No marks]***
Level 1: There is a brief explanation of an advantage or a disadvantage of fossil fuels. ***[1 to 2 marks]***
Level 2: There is some explanation of both advantages and disadvantages of fossil fuels. ***[3 to 4 marks]***
Level 3: There is a clear and detailed explanation of the advantages and disadvantages of using fossil fuels. ***[5 to 6 marks]***
Here are some points your answer may include:
Advantages:
Fossil fuels are reliable.
They are extracted at a fast enough rate that there are always some in stock.
Power plants can respond quickly to peaks in demand.
Running costs of fossil fuel power plants aren't that expensive compared to other energy resources.
Fuel extraction costs are also low.
Disadvantages:
Fossil fuels are slowly running out / they are a non-renewable energy resource.
Burning fossil fuels releases carbon dioxide into the atmosphere.
Carbon dioxide in the atmosphere contributes to global warming.
Burning coal and oil also releases sulfur dioxide, which causes acid rain.
Acid rain can damage soil and trees. This can damage or destroy the habitats of animals.
Coal mining can spoil the view by damaging the landscape.
Oil spillages kill sea life and birds and mammals that live near to the sea.

Page 14 — Trends in Energy Resource Use

1.1 35 + 23 + 5 = 63 %
[2 marks for correct answer, otherwise 1 mark for reading all three values correctly from the graph]

1.2 E.g. the country is using a larger percentage renewable energy resources to generate electricity in 2015 than they were the previous year / overall, they are using a smaller percentage of fossil fuels to generate their electricity in 2015 than they were in 2014 ***[1 mark]***.

2 How to grade your answer:
Level 0: There is no relevant information. ***[No marks]***
Level 1: There is a brief explanation why the UK is using more renewable energy resources.
[1 to 2 marks]
Level 2: There is some explanation of why the UK is using more renewable energy resources and the factors that restrict the increase in their use.
[3 to 4 marks]
Level 3: There is a clear and detailed explanation of why the UK is using more renewable energy resources and the factors that restrict the increase in their use. ***[5 to 6 marks]***
Here are some points your answer may include:
Reasons the UK is using more renewable energy resources:
We understand more about the negative effects that fossil fuels have on the environment, so more people want to use renewable energy resources that have less of an impact on the environment.
Fossil fuel reserves will run out, so we have to find an alternative for them.
Pressure from the public and other countries has lead to government targets for the use of renewable energy resources. This can lead to increased government funding for renewable energy resources.
Pressure from the public and the global community/ other countries has also lead to private companies creating more environmentally-friendly products that use renewable energy resources.
Factors that limit the use of renewable energy resources:
Building new power plants to replace existing fossil fuel powered ones costs money.
Some renewable energy resources are less reliable than fossil fuels.
Research into improving renewable energy resources costs money and will take time.
Personal products that use renewable energy resources, like hybrid cars, are generally more expensive than similar ones that use fossil fuels.

Topic 2 — Electricity

Page 15 — Current and Circuit Symbols

Warm-up
A — cell, B — switch, C — filament lamp, D — fuse.

1.1 There is no source of potential difference ***[1 mark]***

1.2 Current is the rate of flow of **charge** ***[1 mark]***.

2.1 0.5 A ***[1 mark]***

Remember that the current is the same at any point in a single closed circuit loop.

2.2 $Q = I \times t$ ***[1 mark]***

2.3 $t = 2 \times 60 = 120$ s
Charge = 0.5 × 120 ***[1 mark]***
= **60** ***[1 mark]*** **C** ***[1 mark]***

Page 16 — Resistance and V = IR

1 $V = I \times R$
$V = 3 \times 6$ ***[1 mark]*** = **18 V** ***[1 mark]***

2.1 She could have varied the length of the wire between the crocodile clips ***[1 mark]*** and divided the reading on the voltmeter by the reading on the ammeter to find the resistance for each length ***[1 mark]***.

2.2

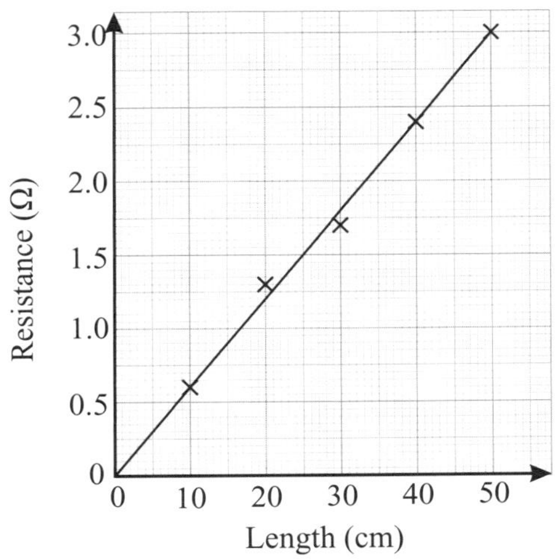

[1 mark for resistance on vertical axis and length on horizontal axis, 1 mark for appropriate values labelled on both axes, 1 mark for correctly plotted points, 1 mark for suitable line of best fit.]

2.3 The resistance is proportional to the length ***[1 mark]***. This is shown by the graph being a straight line through the origin ***[1 mark]***.

Pages 17-19 — Resistance and I-V Characteristics

1.1 C ***[1 mark]***

At a constant temperature, the relationship between pd and current is linear — when this is true, the resistor is said to be ohmic.

1.2 *I-V* characteristic ***[1 mark]***

1.3 A resistor at a constant temperature is an example of an **ohmic** conductor. It is also an example of a **linear** component. ***[1 mark for each correct answer]***

2.1

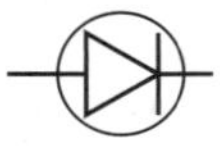

[1 mark]

2.2 A diode only lets current flow through it in one direction ***[1 mark]***.

2.3 The student put the diode/power supply in the circuit the other way around ***[1 mark]***. The resistance of a diode is very large when current goes through it one way and very small when current goes through in the opposite direction ***[1 mark]***.

3.1 It is used to alter the current ***[1 mark]*** so the potential difference can be measured for each current ***[1 mark]***.

3.2 At 3 A the pd is 12 V ***[1 mark]***

$V = I \times R$

$R = V \div I$ ***[1 mark]*** $= 12 \div 3$ ***[1 mark]*** $=$ **4 Ω** ***[1 mark]***

3.3 The resistance increases as the current increases ***[1 mark]***. This is because the increase in current causes the temperature to rise ***[1 mark]***.

3.4 A resistor is ohmic when the relationship between current and potential difference is linear ***[1 mark]***. The graph is linear until approximately 3.5 V, so the resistor is ohmic in this range ***[1 mark]***.

4.1 E.g. adjust the variable resistor to change the current through the circuit. Record the current through the diode using the ammeter, and the potential difference across it using the voltmeter ***[1 mark]***. Use the equation $V = IR$ (in the form $R = V \div I$) to calculate the resistance of the diode at this current using the current and potential difference measurements ***[1 mark]***. Repeat this for a number of different values of current (e.g. at least 6), changing the current by a fixed amount each time (e.g. 1 mA) ***[1 mark]***.

4.2 E.g.

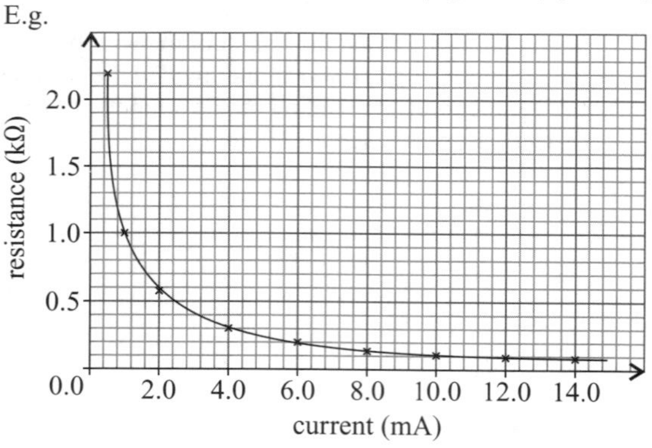

[1 mark for smooth line passing through or close to all points]

4.3 E.g. she has only carried out the experiment for positive values of current / current flowing in one direction ***[1 mark]***. This means she cannot make a conclusion about the effect of the size of the current, because the device may behave differently for current that flows in the opposite direction / because diodes are known to have a very high resistance for one direction of current flow but not the opposite ***[1 mark]***.

Page 20 — Circuit Devices

1.1

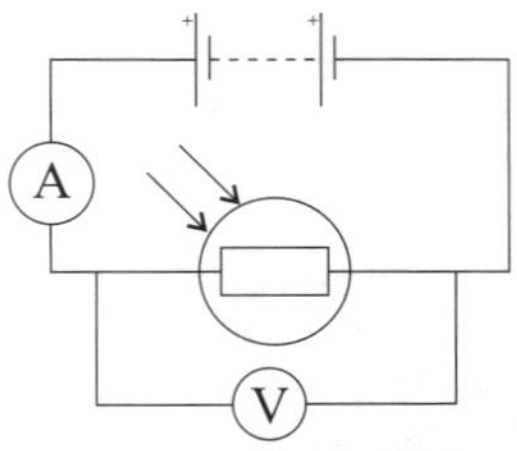

[1 mark for correct LDR symbol, 1 mark for LDR, ammeter and power supply in series, 1 mark for voltmeter in parallel across LDR]

1.2 It decreases ***[1 mark]***

1.3 E.g. automatic night lights / burglar detectors ***[1 mark]***

2 As the temperature increases, the resistance of the thermistor decreases ***[1 mark]***. This means the current in the circuit increases ***[1 mark]***. As the current increases, the brightness of the light increases ***[1 mark]***. When the cooker's surface is cold, the resistance is high and the current is too small to light the bulb ***[1 mark]***.

Page 21 — Series Circuits

1 A ***[1 mark]***.

In a series circuit, there should only be one closed loop of wire.

2.1 $10 + 30 =$ **40 Ω** ***[1 mark]***

2.2 $V = I \times R$

$V = 75 \times 10^{-3} \times 30$ ***[1 mark]*** $=$ **2.25 V** ***[1 mark]***

3 The potential difference across the 8 Ω resistor is:

$6 - 2 = 4$ V ***[1 mark]***

$V = I \times R$, so the current through the 8 Ω resistor is:

$I = V \div R = 4 \div 8$ ***[1 mark]*** $= 0.5$ A ***[1 mark]***

This is the same as the current through R, so the resistance of R is: $R = V \div I = 2 \div 0.5$ ***[1 mark]*** $=$ **4 Ω** ***[1 mark]***

Page 22 — Parallel Circuits

1

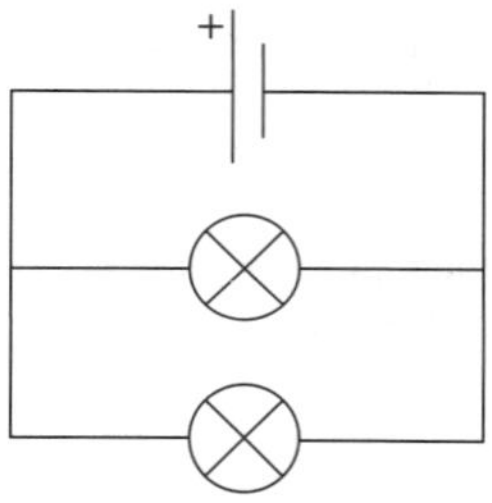

[1 mark]

2.1 6 V ***[1 mark]***

Potential difference is the same across all components in parallel.

2.2 $V = IR$ so $I = V \div R$ ***[1 mark]***

A_1: $I = V \div R = 6 \div 4$ ***[1 mark]*** $=$ **1.5 A** ***[1 mark]***

A_2: $I = V \div R = 6 \div 12$ ***[1 mark]*** $=$ **0.5 A** ***[1 mark]***

2.3 The current from the supply splits into 1.5 A and 0.5 A.

So A_3 reads $1.5 + 0.5 =$ **2 A** ***[1 mark]***

3 How to grade your answer:

Level 0: There is no relevant information. ***[No marks]***

Level 1: There is a brief explanation about the effect of adding resistors in series or parallel. ***[1 to 2 marks]***

Level 2: There is a comparison between adding resistors in series and parallel and an explanation of their effects. ***[3 to 4 marks]***

Level 3: A logical and detailed comparison is given, explaining why adding resistors in series increases the total resistance but adding them in parallel reduces it. ***[5 to 6 marks]***

Here are some points your answer may include:

In series, resistors share the potential difference from the power source.

The more resistors that are in series, the lower the potential difference for each one, and so the lower the current for each one.

Current is the same all around a series circuit, so adding a resistor will decrease the current for the whole circuit.
A decrease in total current means an increase in total resistance.
In parallel, all resistors have the same potential difference as the source.
Adding another resistor in parallel (forming another circuit loop) increases the current flowing in the circuit, as there are more paths for the current to flow through.
An increase in total current means a decrease in total resistance (because $V = IR$).

Page 23 — Investigating Resistance

1.1

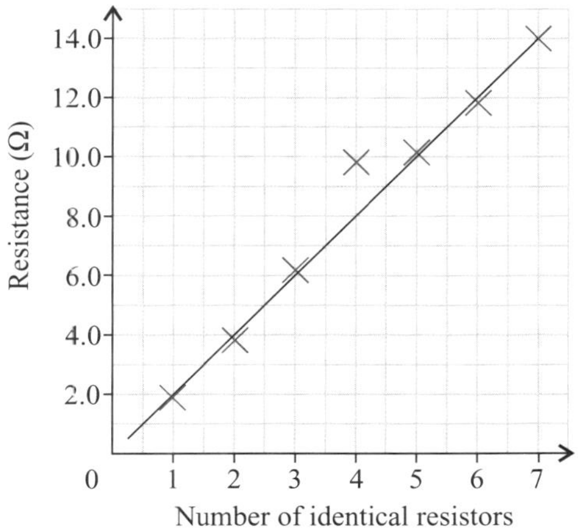

Resistance = **8.0 Ω**
[1 mark for a straight line of best fit that excludes the point plotted for 4 resistors, 1 mark for correct prediction of resistance]

1.2

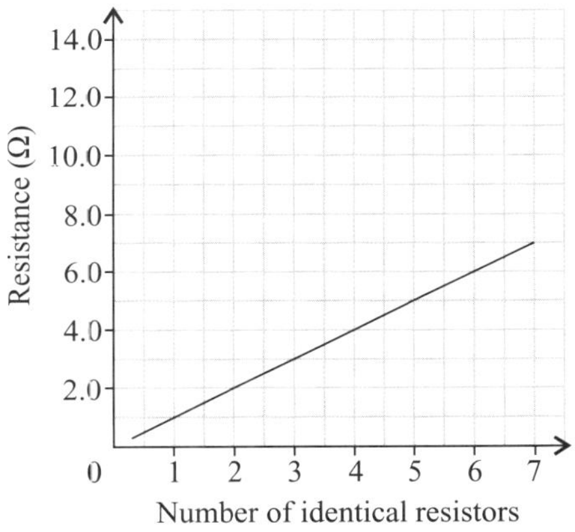

[1 mark for a straight line of best fit with a positive gradient, 1 mark for the gradient of the line being half of the gradient of the line drawn in 1.1]

2 How to grade your answer:
Level 0: There is no relevant information. ***[No marks]***
Level 1: There is a brief description of the techniques used to measure resistance of the circuit. The steps mentioned are not in a logical order.
[1 to 2 marks]
Level 2: There is a good description of the techniques used to measure resistance of the circuit. Most steps are given in a logical order and they could be followed to produced valid results.
A correct circuit diagram may be included.
[3 to 4 marks]
Level 3: A logical and detailed description is given, fully describing the method for investigating the effect of adding resistors in parallel. The method could easily be followed to produce valid results.
A correct circuit diagram may be included.
[5 to 6 marks]

Here are some points your answer may include:
Connect a battery or cell in series with an ammeter and a fixed resistor.
Measure the source potential difference using the voltmeter.
Measure the current through the circuit using the ammeter.
Calculate the resistance of the circuit using $R = V \div I$.
Connect a second identical resistor in parallel with the first resistor.
Do not connect the second resistor across the ammeter.
Measure the current and use this to calculate the resistance of the circuit.
Repeat this for several identical resistors.
Plot a graph of number of identical resistors against overall resistance of the circuit.
A correct circuit diagram, similar to:

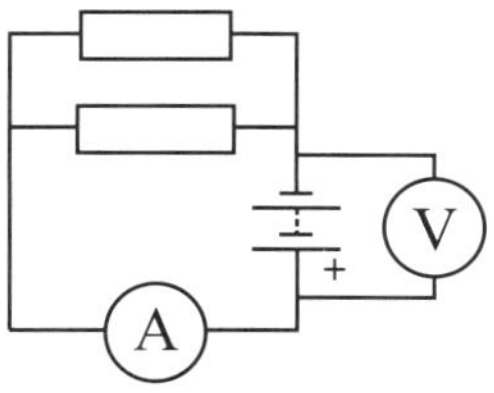

So long as you draw a correct diagram with at least two resistors in parallel, you would get the marks. You could also draw your circuit with several resistors in parallel, all separated with switches.

Page 24 — Electricity in the Home

Warm-up
The live wire is **brown** and is at a potential difference of **230** V.
The earth wire is **green and yellow** and is at a potential difference of **0** V.

1.1 230 V ***[1 mark]***
50 Hz ***[1 mark]***

1.2 How to grade your answer:
Level 0: There is no relevant information. ***[No marks]***
Level 1: There is a brief explanation of the function of the live and neutral wires and some attempt at explaining why the toaster would not work.
[1 to 2 marks]
Level 2: There is a good explanation of the function of the live and neutral wires and why the fault would not allow a current to flow through the toaster.
[3 to 4 marks]

Here are some points your answer may include:
The purpose of the neutral wire is to complete the circuit.
Current flows into the toaster via the live wire, through the toaster, and out of the device by the neutral wire.
The fault means that a closed loop/low-resistance path has been formed between the live and neutral wire before the current in the live wire has reached the toaster.
So no (or very little) current will flow through the toaster.
This means that the toaster will not work.

2.1 To stop an electric current from flowing out of the live wire and potentially causing an electric shock (i.e. for safety) ***[1 mark]***. To make it easy to identify the live wire ***[1 mark]***.

2.2 The man has an electric potential of 0 V ***[1 mark]*** and the wire has an electric potential (of 230 V) so a potential difference exists between them ***[1 mark]***. This causes a current to flow through the man ***[1 mark]***.

2.3 Yes ***[1 mark]***. Although there is no current flowing when it is switched off, there is still a potential difference ***[1 mark]***, so touching the live wire in the socket could cause a current to flow through you to the Earth ***[1 mark]***.

Pages 25-26 — Power of Electrical Appliances

1 The **power** of an appliance is the energy transferred **per second**. Energy is transferred because the **current** does work against the appliance's resistance. ***[1 mark for each correct]***

2.1 $E = P \times t$ ***[1 mark]***

2.2 $E = 50 \times 20$ ***[1 mark]*** = **1000 J** ***[1 mark]***

2.3 The power of the car is higher *[1 mark]*. So more energy is transferred away from the chemical energy store of the battery per second *[1 mark]*.

3.1 Energy is transferred electrically from the power source *[1 mark]* to the thermal energy store of the water *[1 mark]* and the kinetic energy store of the motor *[1 mark]*.

3.2 Work done = power × time ($E = P \times t$)
Work done = 400 × 60 *[1 mark]* = **24 000 J** *[1 mark]*

3.3 Time of economy mode = 160 × 60 = 9600 s
Energy transferred in economy mode
= power × time = 400 × 9600 = 3 840 000 J *[1 mark]*
Time of standard mode = 125 × 60 = 7500 s
Energy transferred in standard mode = 600 × 7500
= 4 500 000 J *[1 mark]*
Energy saved = 4 500 000 – 3 840 000 *[1 mark]*
= **660 000 J** *[1 mark]*

4.1 How to grade your answer:
Level 0: There is no relevant information. *[No marks]*
Level 1: There are some relevant points, but the answer is unclear. There is some description of the experimental set-up, but the details are unclear. There are explanations of the measurements and calculations that should be made, but they may be incomplete. *[1 to 2 marks]*
Level 2: There is a clear description of how the equipment listed should be set up and used to carry out an experiment safely. There are full explanations of the measurements and calculations that should be made to determine the useful output power of the motor. *[3 to 4 marks]*
Here are some points your answer may include:
Securely attach the clamp stand to the edge of a bench/worktop.
Set up the motor so that it is connected to the circuit, and clamped to the clamp stand. Make sure there is at least a metre of clear space between the motor and the ground.
Attach one end of the string to the axle of the motor (so that it will wind around the axle when the motor spins).
Attach the other end of the string to the 1 kg mass securely, so it hangs from the string.
Set up the ruler to stand vertically, parallel to the string.
Attach a marker to the bottom of the mass so that the distance moved by the mass can be accurately measured.
Turn on the motor, and, using the stopwatch, record the time taken for the motor to lift the mass through a fixed vertical height, e.g. 60 cm, measured by the metre ruler.
Repeat this at least two more times, and calculate an average value of the time taken from the three results.
Use the height to calculate the change in gravitational potential energy of the mass, and so the useful energy transferred by the motor.
Calculate the useful power by dividing this value of energy by the average value of time taken.

4.2 0.01 s *[1 mark]*.

4.3 The errors in the student's time measurements will mostly be caused by human error and her reaction time *[1 mark]*. Human reaction times are typically much larger than the smallest time measured by the stopwatch (0.2-0.9 s compared to 0.01 s) *[1 mark]*.

Page 27 — More on Power

Warm-up
A power source supplies **energy** to a charge. When a charge passes through a component with **resistance**, it does **work**, so the charge's energy **decreases**.

1.1 $E = V \times Q$ *[1 mark]*

1.2 $E = 6 \times 2$ *[1 mark]* = **12 J** *[1 mark]*

1.3 Multiplying the potential difference by the current gives the power *[1 mark]*. In 1.2 the energy was transferred by the two coulombs of charge in one second *[1 mark]*. This is the same as the power *[1 mark]*.

2.1 $P = I \times V$
so $I = P \div V = 75 \div 230$ *[1 mark]* = 0.3260...
= **0.33 A (to 2 s.f.)** *[1 mark]*

2.2 $P = I^2 \times R$
so $R = P \div I^2 = 2.5 \div 0.50^2$ *[1 mark]* = **10 Ω** *[1 mark]*

Page 28 — The National Grid

1.1 Potential Difference *[1 mark]*, Current *[1 mark]*

1.2 A step-up transformer increases the potential difference, a step-down transformer decreases it *[1 mark]*.

2.1 Transformer A = step-up transformer *[1 mark]*
Transformer B = step-down transformer *[1 mark]*

2.2 How to grade your answer:
Level 0: There is no relevant information. *[No marks]*
Level 1: There is a brief explanation of the function of the step-up transformer and how this results in smaller energy losses. *[1 to 2 marks]*
Level 2: There is a good explanation of the function of the step-up transformer and how reducing the energy lost increases the efficiency of the national grid. *[3 to 4 marks]*
Here are some points your answer may include:
Transformer A increases the potential difference.
This decreases the current at a given power.
This decrease in current decreases energy lost to the thermal energy stores of the cables and surroundings.
Efficiency is useful output energy transfer ÷ total input energy transfer, so reducing the energy lost to thermal stores makes the transmission of electricity more efficient.

2.3 The potential difference across the power cables is very high and too large for domestic devices *[1 mark]*. Transformer B reduces the potential difference to lower, usable levels *[1 mark]*.

Page 29 — Static Electricity

1.1 The charges are alike *[1 mark]*. The balloons are repelling each other *[1 mark]*.

1.2 The balloons were rubbed against something, e.g. clothing/hair *[1 mark]*.
This wouldn't work if the balloons were rubbed against each other, as that would charge them up with opposite charges

2.1 Electrons *[1 mark]* are removed from the dusting cloth and transferred to the polythene rod *[1 mark]*.

2.2 The student could bring the dusting cloth towards one end of the rod *[1 mark]*. The rod should turn towards the cloth *[1 mark]*.

3.1 The man is charged, so there is a potential difference between him and the rail *[1 mark]*. When the potential difference is high enough, electrons jump across the gap to the rail, producing a spark *[1 mark]*.

3.2 Negatively charged *[1 mark]*. Only negative charges/electrons can move *[1 mark]* and they will move from an area of negative charge to an earthed area *[1 mark]*.

Page 30 — Electric Fields

1.1
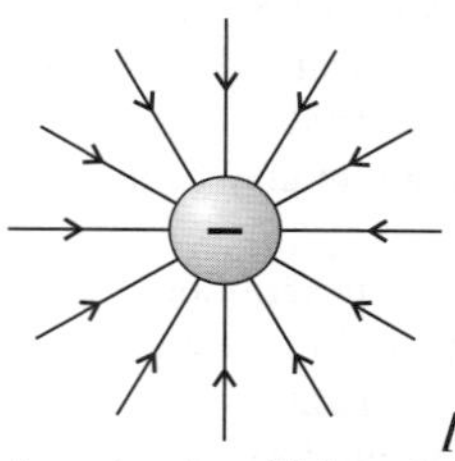

[1 mark]

1.2 A region in which a charged object will experience a force *[1 mark]*.

1.3 It decreases *[1 mark]*.

1.4 The second sphere is not charged ***[1 mark]***.
2.1 The size of the force increases ***[1 mark]***.
2.2 The negative charges are attracted towards the positive sphere, while the positive charges are attracted towards the negative sphere ***[1 mark]***. So parts of the particle are pulled away from each other ***[1 mark]***. When the potential difference is high enough, the force becomes large enough to break the particle apart ***[1 mark]***.

Topic 3 — Particle Model of Matter

Pages 31-32 — Density of Materials

Warm-up
From left to right: liquid, solid, gas

1.1 $\rho = m \div v$ ***[1 mark]***
1.2 $\rho = 10\,000 \div 0.5$ ***[1 mark]*** = **20 000 kg/m³** ***[1 mark]***
1.3 The density is the same for the whole block, so $\rho = 20\,000$ kg/m³
$\rho = m \div v$ so $m = \rho \times v$ ***[1 mark]***
$= 20\,000 \times 0.02$ ***[1 mark]*** = **400 kg** ***[1 mark]***
2 There is a smaller mass (and so fewer particles) in a given volume of ice than of water ***[1 mark]***. So the water molecules are further apart in ice than they are in liquid water ***[1 mark]***.

Substances are usually more dense as a solid than as a liquid, but water is an exception to this.

3.1 How to grade your answer:
Level 0: There is no relevant information. ***[No marks]***
Level 1: There is a brief description of how to measure the mass of the object and how to use this along with its volume to calculate its density. ***[1 to 2 marks]***
Level 2: There is a clear description of how to measure both the mass and volume of the object and how to use these values to calculate its density. ***[3 to 4 marks]***
Here are some points your answer may include:
First measure the mass of the object using a mass balance.
Then submerge the object in the water.
Measure the volume of water displaced using the scale on the measuring cylinder.
The volume of the displaced water in the measuring cylinder is equal to the volume of the object.
Use density = mass ÷ volume to calculate the density of the object.
3.2 $\rho = m \div v$
1 ml of water = 1 cm³ ***[1 mark]***
A: $\rho = 5.7 \div 0.30 = 19$ g/cm³. So A is gold. ***[1 mark]***
B: $\rho = 2.7 \div 0.60 = 4.5$ g/cm³. So B is titanium. ***[1 mark]***
C: $\rho = 3.0 \div 0.30 = 10$ g/cm³. So C is silver. ***[1 mark]***
4 Volume of empty aluminium can
= volume displaced by full can – volume of cola
= 337 – 332 = 5 ml ***[1 mark]***
5 ml = 5 cm³ ***[1 mark]***
$\rho = m \div v = 13.5 \div 5$ ***[1 mark]*** = **2.7 g/cm³** ***[1 mark]***

Page 33 — Internal Energy and Changes of State

1 When a system is heated, the internal energy of the system **increases**. This either increases the **temperature** of the system or causes a change of state. During a change of state the temperature and **mass** of the substance remain constant.
[2 marks for all correct, otherwise 1 mark for two correct]
2.1 Gas to liquid: condensing
Liquid to gas: evaporating/boiling ***[1 mark for both correct]***
2.2 E.g. a change where you don't end up with a new substance / you end up with the same substance in a different form ***[1 mark]***.
3.1 E.g. the energy stored in a system by its particles. / The sum of the energy in the particles' kinetic and potential energy stores ***[1 mark]***.
3.2 Any two from: mass, specific heat capacity, total energy transferred to the system ***[2 marks]***
4 10 g ***[1 mark]*** E.g. because when a substance changes state, its mass doesn't change. So the mass of the water vapour equals the mass of the water originally in the test tube ***[1 mark]***.

Pages 34-35 — Specific Latent Heat

1.1 The amount of energy required to change the state of one kilogram of a substance with no change in temperature ***[1 mark]***.
1.2 $E = mL$ so $L = E \div m$ ***[1 mark]***
$L = 1.13 \div 0.5$ ***[1 mark]*** = **2.26 MJ/kg** ***[1 mark]***
2.1 The substance is melting ***[1 mark]***.
2.2 As the substance is heated, its internal energy increases ***[1 mark]***. As the substance melts (during 3-8 minutes), all of this energy is used to break apart intermolecular bonds ***[1 mark]*** so there is no increase in the substance's temperature as it changes state ***[1 mark]***.
2.3 Melting point = –7 °C ***[1 mark]***
Boiling point = 58 °C ***[1 mark]***
3.1 Any two from: e.g. take temperature measurements at smaller time intervals / continue measuring after the first non-zero temperature measurement to be sure the ice has finished melting / find the mass of any remaining solid ice at the end of the experiment to determine the exact mass of ice that melted / use a temperature probe to automatically record temperature values at accurate times ***[2 marks]***.
3.2 Total energy required to melt the ice is given by $E = mL$
$E = 0.05 \times 334\,000 = 16\,700$ J ***[1 mark]***
The time in which energy was transferred to the ice and only caused the ice to melt is given by the flat part of the graph, since this is where the temperature didn't change. The flat part of the graph starts at 3 minutes, and finishes at 142 minutes. So the total time for the flat section
= 142 – 3 = 139 minutes = 139 × 60 = 8340 s ***[1 mark]***
So, average rate of energy transfer
= total energy transferred ÷ time taken for energy transfer
= 16 700 ÷ 8340 ***[1 mark]***
= 2.002...
= **2 J/s (to 1 s.f.)** ***[1 mark]***
3.3 The student is incorrect. For the second experiment to be a valid test of the experiment's repeatability, it has to be identical to the first experiment ***[1 mark]***. Since the student has used ice in a different form for the second experiment, the method and conditions are not the same, so the student cannot make conclusions about the first experiment's repeatability from the results ***[1 mark]***.

Pages 36-37 — Particle Motion in Gases

Warm-up
They are constantly moving in random directions at random speeds.

1 When the temperature of a gas increases, the average energy in the **kinetic** energy stores of the gas molecules increases. This **increases** the **average** speed of the gas molecules. If the gas is kept at a constant volume, increasing the temperature **increases** the pressure.
[3 marks for all correct, otherwise 1 mark for two correct or 2 marks for three correct]
2.1 pV = constant
$8.0 \times 10^{-4} \times 50 \times 10^{3} = 40$ ***[1 mark]***
So $p = 40 \div (1.6 \times 10^{-4})$ ***[1 mark]*** = 250 000 = **250 kPa** ***[1 mark]***

2.2

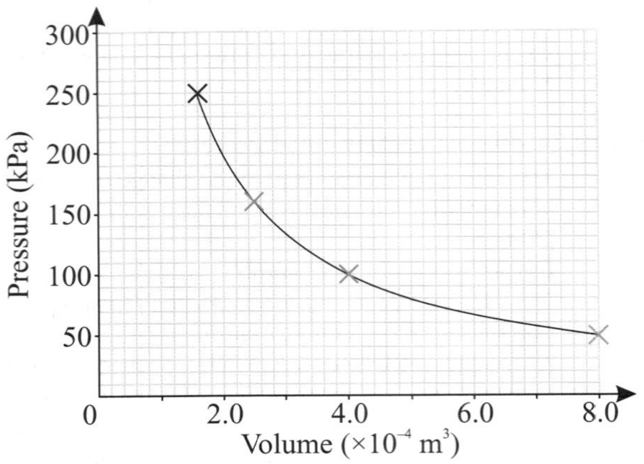

[1 mark for correctly plotted point, 1 mark for a curved line connecting them]

3 E.g. a gas is made of particles ***[1 mark]***. The particles collide with each other and the sides of the container they are in, which exerts a force on the sides of the container ***[1 mark]***. The total force per unit area exerted on the container is the gas pressure ***[1 mark]***. As the volume is increased, the gas particles spread out more ***[1 mark]***. This means that there are fewer collisions with the sides of the container in a given time, so the pressure is lower ***[1 mark]***.

4 How to grade your answer:
Level 0: There is no relevant information. ***[No marks]***
Level 1: There is a brief explanation of how work is done on the air. ***[1 to 2 marks]***
Level 2: There is some explanation of how doing work on the air increases its temperature.
[3 to 4 marks]
Level 3: There is a clear and detailed explanation of how doing work on the air transfers energy to the particles in the air and how it causes an increase in temperature.
[5 to 6 marks]
Here are some points your answer may include:
To compress the air, work must be done.
This work is done against the force caused by the pressure of the air in the piston.
Doing work causes a transfer of energy.
Energy is transferred to the internal energy of the system.
So energy is transferred to the kinetic energy stores of the air particles in the system.
This increases the temperature of the air/gas.
Because temperature of a gas is related to the average energy in the kinetic energy stores of the gas molecules.
So doing work on the gas increases its temperature.

Topic 4 — Atomic Structure

Pages 38-39 — Developing the Model of the Atom

Warm-up
1×10^{-10} m
10 000

1.1 Our current model shows that the atom can be broken up (into protons, neutrons and electrons) ***[1 mark]***.

1.2 The plum pudding model ***[1 mark]***. This was where an atom was thought to be a sphere of positive charge, with electrons spread throughout it ***[1 mark]***.

1.3 The neutron ***[1 mark]***.

2.1 An electron can move into a higher energy level / further from the nucleus, by absorbing EM radiation ***[1 mark]***, and move into a lower energy level / closer to the nucleus, by emitting EM radiation ***[1 mark]***.

2.2 ion ***[1 mark]***

2.3 Positive (or +1) ***[1 mark]***

An atom is neutral. Losing an electron takes away negative charge, so the remaining ion is positive.

3 Level 0: There is no relevant information. ***[No marks]***
Level 1: There is only one correct discovery mentioned with a brief description of the observation that led to it.
[1 to 2 marks]
Level 2: Two correct discoveries are given with a detailed description of how observations led to them.
[3 to 4 marks]
Here are some points your answer may include:
Discovery: The atom is mostly made up of empty space / most of the atom's mass is concentrated at the centre in a tiny nucleus.
Observation: Most of the alpha particles fired at the thin gold foil passed straight through.
Discovery: The atom has a positively charged central nucleus.
Observation: Some of the positive alpha particles were deflected back towards the emitter, so they were repelled by the nucleus.

4.1 Proton: (+)1 ***[1 mark]***
Neutron: 0 ***[1 mark]***

4.2 The protons and neutrons are in the central nucleus ***[1 mark]*** and the electrons surround the nucleus (arranged in shells) ***[1 mark]***.

4.3 26 electrons ***[1 mark]***. Atoms are neutral ***[1 mark]***. Protons and electrons have equal but opposite charges. For these charges to cancel, there must be the same number of each ***[1 mark]***.

Pages 40-42 — Isotopes and Nuclear Radiation

Warm-up
Gamma — weakly ionising, alpha — strongly ionising,
beta — moderately ionising.

1.1 radioactive decay ***[1 mark]***

1.2 Atoms with the same number of protons ***[1 mark]*** but different numbers of neutrons (in their nucleus) ***[1 mark]***

1.3 An atom losing (or gaining) at least one electron ***[1 mark]***.

1.4 Alpha decay ***[1 mark]***

2 E.g. Alpha particles have a small range in air and will be stopped by a thin sheet of material ***[1 mark]***. So the alpha radiation inside the detector cannot escape the detector ***[1 mark]***.

3.1 23 ***[1 mark]***

Remember that the mass number is the little number in the top-left. It's the total number of protons and neutrons in the nucleus.

3.2 23 – 11 = 12 neutrons ***[1 mark]***

The number of neutrons is the difference between the mass number and the atomic number.

3.3 ${}^{24}_{11}\text{Na}$ ***[1 mark]***

An isotope has the same number of protons (so the same atomic number), but a different number of neutrons (so a different mass number).

3.4 The atomic number of the neon isotope is lower, so there are fewer protons in the neon isotope ***[1 mark]***. So the charge on the neon isotope's nucleus is lower than the charge on the sodium isotope's nucleus ***[1 mark]***.

4 How to grade your answer:
Level 0: There is no relevant information. ***[No marks]***
Level 1: There is a brief explanation of the method of locating the leak and of the radiation used.
[1 to 2 marks]
Level 2: There is some explanation of the method of locating the leak and of the radiation used.
[3 to 4 marks]
Level 3: There is a clear and detailed explanation of the method of locating the leak and of the radiation used. ***[5 to 6 marks]***
Here are some points your answer may include:
The isotope travels along the pipe.
If there is no leak, the radiation doesn't escape the pipe/not much radiation can escape the pipe/some of the radiation is blocked by the pipe.
If there is a leak, the isotope escapes the pipe and some/more radiation can reach the detector.

This causes the count-rate to increase.
An increase in count-rate indicates a leak.
The isotope could be beta-emitting because beta radiation would be blocked by the pipe but would not be blocked by the small amount of ground above the pipe.
OR The isotope could be gamma-emitting because it can escape the pipe and reach the detector, and more gamma radiation would get to the detector if there was a leak.

5.1 For 0.5 mm thickness:
uncertainty = range ÷ 2 = (122 – 99) ÷ 2 = **11.5** ***[1 mark]***
For 0.6 mm thickness:
mean = (93 + 95 + 98) ÷ 3
= 95.33... = **95 (to nearest whole number)** ***[1 mark]***

5.2 The results for a thickness of 0.6 mm are the most precise, as they have the smallest range / they have the smallest uncertainty / the individual results are closest to the mean value for count-rate ***[1 mark]***. It's not possible to know whether they are the most accurate, as you can't tell from the data how close to the true value the measurements are ***[1 mark]***.

5.3 E.g. the thicker the paper, the less beta radiation reaches the detector / the more beta radiation is absorbed by the paper ***[1 mark]***.

5.4 If the half-life was shorter than or close to the duration of the experiment, the count-rate would reduce significantly during the experiment ***[1 mark]***, and it would not be possible to conclude if a decrease in count-rate was due to the paper or the decay of the substance ***[1 mark]***.

Page 43 — Nuclear Equations

1.1 It increases the positive charge on the nucleus / makes the nucleus 'more positive' ***[1 mark]***.

1.2 The atomic number increases ***[1 mark]*** but the mass number stays the same ***[1 mark]***. This is because emitting an electron (beta decay) involves a neutron turning into a proton ***[1 mark]***.

Remember that a neutron turns into a proton in order to increase the positive charge on the nucleus. (Because emitting the electron has taken away some negative charge.)

1.3 No effect ***[1 mark]***

When an electron moves to a lower energy level, it loses energy in the form of an EM wave, which doesn't change the charge or mass of the nucleus.

2.1 The atomic numbers on each side are not equal ***[1 mark]***.

2.2 ${}^{0}_{-1}\text{e}$ ***[1 mark]***

The other particle must be an electron (a beta particle), as this will balance the equation.

2.3 ${}^{226}_{88}\text{Ra} \longrightarrow {}^{222}_{86}\text{Rn} + {}^{4}_{2}\text{He}$

[3 marks in total — 1 mark for each correct symbol]

You know that the mass number of the radium is 226 (that's what 'radium-226' means). You also know that an alpha particle is ${}^{4}_{2}He$, so you can find the mass and atomic numbers of radon by balancing the equation.

2.4 Rn-222 has 222 – 86 = 136 neutrons ***[1 mark]***
2 alpha decays = 2 × 2 = 4 neutrons released ***[1 mark]***
136 – 4 = **132** ***[1 mark]***

Pages 44-45 — Half-life

1.1 E.g. the time taken for the count-rate of a sample to halve ***[1 mark]***.

1.2 75 seconds ***[1 mark]***

The initial count-rate is 60 cps. Half of this is 30 cps, which corresponds to 75 seconds on the time axis.

1.3 After 1 half-life, there will be 800 ÷ 2 = 400 undecayed nuclei remaining. After 2 half-lives, there will be 400 ÷ 2 = 200 undecayed nuclei remaining.
So 800 – 200 = **600** nuclei will have decayed.
[2 marks for correct answer, otherwise 1 mark for calculating the number of decayed/undecayed nuclei after one half-life]

1.4 After 2 half-lives, there are 200 undecayed nuclei.
The ratio is 200:800,
which simplifies to **1:4** ***[1 mark]***

You don't even need the numbers to work out this ratio. For any radioactive isotope, after two half lives, the initial number of undecayed nuclei will have halved and then halved again. It will be one quarter of the original number, so the ratio is always 1:4.

2 Isotope 1, because more nuclei will decay per second ***[1 mark]***.

3.1 It takes a total of 2 hours and 30 minutes for the activity to halve from 8800 Bq to 4400 Bq,
so its half-life = (2 × 60) + 30 = **150 minutes** ***[1 mark]***

3.2 Check how many half-lives pass during 6 hours and 15 minutes:
6 hours and 15 minutes = (6 × 60) + 15 = 375 minutes
375 ÷ 150 = 2.5 half-lives
The activity can only be worked out if a whole number of half-lives have passed, so calculate how many half-lives have passed from the time when activity = 6222 Bq:
1 hour 15 minutes = 60 + 15 = 75 minutes
375 – 75 = 300 minutes
300 ÷ 150 = 2 half-lives.
So now you can calculate the activity after 2 half-lives, with an initial activity of 6222 Bq:
After 1 half-life, the activity will be 6222 ÷ 2 = 3111 Bq
After 2 half-lives, the activity will be 3111 ÷ 2 = 1555.5 Bq
1555.5 = **1600 Bq (to 2 s.f.)**
[2 marks for correct answer, otherwise 1 mark for finding how many half-lives will have passed between 1 hour and 15 minutes and 6 hours and 15 minutes]

4.1

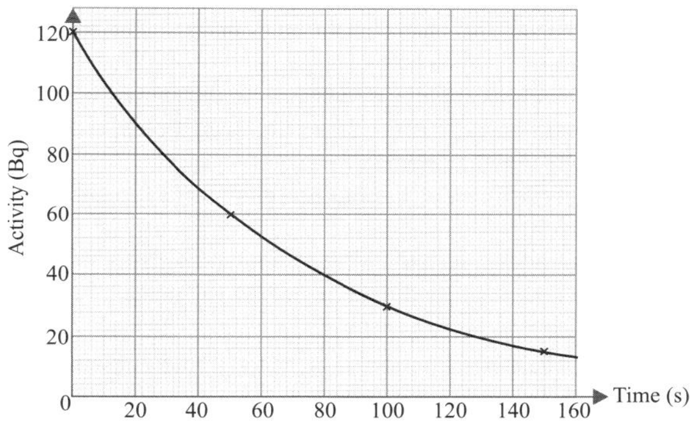

[3 marks in total — 2 marks for all points plotted correctly, otherwise 1 mark for three points plotted correctly, 1 mark for smooth curve.]

Start the graph at 120 Bq. After 50 s, this will have halved to 60 Bq. After another 50 s (i.e. 100 s altogether), it will have halved again, to 30 Bq. Plot these points, then join them up with a nice smooth curve.

4.2 70 Bq (accept between 68 Bq and 72 Bq)
[1 mark for correct value from your graph]

4.3 After 200 s, 15 ÷ 2 = 7.5 Bq
After 250 s, 7.5 ÷ 2 = **3.75 Bq** ***[1 mark]***
E.g. radioactive decay is random ***[1 mark]*** and the effect of randomness on the activity will be greater for lower activities ***[1 mark]***.

Pages 46-48 — Background Radiation and Contamination

Warm-up
E.g. cosmic rays / rocks

1 Any two from: e.g. using shielding / working in a different room to the radioactive source / using remote-controlled arms to handle sources / wearing protective suits ***[2 marks]***

2.1 Low-level radiation which is around us all of the time.
[1 mark]

2.2 Systematic error *[1 mark]*. If she doesn't subtract the background radiation, her results will all be too large by the same amount *[1 mark]*.

This assumes that the background level is constant for the duration of her experiment. This is a reasonable assumption, as long as she carries out the experiment in the same location under the same conditions each time.

2.3 Radiation dose ***[1 mark]***

2.4 E.g. Where you live / your job ***[1 mark for both correct]***

3.1 Contamination is when unwanted radioactive particles get onto an object ***[1 mark]***. Irradiation is when an object is exposed to radiation ***[1 mark]***.

3.2 E.g. keeping the sample in a protective box / standing behind a protective barrier ***[1 mark]***

3.3 Any two from: e.g. wearing protective gloves / using tongs / wearing a protective suit or mask ***[2 marks]***.

4 How to grade your answer:
Level 0: There is no relevant information. ***[No marks]***
Level 1: There is a brief explanation of the dangers of contamination or radiation. ***[1 to 2 marks]***
Level 2: There is some explanation of the dangers and risks of contamination and radiation. ***[3 to 4 marks]***
Level 3: There is a clear and detailed explanation of the dangers and risks of contamination and radiation, used to justify the conclusion that the clockmaker should be more concerned about contamination. ***[5 to 6 marks]***
Here are some points your answer may include:
Alpha particles are strongly ionising.
Alpha particles are stopped by skin or thin paper.
Being irradiated won't make the clockmaker radioactive.
But irradiation may do some damage to his skin.
However, the radiation cannot penetrate his body and cause damage to his tissue or organs.
If the clockmaker's hands get contaminated with radium-226, he will be exposed to more alpha particles, close to his skin.
Or he may accidentally ingest (eat) some.
Or if particles of the radium get into the air, he could breathe them in.
The radium will then decay whilst inside his body.
This means that the alpha particles can do lots of damage to nearby tissue or organs.
So he should be more concerned about contamination.

5.1 E.g. the student's radioactive source could contribute to the count-rate recorded, but would not be present during the scientist's experiment, causing an overestimate in the background count-rate ***[1 mark]***.

5.2 First, find the mean counts in 5 minutes.
Mean counts = (598 + 641 + 624) ÷ 3 ***[1 mark]***
= 621 ***[1 mark]***
To get count-rate in cps, divide by the number of seconds in 5 minutes.
mean count-rate = 621 ÷ (5 × 60) = **2.07 cps** ***[1 mark]***

Alternatively, you could add the three counts together and divide by the number of seconds in fifteen minutes — i.e. combining the steps.

5.3 E.g. put the radioactive substance back into its storage case while replacing the Geiger-Muller tube / place a shielding barrier around the radioactive substance while replacing the Geiger-Muller tube ***[1 mark]***.

5.4 The scientist's results will be less valid, as changing the distance may change the count-rate detected / the distance between the substance and the Geiger-Muller tube was a control variable in the experiment ***[1 mark]***, so the results won't be valid as a measure of only how the count-rate varies with time, and cannot be used to accurately calculate the half-life ***[1 mark]***.

Page 49 — Uses and Risk

Warm-up

Radiation can cause cells to **mutate** or **die**, which can cause cancer or radiation sickness. Radiation can also be used to treat **cancer** and to **diagnose** illnesses.

1.1 Gamma ***[1 mark]***

1.2 E.g. the gamma rays could cause damage to healthy cells ***[1 mark]***. Rotating the beam ensures healthy cells nearby get a lower dose of radiation ***[1 mark]***.

2.1 Iodine-123 could be injected into or swallowed by the patient, where it would be absorbed by their thyroid ***[1 mark]***. The iodine would then decay, giving off radiation that could be detected outside the body ***[1 mark]***. The amount of radiation detected could then be used to find how much iodine has been absorbed by the thyroid, to check whether or not the thyroid is overactive ***[1 mark]***.

2.2 Because alpha radiation would be too dangerous inside the body ***[1 mark]*** and it would not be detectable outside the body, as it cannot penetrate tissue ***[1 mark]***.

2.3 A short half-life means the activity will quickly drop, so the patient will not be exposed to radiation for too long ***[1 mark]***.

Page 50 — Fission and Fusion

1 Both statements are true ***[1 mark]***.

2 Similarity: E.g. they both release energy ***[1 mark]***.
Difference: E.g. fission is the splitting of a large nucleus to form a smaller nuclei, whereas fusion is the joining of smaller nuclei to form a larger one ***[1 mark]***.

3.1 How to grade your answer:
Level 0: There is no relevant information. ***[No marks]***
Level 1: There is a brief explanation of nuclear fission and that a neutron can start the fission reaction. ***[1 to 2 marks]***
Level 2: There is a detailed explanation of how a neutron starts a forced fission reaction, what a fission reaction is and how this leads to a chain reaction. ***[3 to 4 marks]***
Here are some points your answer may include:
Absorbing a neutron makes the nucleus more unstable.
The unstable nucleus undergoes fission.
Fission is the splitting of an unstable nucleus into two lighter elements and releasing two or three neutrons.
These neutrons can be absorbed by other nuclei, causing more fission.
Each decay can cause another decay to happen, which is a chain reaction.

3.2 E.g. each fission decay releases energy ***[1 mark]*** so an uncontrolled chain reaction would release lots of energy, which could lead to reactor meltdown/an explosion ***[1 mark]***.

Topic 5 — Forces

Page 51 — Contact and Non-Contact Forces

Warm-up

Scalar — mass, time, temperature

Vector — acceleration, weight, force

1 Vector quantities have both magnitude and direction. ***[1 mark]***

2 Contact force: e.g. friction / tension / normal contact force / air resistance ***[1 mark]***
Non-contact force: e.g. weight / gravitational force ***[1 mark]***

3.1

[1 mark for correct arrow length, 1 mark for correct direction]

3.2 Both arrows need to be longer (to indicate the stronger interaction) ***[1 mark]***.
The arrows need to be the same size as each other ***[1 mark]***.

Pages 52-53 — Weight, Mass and Gravity

1 **Mass** is the amount of matter in an object. **Weight** is a force due to gravity. Mass is measured **kilograms** whilst weight is measured in **newtons**. The weight of an object is **directly** proportional to its mass. ***[3 marks for all correct, 2 marks for 3-4 correct, 1 mark for 1-2 correct]***

2 A point at which you can assume the whole mass of an object is concentrated. / The point from which the weight of an object can be assumed to act. ***[1 mark]***

3.1 $W = mg$ ***[1 mark]***

3.2 $W = 350 \times 9.8$ ***[1 mark]*** = **3430 N** ***[1 mark]***

3.3 New mass = 350 – 209 = 141 kg ***[1 mark]***
$W = mg = 141 \times 3.8$ ***[1 mark]*** = 535.8
= **536 N (to 3 s.f.)** ***[1 mark]***

4.1 E.g. the standard mass may no longer have the same mass as it is labelled with ***[1 mark]***.

This is because some of the rusted standard mass is made of a different substance (the rust) instead of pure iron as when it was originally measured and labelled. Also, the rust could flake off the standard mass, leaving it with a lower mass than before.

4.2 Systematic error ***[1 mark]***, because the weight of the plastic tray will be included in each of the weight measurements, making them all too large by the same amount ***[1 mark]***.

4.3 E.g.

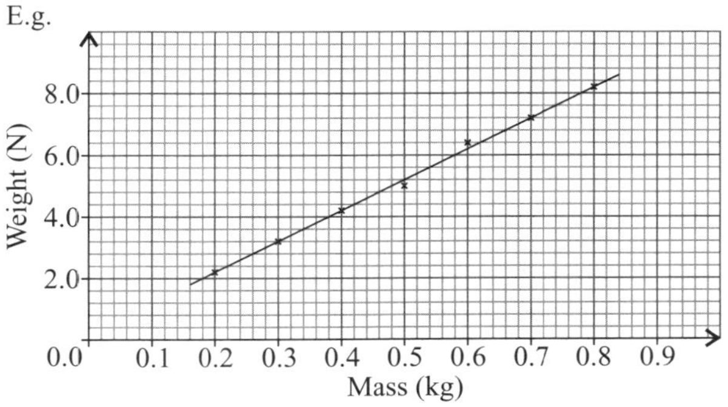

[1 mark for all points plotted correctly and 1 mark for a straight line of best fit drawn through or close to all points]

4.4 Since $W = mg$, by comparing this to the equation for a straight-line graph, $y = mx + c$, you can see that the gravitational field strength, g, is equal to the gradient of the graph, m ***[1 mark]***.

E.g. $g = \frac{\text{change in } y}{\text{change in } x} = \frac{8.4 - 2.0}{0.82 - 0.18}$ ***[1 mark]***
= **10 N/kg** ***[1 mark]***

You'll get the calculation marks here as long as your calculation of the gradient is correct for your line of best fit.

Page 54 — Resultant Forces and Work Done

1 C ***[1 mark]***

The resultant force is the sum of the two forces acting on each runner, taking into account the direction. For runner C, the resultant force is 130 N – 100 N = 30 N.

2.1 $W = Fs = 50 \times 15$ ***[1 mark]*** = **750** ***[1 mark]***
Unit: **J** or **Nm** ***[1 mark]***

2.2 The temperature of the suitcase increases ***[1 mark]*** because doing work causes some energy to be transferred to the thermal energy store of the suitcase ***[1 mark]***.

3.1 100 N ***[1 mark]***

As the ladder isn't moving, the resultant force is zero, and so the weight of the ladder is equal to the normal contact force acting on the ladder.

3.2

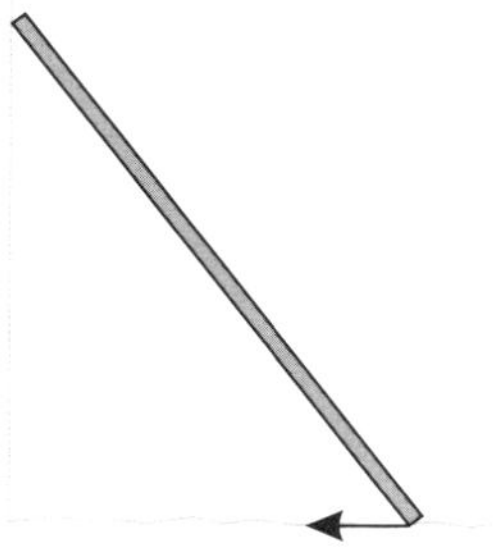

[1 mark for correct arrow length (same as 30 N arrow length), 1 mark for correct direction]

Page 55 — Calculating Forces

Warm-up

Horizontal component = 4 N

Vertical component = 3 N

1.1 1 cm = 100 N ***[1 mark]***

1.2

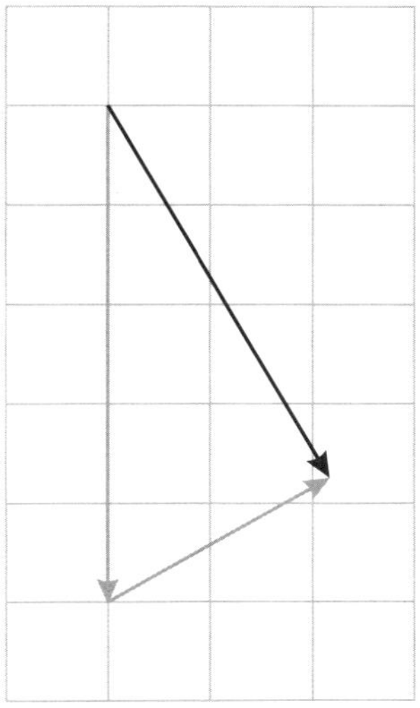

Magnitude = **430 N**

[1 mark for correct construction of resultant force, 1 mark for correct magnitude]

Page 56 — Forces and Elasticity

1.1 Elastic deformation is when an object returns to its original size after the deforming force is removed ***[1 mark]***. Inelastic deformation is when an object has been deformed such that it cannot return to its original size or shape after the deforming force is removed ***[1 mark]***.

1.2 Compressing, bending ***[1 mark for both correct]***

2.1 $F = ke$ so $k = F \div e$
e = 20 cm = 0.2 m
so $k = 250 \div 0.2$ ***[1 mark]*** = **1250** ***[1 mark]***
Unit = **N/m** ***[1 mark]***

2.2 E.g. Agree — the extension will be 40 cm, because force is proportional to extension, so doubling the force doubles the extension ***[1 mark]***, assuming that the spring hasn't gone past its limit of proportionality ***[1 mark]***.

Page 57 — Investigating Springs

1.1

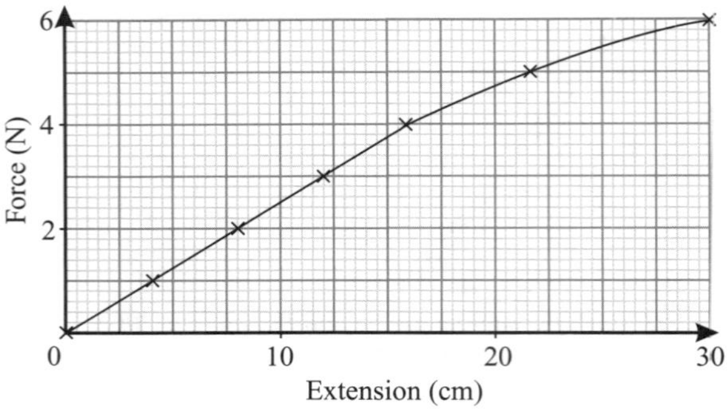

[1 mark for points plotted correctly, 1 mark for line of best fit showing linear relationship at the start, 1 mark for curved line of best fit towards the end of the graph]

1.2 Spring constant = Force ÷ Extension
= gradient of the linear section of the graph
$k = 3 \div 0.12 =$ **25 N/m**
[2 marks for correct answer between 24 and 26 N/m, otherwise 1 mark for correct calculation]

2 Work done on spring = energy stored in the spring's elastic potential energy store
$E = \frac{1}{2}ke^2 = \frac{1}{2} \times 25 \times 0.08^2$ ***[1 mark]*** = **0.08 J** ***[1 mark]***

Pages 58-59 — Moments

1 $M = Fd = 50 \times 0.12$ ***[1 mark]*** = **6 Nm** ***[1 mark]***

2.1 Gear B: clockwise ***[1 mark]***
Gear C: anticlockwise ***[1 mark]***

2.2 faster than gear A ***[1 mark]***

3 Anticlockwise moment:
$320 \times 1 = 320$ Nm
$365 \times (1 + 1) = 730$ Nm
$320 + 730 = 1050$ Nm ***[1 mark]***
Total anticlockwise moment must equal the total clockwise moment for the seesaw to balance.
$Fd = 1050$ Nm ***[1 mark]***
$d = 1050 \div 350 =$ **3 m** ***[1 mark]***

4.1 How to grade your answer:
Level 0: There is no relevant information. ***[No marks]***
Level 1: There is some description of the experimental set-up and the measurements that should be made, but it may be incomplete and the details are unclear. ***[1 to 2 marks]***
Level 2: There is a description of how the equipment shown should be used to carry out an experiment. There is a discussion of the measurements and calculations that should be made to confirm the principle of moments. The points made may not be in a logical order. ***[3 to 4 marks]***
Level 3: There is a clear and logical description of how the equipment shown should be used to carry out an experiment. There is a full explanation of the measurements and calculations that should be made to confirm the principle of moments. ***[5 to 6 marks]***

Here are some points your answer may include:
Hang a 100 g hanging mass on the left arm of the bar, and record its mass and distance from the pivot.
Hang another 100 g hanging mass from the right arm of the bar at any distance from the pivot. Observe whether the bar becomes balanced (i.e. becomes horizontal).
Move the mass on the right arm of the bar to hang at different distances from the pivot. Record the mass and any distance from the pivot where the mass balances the bar.
Add another 100 g mass to the hanging mass (so the total mass is 200 g) on the right arm. Again, move this mass along the right bar until the bar is balanced. Record the mass and the distance from the pivot.
Repeat the balancing process for different masses hung on the right arm of the bar (by adding more 100 g masses to the hanging mass on the right arm).
Change the distance of the mass on the left arm of the bar, or the mass hanging from the left arm of the bar, and repeat the whole balancing process by adding and moving masses to the right arm of the bar.
Repeat this for a number (e.g. 3-5) of different distances or masses on the left arm of the bar.
Calculate the moments for each pair of balanced masses you recorded using $M = FD$. (Masses placed on the left arm will produce anticlockwise moments, masses on the right arm will produce clockwise moments.)
Compare each anticlockwise moment to the clockwise moments that balanced it.
Each clockwise moment should equal the anticlockwise moment.
This confirms the principle of moments.

4.2 It will make sure that the bar is able to rotate freely about the pivot ***[1 mark]***, so the bar can only be balanced due to the moments that are being applied by the student (rather than any resistive forces acting at the pivot) ***[1 mark]***.

Pages 60-61 — Fluid Pressure

Warm-up
Liquids and **gases** are both fluids. Fluid pressure is the force exerted **perpendicular** to a surface, per unit **area**. The unit of pressure is **pascals**.

1.1 $p = F \div A$ ***[1 mark]***

1.2 $p = 12 \div 0.15$ ***[1 mark]*** = **80 Pa** ***[1 mark]***

2 Pressure increases with depth ***[1 mark]*** because at a greater depth there are more water molecules above a surface and their weight contributes to the pressure ***[1 mark]***. This causes the force pushing the water out of the spouting tank to be larger, so more water leaves the lowest spout in a given time ***[1 mark]***.

3 Pressure at a given depth depends on the density of the liquid ***[1 mark]***. Sea water has a higher density than fresh water, so the diver experiences a higher pressure ***[1 mark]***.

4.1 $A = 0.025 \times 0.025 = 0.000625$ m^2 ***[1 mark]***
$p = F \div A = 100 \div 0.000625$ ***[1 mark]***
= **160 000 Pa** ***[1 mark]***

4.2 $F = p \times A = 160\,000 \times 0.005$ ***[1 mark]*** = 800 N
800×4 ***[1 mark]*** = **3200 N** ***[1 mark]***

5 $p = h\rho g$
p at X = $0.040 \times 1.0 \times 10^3 \times 9.8 = 392$ Pa ***[1 mark]***
p at base = $0.300 \times 1.0 \times 10^3 \times 9.8 = 2940$ Pa ***[1 mark]***
$2940 - 392 = 2548 =$ **2500 Pa (to 2 s.f.)** ***[1 mark]***

Page 62 — Upthrust and Atmospheric Pressure

1 In a liquid, pressure **increases** with depth. This means that the force acting on the bottom of a submerged object is **larger** than the force acting on the top of the object. This leads to a resultant force called **upthrust**.
[2 marks for all three correct, otherwise 1 mark for one or two correct]

2 When the ball is submerged in the water, upthrust acts upon the ball ***[1 mark]***. This is a force that acts in the opposite direction to the ball's weight ***[1 mark]*** so combining these forces leads to the ball appearing to weigh less ***[1 mark]***.

3 The upthrust acting on the necklace is equal to the weight of the water that the necklace displaces ***[1 mark]***. Water has a much lower density than silver, so the weight of the displaced water is less than the weight of the necklace ***[1 mark]***. This means that the upthrust acting on the necklace is less than its weight, so it sinks ***[1 mark]***.

4 How to grade your answer:
Level 0: There is no relevant information. ***[No marks]***
Level 1: There is a brief explanation of the cause of atmospheric pressure. ***[1 to 2 marks]***

Level 2: There is some explanation of why atmospheric pressure decreases with altitude. ***[3 to 4 marks]***
Level 3: There is a clear and detailed explanation of why atmospheric pressure decreases with altitude. ***[5 to 6 marks]***
Here are some points your answer may include:
The atmosphere is a relatively thin layer of air around the earth.
Atmospheric pressure is caused by air molecules colliding with a surface, which exerts a force on the surface.
As altitude increases, the atmosphere gets less dense (there are fewer air molecules in a given volume).
This means that there are fewer air molecules to collide with a surface, so the force and pressure exerted decrease.
The weight of the air molecules above a surface also contributes to atmospheric pressure.
Because there are fewer air molecules as altitude increases, the weight of the air above a surface will also decrease. So the atmospheric pressure decreases too.

Pages 63-64 — Distance, Displacement, Speed and Velocity

Warm-up
Displacement and **velocity** are both **vector** quantities. This means they have both a size and a direction. Speed and **distance** are both **scalar** quantities. They do not depend on direction.

1.1 7 m ***[1 mark]***
1.2 12 m ***[1 mark]***
1.3

[1 mark for arrow of correct length in the correct direction]

1.4 2 m ***[1 mark]***
2 330 m/s ***[1 mark]***
3 Any three from: fitness / age / distance travelled / terrain ***[3 marks — 1 mark for each correct answer]***
4 No — velocity is speed in a given direction ***[1 mark]***. The satellite travels at a constant speed, but is always changing direction so its velocity is always changing ***[1 mark]***.
5.1 $s = vt$ ***[1 mark]***
5.2 Typical walking speed = 1.5 m/s (accept 1-2 m/s) ***[1 mark]***
$t = s \div v = 6000 \div 1.5$ ***[1 mark]***
$= \mathbf{4000\ s}$ (accept 3000-6000 s) ***[1 mark]***
5.3 Typical cycling speed = 6 m/s (accept 5-7 m/s) ***[1 mark]***
$s = vt$ so $t = s \div v = 6000 \div 6$ ***[1 mark]*** = 1000 s ***[1 mark]***
4000 – 1000 = **3000 s** (accept 1800-5200) ***[1 mark]***
5.4 $t = 20 \times 60 = 1200$ s ***[1 mark]***
$s = vt$ so $v = s \div t = 9600 \div 1200$ ***[1 mark]*** = **8 m/s** ***[1 mark]***
6 Speed of sound = 331 + (0.6 × –60) = 295 m/s ***[1 mark]***
Jet speed = 0.80 × 295 = 236 m/s ***[1 mark]***
$s = vt$
$= 236 \times 5.0 \times 10^4$ ***[1 mark]***
= 11 800 000 m = **11 800 km** ***[1 mark]***

Page 65 — Acceleration

Warm-up
A sprinter starting a race — 1.5 m/s^2
A falling object — 10 m/s^2
A bullet shot from a gun — 2×10^5 m/s^2

1 The object is slowing down ***[1 mark]***.
2.1 $a = \Delta v \div t$ ***[1 mark]***
2.2 $a = \Delta v \div t = 4 \div 1$ ***[1 mark]*** = **4 m/s^2** ***[1 mark]***
3 $a = \Delta v \div t$
$t = \Delta v \div a$ ***[1 mark]*** $= 20 \div 2.5$ ***[1 mark]*** = **8 s** ***[1 mark]***
4 $v^2 - u^2 = 2as$ so
$a = (v^2 - u^2) \div 2s = (18^2 - 32^2) \div (2 \times 365)$ ***[1 mark]***
= –0.9589...
So deceleration = 1.0 m/s^2 (to 2 s.f.) ***[1 mark]***

Pages 66-69 — Distance-Time and Velocity-Time Graphs

1.1

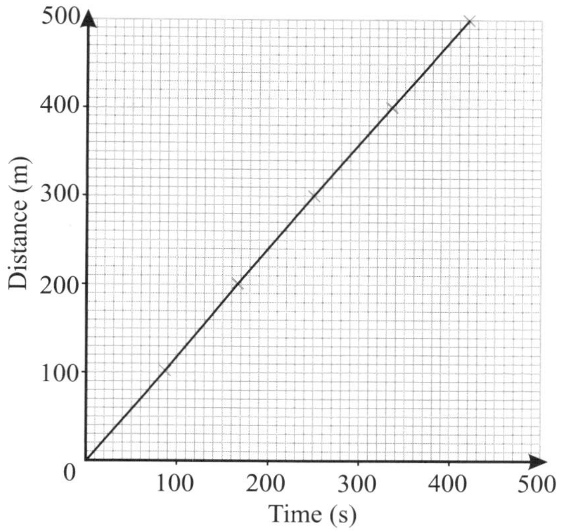

[3 marks for graph plotted correctly, otherwise 1 mark for three points correct, 1 mark for any suitable straight line]

1.2 360 m (accept between 350 m and 370 m) ***[1 mark]***
1.3 210 s (accept between 200 s and 220 s) ***[1 mark]***
1.4 E.g. refer to the same point on the boat / make sure that the timings are measured from exactly level with the posts / make sure timings are made close to the posts to avoid parallax / use a stopwatch instead of a watch ***[1 mark for any correct answer]***
2.1 12 minutes ***[1 mark]***
2.2 Accelerating ***[1 mark]***
3.1 $v = \Delta s \div t$ = gradient of line
Speed = (92 – 20) ÷ (6 – 3) = 72 ÷ 3 = **24 m/s**
(accept between 23 m/s and 25 m/s)
[3 marks for correct answer, otherwise 1 mark for realising speed is the gradient of the line, 1 mark for correct calculation]
3.2 Speed = gradient of a tangent to the line
$v = \Delta s \div \Delta t = (16 - 0) \div (3 - 1) = 16 \div 2 =$ **8 m/s**
(accept between 6 m/s and 10 m/s)
[3 marks for correct answer, otherwise 1 mark for a correct tangent to the line, 1 mark for correct calculation]
4.1

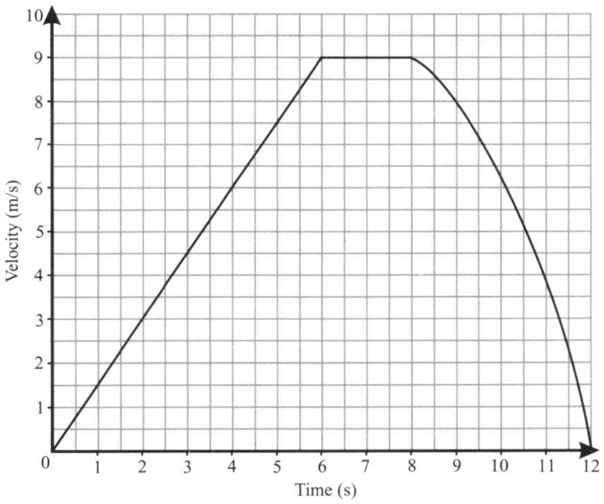

[1 mark for correct shape of graph, 1 mark for graph ending at 0 m/s]

4.2 $a = \Delta v \div t$ = gradient of the line
Acceleration = (9 – 0) ÷ (6 – 0) = **1.5 m/s^2**
[2 marks for correct answer, otherwise 1 mark for correct calculation]
4.3 $s = vt$ = area under the line ***[1 mark]***
0-6 s: area = ½bh = ½ × 6 × 9 = 27 m ***[1 mark]***
6-8 s: area = bh = 2 × 9 = 18 m ***[1 mark]***
Total distance in 8 s = 27 + 18 = **45 m** ***[1 mark]***

4.4 1 square is worth 0.5 s on the x-axis (time)
1 square is worth 0.5 m/s on the y-axis (velocity)
[1 mark for both correct]
$s = vt = 0.5 \times 0.5 = 0.25$ m ***[1 mark]***
Squares under the line between 8 s and 12 s = 91 ***[1 mark]***
$91 \times 0.25 = 22.75$ m ***[1 mark]***
Total distance = 45 + 22.75 = 67.75 = **68 m** ***[1 mark]***
(accept between 63 and 72 m)

5.1 The instantaneous acceleration can be found by finding the gradient of a tangent drawn at that point. So, draw a tangent at $t = 26$ s
E.g.

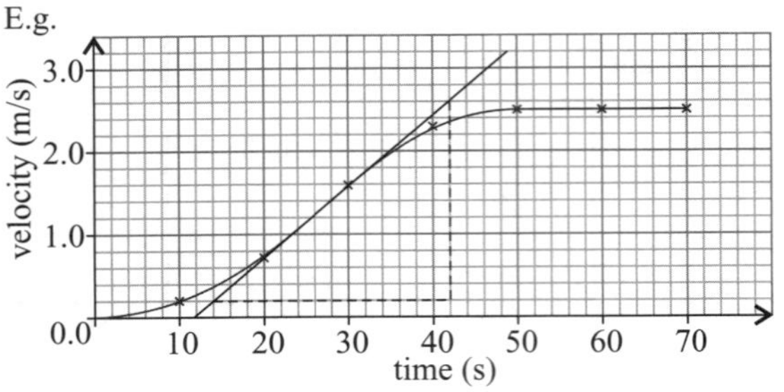

[1 mark]

gradient = $\dfrac{\text{change in } y}{\text{change in } x} = \dfrac{2.6 - 0.2}{42 - 14}$ ***[1 mark]***
$= 0.0857...$
$=$ **0.086 m/s² (to 2 s.f.)** ***[1 mark]***

You'll get the marks here as long as you've drawn a sensible tangent at t = 26 s, and your calculation of the gradient is correct for the tangent you've drawn.

5.2 Advantage of light gates: e.g. the light gates will be able to measure both the speed of the car and the time very accurately / the light gates will be able to measure both the speed of the car and the time to a high resolution ***[1 mark]***.
Disadvantage of light gates: e.g. the measurement points have to be marked out every 50 cm, so some changes in acceleration may be missed between measurements / the car has to be kept travelling in a straight line to easily pass through the gate and provide an accurate measurement ***[1 mark]***.
Advantage of the ticker tape method: e.g. it will provide many potential data points, taken at regular time intervals / the results are less affected by deviations in the straight line path of the car ***[1 mark]***.
Disadvantage of the ticker tape method: e.g. speeds have to be calculated manually from the distance measured between marks, which may introduce errors into the values / the tape may provide a resistive force against the motion of the car, causing the car to have a lower acceleration than it would without the tape ***[1 mark]***

Page 70 — Terminal Velocity

1 The resultant vertical force on an object falling at its terminal velocity is zero. Terminal velocity is the maximum velocity an object can fall at. ***[1 mark for both correct]***

2

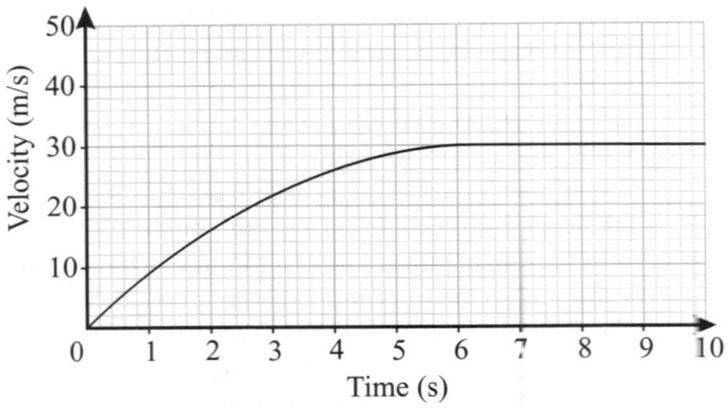

[1 mark for curved shape of graph up to 6 s, 1 mark for straight line at 30 m/s after 6 s]

3 As both objects fall, they accelerate due to gravity ***[1 mark]***. As their velocities increase, so does the air resistance acting on them ***[1 mark]***. The air resistance acts in the opposite direction to the acceleration, reducing the resultant forces acting on each object. Eventually the resultant forces on the objects are zero and they fall at constant velocities ***[1 mark]***. The book has a larger surface area than the ball, so experiences more air resistance ***[1 mark]***. This means that the resultant force on the book reaches zero sooner, and so it has a lower terminal velocity ***[1 mark]***.

Pages 71-72 — Newton's First and Second Laws

1 If the resultant force on a stationary object is zero, the object will remain stationary ***[1 mark]***.

2 Newton's Second Law states that the acceleration of an object is **directly** proportional to the **resultant** force acing on the object and **inversely** proportional to the **mass** of the object. ***[3 marks for all correct, 2 marks for 2-3 correct, 1 mark for one correct]***

3.1 E.g. friction ***[1 mark]***, air resistance / drag ***[1 mark for either]***

3.2 Resultant force on an object at a constant velocity is zero.
so 5000 = 3850 + second force
Second force = 5000 – 3850 = **1150 N**
[1 mark for correct answer]

4.1 $F = ma$ ***[1 mark]***

4.2 $F = 5.0 \times 9.8$ ***[1 mark]*** = **49 N** ***[1 mark]***

5 $a = \Delta v \div t$, so $a = 24 \div 9.2$ ***[1 mark]*** = 2.6... m/s² ***[1 mark]***
$F = ma$, so $F = 1450 \times 2.6...$ ***[1 mark]*** = 3782.6...
= **3800 N (to 2 s.f.)**
[1 mark]

6 Typical speed of a lorry is 25 m/s
(accept 20-30 m/s) ***[1 mark]***
$v^2 - u^2 = 2as$
$a = (v^2 - u^2) \div 2s = (0^2 - 25^2) \div (2 \times 50)$ ***[1 mark]***
$= -625 \div 100 = -6.25$ m/s² (accept 4-9 m/s²) ***[1 mark]***
$F = ma = 7520 \times -6.25$ ***[1 mark]***
= **(–) 47 000 N** (accept 30 100-67 700 N) ***[1 mark]***

Page 73 — Inertia and Newton's Third Law

Warm-up
When two objects interact, they exert equal and opposite forces on each other.

1.1 320 N ***[1 mark]***

1.2 Normal contact force ***[1 mark]***

1.3 640 N ***[1 mark]***

Weight is the force exerted by the Earth on the gymnast (because of the gymnast and the Earth interacting). An equal but opposite force acts on the Earth because of the gymnast.

2.1 The tendency to continue in the same state of motion
[1 mark]

2.2 E.g. how difficult it is to change the velocity of an object / ratio of force over acceleration / $m = F \div a$
[1 mark for any correct definition]

Page 74 — Investigating Motion

1.1 E.g. as force increases, so does acceleration / acceleration is proportional to force
[1 mark for any correct conclusion]

1.2 $F = ma$ ***[1 mark]***

1.3 At a force of 4.0 N, the acceleration is 2.25 m/s^2
So $m = F \div a$ ***[1 mark]*** $= 4.0 \div 2.25$ ***[1 mark]***
$= 1.77... =$ **1.8 kg** ***[1 mark]***

You'll still get the marks if you took readings from a different part of the graph, so long as you get the correct final answer.

2 To test the effect of varying the mass of the trolley, the force on the trolley has to remain constant ***[1 mark]***. Adding masses to the trolley increases both the force on and mass of the trolley, so the effect of varying the mass cannot be found ***[1 mark]***.

Page 75 — Stopping Distances

1.1 The distance travelled during the driver's reaction time ***[1 mark]***

1.2 The distance travelled under the braking force of the vehicle ***[1 mark]***

2 Stopping distance = thinking distance + braking distance
12 + 24 = **36 m** ***[1 mark]***

3 Work is done by friction between the brakes and the wheels ***[1 mark]***. This causes energy to be transferred to the thermal energy stores of the brakes, so they increase in temperature ***[1 mark]***.

4 Level 0: There is no relevant information. ***[No marks]***
Level 1: There is a brief explanation of why good brakes and tyres are important. ***[1 to 2 marks]***
Level 2: There is an explanation of why good brakes and tyres are important with some explanation as to the safety implications of poor brakes or tyres. ***[3 to 4 marks]***
Level 3: A logical and detailed explanation is given which includes at least 2 examples of explaining the importance of having the tyres and brakes in good condition, at least 2 safety implications and at least 1 effect on stopping distance. ***[5 to 6 marks]***

Here are some points your answer may include:
A good tread depth on tyres removes water.
This means there is a large amount of grip (friction) between the road and the tyres.
This decreases the braking (and so stopping) distance in wet conditions.
It also means the car will be less likely to skid in wet conditions.
Brakes that are in good condition allow a larger braking force to be applied.
This means that the braking distance of the car is shorter.
Brakes that are in good condition are also less likely to overheat under a large braking force.
So the car is less likely to go out of control or cause a crash.

Pages 76-77 — Reaction Times

1 0.2 - 0.9 s ***[1 mark]***

2 Any three from: tiredness / alcohol / drugs / distractions
[3 marks — 1 mark for each correct answer]

3.1 E.g. clicking a mouse when a computer screen changes colour ***[1 mark]***

3.2 Student A: $(7.0 + 7.1 + 6.9) \div 3 =$ **7.0 cm** ***[1 mark]***
Student B: $(8.4 + 8.2 + 8.3) \div 3 =$ **8.3 cm** ***[1 mark]***

3.3 Student A, because the average distance fallen by the ruler was less for Student A than Student B ***[1 mark]***.

3.4 E.g. use the same ruler, always have the same person dropping the ruler. ***[2 marks — 1 mark for each correct answer]***

3.5 Their reaction times will get longer ***[1 mark]***.

4 Hold a ruler between the open forefinger and thumb of the person being tested ***[1 mark]***. Align their finger to the zero line of the ruler, then drop the ruler without warning ***[1 mark]*** and have the test subject close their thumb and finger to catch the ruler ***[1 mark]***. The distance the ruler falls can be read from the ruler ***[1 mark]***. The time taken for it to fall can be calculated, as the acceleration (due to gravity) is constant. This is the reaction time of the test subject ***[1 mark]***.

5 Level 0: There is no relevant information. ***[No marks]***
Level 1: There is a brief explanation of how the man's reaction time may be affected and at least one mention of an implication this has for safety. ***[1 to 2 marks]***
Level 2: There is an explanation of how the man's reaction time may be affected and the implications this has for safety. ***[3 to 4 marks]***

Here are some points your answer may include:
Listening to loud music may mean that the driver is distracted.
This may increase his reaction time.
An increased reaction time means an increased thinking distance.
Driving quicker also increases the distance the car travels during the man's reaction time.
All of these things increase stopping distance, which means the man may not be able to stop in time to avoid hitting a hazard.
He may be unable to see an upcoming hazard because it is dark.
Driving late at night might mean that the man is tired.
He may not be able to hear an upcoming hazard because of the loud music.
This reduces the stopping distance required to avoid hitting a hazard and may lead to the driver having a collision.

6 $v^2 - u^2 = 2as$
$v^2 = 0 + (2 \times 9.8 \times 0.45)$ ***[1 mark]*** $= 8.82$
$v = 2.969...$ m/s ***[1 mark]***
$a = \Delta v \div t$, so $t = \Delta v \div a = 2.969... \div 9.8$ ***[1 mark]***
$= 0.303... =$ **0.30 s (to 2 s.f.)** ***[1 mark]***

Page 78 — More on Stopping Distances

1.1

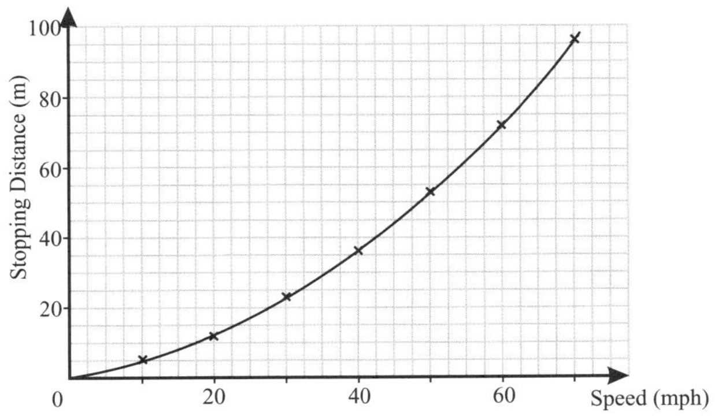

[1 mark for each correctly plotted point, 1 mark for correct line of best fit]

1.2 30 m (accept between 28 m and 32 m) ***[1 mark]***

1.3 83 – 30 = **53 m** (accept between 50 m and 56 m)
[2 marks for correct answer, otherwise 1 mark for reading a value correctly from the graph for 65 mph]

2 $s = vt = 18 \times 0.5 = 9$ m ***[1 mark]***, so thinking distance is 9 m.
45 – 9 = 36 m ***[1 mark]***, so braking distance is 36 m.
If the speed doubles, the thinking distance doubles
9 × 2 = 18 m ***[1 mark]***
If the speed doubles, braking distance increases four-fold (2^2): $36 \times 2^2 = 144$ m ***[1 mark]***
Stopping distance = 18 + 144 = **162 m** ***[1 mark]***

Pages 79-80 — Momentum

Warm-up
1: Momentum is a property of...
2: ...moving objects.
3: It is a...
4: ...vector quantity and is equal to...
5: ...mass × velocity.

1.1 $p = mv$ ***[1 mark]***

1.2 $m = p \div v$ ***[1 mark]*** = 5500 ÷ 25 ***[1 mark]*** = **220 kg** ***[1 mark]***

2 In Figure 1, the total momentum of the system is equal to the mass of the moving ball multiplied by its velocity ***[1 mark]***. As it hits the line of balls, it transfers this momentum to them and comes to a stop. All of this momentum is transferred along the line of balls to the ball at the end of the line, which is why the middle balls don't move ***[1 mark]***. This final ball has the same momentum as the first ball, causing it to move with the same velocity (because all of the balls have the same mass) that the moving ball in Figure 1 had ***[1 mark]***. In Figure 2, the total momentum of the system is equal to the total momentum in Figure 1 ***[1 mark]***.

3.1 Trial 6 ***[1 mark]***.

3.2 E.g. it will be difficult for the student to set vehicle A moving with a consistent speed, so it may take many trials to get another measurement of the same speed ***[1 mark]***.

3.3 E.g. if the mass of vehicle B gets too large, it may not be held up by the air jets on the air track any more ***[1 mark]***. This would cause the vehicle to come into contact with the track, and experience friction, making the results for the speed of vehicle B less accurate ***[1 mark]***.

Also, if the mass of vehicle B gets too big it could also move too slowly to be measured accurately by the light gate. Or it could cause vehicle A to come to a stop before it passes through the gate.

Page 81 — Changes in Momentum

1 The resultant force acting on the object. ***[1 mark]***

2 $F = (m\Delta v) \div \Delta t = 10 \div 0.1 =$ **100 N**
[2 marks for correct answer, otherwise 1 mark for correct calculation]

3 The air bag increases the time taken for the driver to stop ***[1 mark]***. This decreases the rate of change of momentum ***[1 mark]***. The force exerted on the driver equals the rate of change of momentum so the force on the driver is reduced ***[1 mark]***. A lower force on the driver means a reduced risk of injury ***[1 mark]***.

4 $p = mv$
Before tackle:
Momentum of first player = 80 × 8.0 = 640 kg m/s
Momentum of second player = 100 × –5.5 = –550 kg m/s

The velocity (and so momentum) is negative for the second player because he is moving in the opposite direction to the first player. For this question, I've taken to the right to be positive.

Total momentum = 640 – 550 = 90 kg m/s ***[1 mark]***
After tackle:
Mass = 80 + 100 = 180 kg
Momentum = 180 × v ***[1 mark]***
Momentum before = momentum after, so
90 = 180 × v ***[1 mark]***
v = 90 ÷ 180 = 0.5 m/s
Magnitude of velocity = 0.5 m/s ***[1 mark]***
Direction = to the right ***[1 mark]***

Topic 6 — Waves

Page 82 — Transverse and Longitudinal Waves

1.1 Spring A: transverse wave ***[1 mark]***
Spring B: longitudinal wave ***[1 mark]***

1.2 E.g.

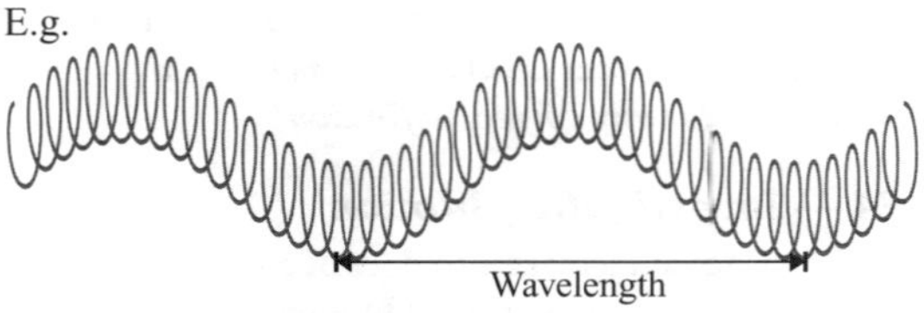

[1 mark for correctly labelled wavelength]

1.3 Amplitude is the maximum displacement of a point on a wave from its undisturbed position ***[1 mark]***.

1.4 E.g. ripples on the surface of water / light / any other electromagnetic wave ***[1 mark]***

2.1 Horizontal arrow drawn pointing away from the loudspeaker ***[1 mark]***

2.2 $T = 1 \div f = 1 \div 200$ ***[1 mark]*** = **0.005 s** ***[1 mark]***

2.3 In longitudinal waves, the oscillations/vibrations are parallel to the wave's direction of energy transfer ***[1 mark]***, but in transverse waves, the oscillations/vibrations are perpendicular/at right angles to the wave's direction of energy transfer ***[1 mark]***.

Page 83 — Experiments with Waves

1.1 E.g. the student could use a strobe light ***[1 mark]***. When the frequency of the strobe light matches that of the wave, the wave fronts will appear stationary (and the student can then measure the stationary wave) ***[1 mark]***.

1.2 There are 9 wavelengths in the distance of 18 cm.
Therefore, wavelength = 18 cm ÷ 9 = 2 cm ***[1 mark]***
$v = f\lambda = 12 \times 0.02$ ***[1 mark]*** = **0.24 m/s** ***[1 mark]***

2 How to grade your answer:
Level 0: There is no relevant information. ***[No marks]***
Level 1: A simple method to find the speed of waves on a string is partly outlined. ***[1 to 2 marks]***
Level 2: A method to find the speed of waves on a string is outlined in some detail. ***[3 to 4 marks]***
Level 3: A method to find the speed of waves on a string is fully explained in detail. ***[5 to 6 marks]***
Here are some points your answer may include:
Connect a string over a pulley to a vibration transducer.
Connect a signal generator to the vibration transducer and switch it on.
Adjust the frequency of the signal generator to produce clear waves on the string.
For as many half-wavelengths on the string as you can, measure the distance they cover.
Divide this by the number of half-wavelengths to find the average half-wavelength of the waves on the string.
Double this value to find the wavelength, λ, and note down the frequency of the frequency generator, f.
Use the formula $v = f\lambda$ to calculate the speed of the waves on the string, v.
To get more accurate results the experiment can be repeated for different frequencies and a mean value calculated.

Pages 84-85 — Reflection

Warm-up
wave is reflected — it bounces back off the material
wave is absorbed — it transfers all energy to the material
wave is transmitted — it passes through the material

1

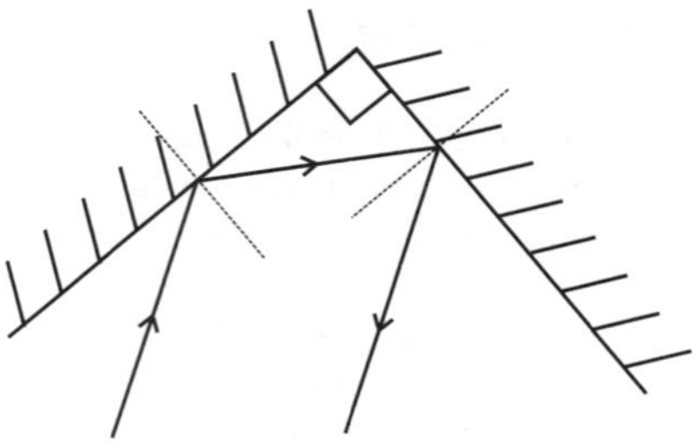

[1 mark for normal lines drawn correctly, 1 mark for the path of the light ray drawn correctly]

2.1 Some of the light is reflected back ***[1 mark]*** and some of the light is transmitted through the lens ***[1 mark]***.

2.2 The damaged lens has a rough surface so it will reflect light in many different directions (diffuse reflection) ***[1 mark]***. Therefore, no clearly reflected image will be visible in the damaged lens ***[1 mark]***. A clear reflection is seen in the undamaged lens because light is reflected in a single direction by a smooth surface (specular reflection) ***[1 mark]***.

3.1 E.g. as the beam is narrower than the distance between the markers on the protractor's scale, it will be easier to measure angles to the nearest degree ***[1 mark]***, so it is less likely that there will be human errors (due to judgement) in the results ***[1 mark]***. This means their results will be more accurate ***[1 mark]***.

3.2 E.g.

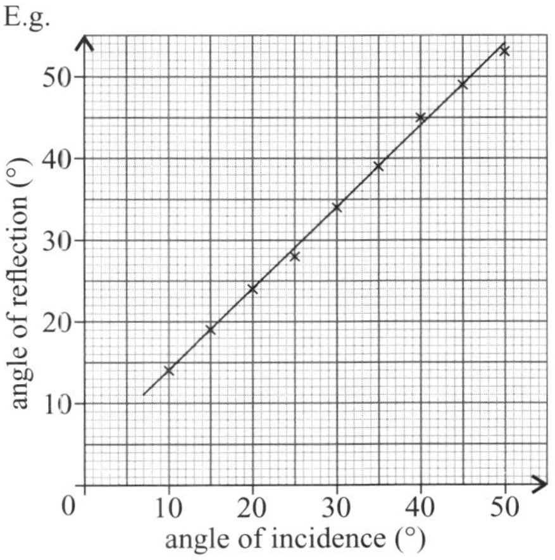

[1 mark for correctly labelled axes with a sensible scale, 1 mark for all points plotted correctly, 1 mark for a straight line of best fit that passes through or close to all the points]

3.3 The graph shows it does not agree with the law of reflection because e.g. the data/line of best fit does not fall along the line angle of incidence = angle of reflection ***[1 mark]***. The error could have been caused by e.g. the normal not being drawn perpendicular/at 90 °C to the mirror ***[1 mark]***.

Page 86 — Electromagnetic Waves and Refraction

1.1 All waves in the electromagnetic spectrum are **transverse**. ***[1 mark]***. All electromagnetic waves travel at the same speed in a vacuum. ***[1 mark]***

1.2 microwaves ***[1 mark]***

1.3 E.g. energy is transferred from the thermal energy store of a toaster's heating element ***[1 mark]*** by (infrared) radiation to the thermal energy store of bread inside the toaster ***[1 mark]***.

2.1

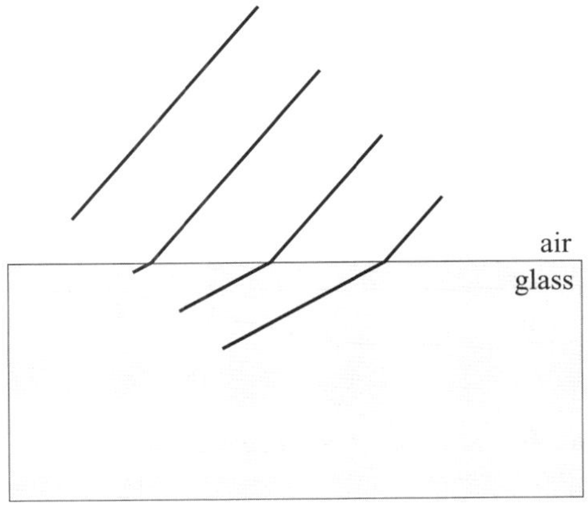

[1 mark for wave fronts bending in the correct direction, 1 mark for wave fronts inside the glass being joined up with those in the air]

2.2

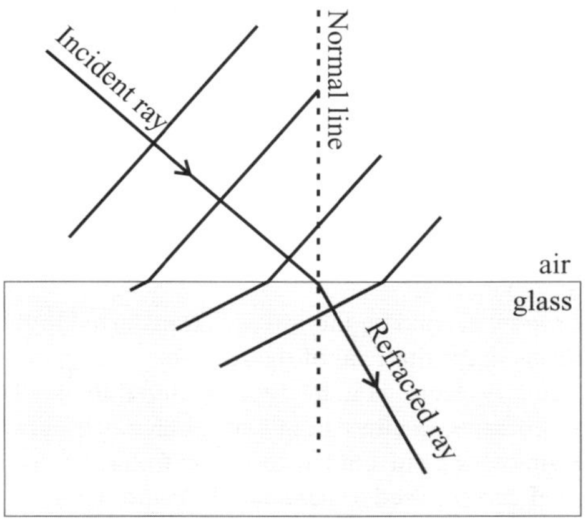

[1 mark for incident ray drawn and labelled correctly, 1 mark for normal line drawn and labelled correctly, 1 mark for refracted ray drawn and labelled correctly.]

Pages 87-88 — Investigating Light

1.1 The angle of incidence and angle of reflection should be equal ***[1 mark]***.

1.2 At the mirror: specular reflection ***[1 mark]***.
At the card: diffuse reflection ***[1 mark]***.

1.3 The rough surface means that the angle of incidence is different for each ray across the width of the beam ***[1 mark]***. This means each ray is reflected in a different direction, so the light is scattered ***[1 mark]***.

1.4 A ray box was used to provide a thin beam of light ***[1 mark]*** so that the angles of incidence and reflection could be easily and accurately measured ***[1 mark]***. A laser could also have been used to produce similar results ***[1 mark]***.

2.1

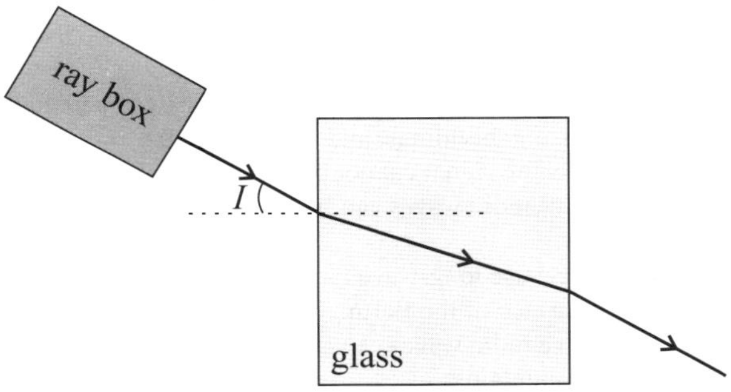

[1 mark for straight line with correct arrow drawn, connecting the two rays at the edge of the block]

2.2 18° ***[1 mark for an answer in the range 17° to 19°]***

2.3 The speed of the light ray decreases ***[1 mark]*** as the angle of refraction, *R*, is smaller than the angle of incidence, *I*, i.e. it is bent towards the normal ***[1 mark]***.

2.4 The speed of the light ray changes least in water ***[1 mark]***. Water has the largest angle of refraction ***[1 mark]***, so has bent the light the least (so has slowed the light down the least) ***[1 mark]***.

2.5 The material of the container will also refract light ***[1 mark]***. The thinner the walls of the container, the less this will affect the results ***[1 mark]***.

Page 89 — Radio Waves

Warm-up

True, True, False, True.

1 How to grade your answer:

Level 0: There is no relevant information. ***[No marks]***

Level 1: A simple method of generating radio waves is described. ***[1 to 2 marks]***

Level 2: A method of generating radio waves and how these waves generate an electrical signal in a distant TV aerial is described. ***[3 to 4 marks]***

Here are some points your answer may include:
An alternating current flows in the circuit the transmitter is connected to.
Alternating currents are made up of oscillating charges/electrons.
As the electrons oscillate in the transmitter, they produce oscillating electric and magnetic fields/radio waves.
Radio waves are transmitted to and then absorbed by the distant TV aerial.
The energy carried by the waves is transferred to the electrons in the material of the receiver.
This causes electrons in the receiver aerial to oscillate.
This generates an alternating current/an electrical signal.
This alternating current has the same frequency as the original current used to generate the radio wave.

2 How to grade your answer:
Level 0: There is no relevant information. ***[No marks]***
Level 1: There is a brief explanation of the differences between radio wave types used for broadcasting ***[1 to 2 marks]***
Level 2: There is some explanation of the differences between radio wave types used for broadcasting, including their different ranges and how this affects which broadcast can be heard. ***[3 to 4 marks]***
Level 3: There is a clear and detailed explanation of the differences between radio wave types used for broadcasting, including their different ranges and how this affects which broadcast can be heard. ***[5 to 6 marks]***
Here are some points your answer may include:
FM radio is transmitted using very short wavelength radio waves.
These radio waves can only be received while the receiver is in direct sight of the transmitter.
This is because these wavelengths are easily absorbed by obstacles, e.g. buildings, and cannot diffract.
Therefore, the signal cannot be received in France.
Long-wave radio waves can be transmitted over long distances.
This is because long-wave radio waves diffract around the curved surface of the Earth.
Long-wave radio waves can also diffract around obstacles such as mountains.
Hence the signal can be received in France.

Page 90 — EM Waves and Their Uses

1.1 The microwaves are absorbed by water molecules in the potato ***[1 mark]***. This transfers energy to the water molecules, causing the water in the potato to heat up ***[1 mark]***. The water molecules transfer the energy they have absorbed to the rest of the molecules in the potato, cooking it ***[1 mark]***.
1.2 The glass plate does not absorb any microwaves ***[1 mark]*** as it does not contain any water molecules, and so it is only heated by (conduction from) the potato ***[1 mark]***.
1.3 infrared ***[1 mark]***
2 It is dark so there is very little visible light for a normal camera to pick up ***[1 mark]***. The person trying to hide is warmer than the surroundings and so emits more infrared radiation ***[1 mark]***. This makes the person stand out from the surroundings if observed through infrared radiation ***[1 mark]***.

Page 91 — More Uses of EM Waves

Warm-up
UV Rays: A, C, D
Visible Light: B, C
X-rays: E, F
Gamma Rays: F

1.1 E.g. the patient is injected with a gamma-emitting source ***[1 mark]***. Gamma radiation is detected outside of the body, which is used to follow the source's progress around the patient's body ***[1 mark]***.
1.2 E.g. they can pass out of the patient's body / they can be detected outside of the patient's body ***[1 mark]***.
1.3 X-rays are directed at the patient. The X-rays are absorbed by bones ***[1 mark]***, but transmitted by less dense body material, such as flesh ***[1 mark]***. A screen behind the patient detects the X-rays and a negative image is formed with brighter areas where fewer X-rays are detected ***[1 mark]***.
1.4 E.g. wear lead aprons / stand behind lead screens / leave the room whilst treatment is taking place ***[1 mark]***.

Page 92 — Dangers of Electromagnetic Waves

1.1 X-rays and gamma rays transfer so much energy to living cells that they can knock off electrons (ionise atoms) ***[1 mark]***. This can cause mutation of genes, leading to cancer ***[1 mark]***.
1.2 Any two from: sunburn / premature aging / blindness / (increased risk of) skin cancer ***[2 marks]***
2.1 Compare risk of chest scan to risk of head scan,
$10\,000 \div 2500 = 4$
Risk is 4 times greater, so dose is 4 times greater ***[1 mark]***.
Dose = $2 \times 4 =$ **8 mSv** ***[1 mark]***
2.2 How to grade your answer:
Level 0: There is no relevant information. ***[No marks]***
Level 1: The risks and benefits are identified but no comparison is made about whether one outweighs the other. ***[1 to 2 marks]***
Level 2: There is some discussion about balancing the benefits with the risks. ***[3 to 4 marks]***
Level 3: There is a detailed explanation of the benefits and risks, and an informed explanation of why the procedure may go ahead. ***[5 to 6 marks]***
Here are some points your answer may include:
The radiation dose is large, so the risk of developing cancer from the procedure is higher than in some other procedures.
However, the procedure might better inform a decision on future treatment.
So future treatment may be more effective.
The benefit of treating the condition needs to be compared with the risk of the procedure (and any subsequent treatment).
An assessment needs to be made about the risk of dying (or poor quality of life) from the underlying condition and the potential benefits for treatment.
Other less risky procedures might lead to similar benefits and these need to be considered.
If the benefits outweigh the risks considerably, then it is worth carrying on with the procedure.

Page 93 — Lenses

1.1

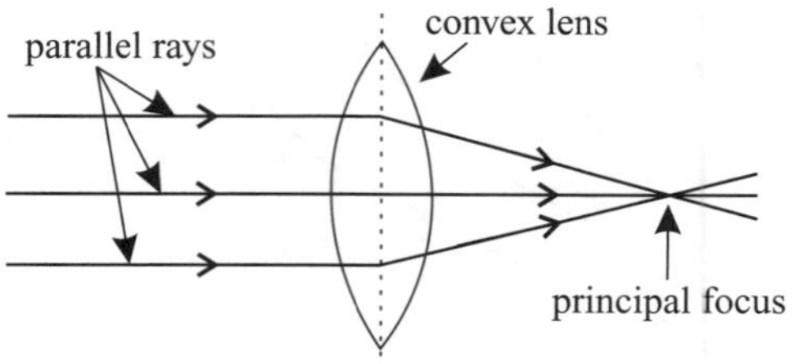

[3 marks — 1 mark for each correct label]

Note: There is another principle focus on the other side of the lens. Labelling either is fine.

1.2 4.5 cm (allow 4.3 — 4.7 cm) ***[1 mark]***
1.3 ...refracting light ***[1 mark]***
Lenses form images by changing the direction of rays of light.

2 E.g.

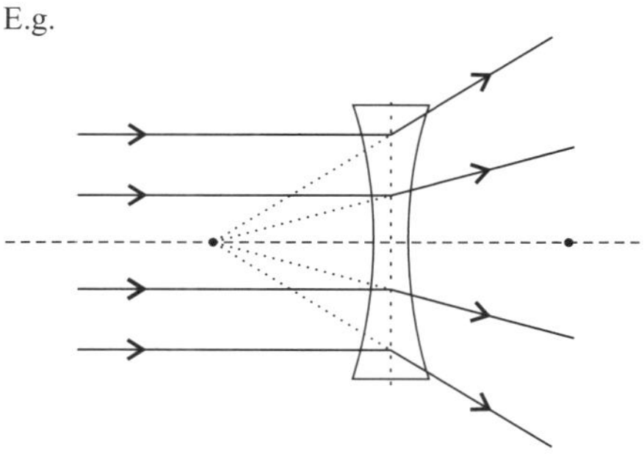

[1 mark for non-central rays diverging once they have passed through the lens, 1 mark for correct construction of refracted rays that are traced back to the principal focus on the correct side]

You could also draw the light rays refracting at each side of the lens — both when they're entering the lens and leaving it. You just need to make sure the light rays leaving the lens trace back to the principal focus.

Page 94 — Images and Ray Diagrams

1.1

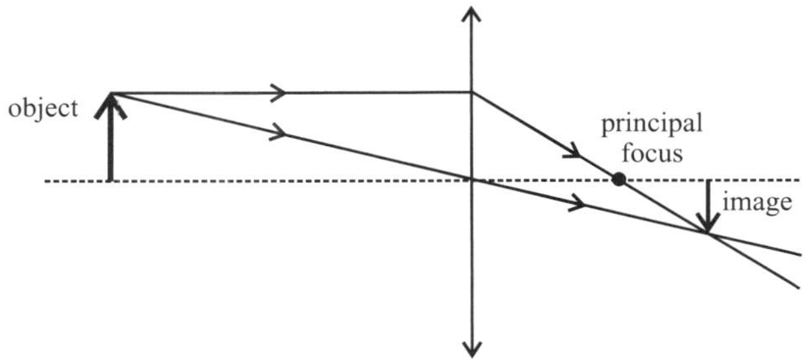

[1 mark for ray through middle of the lens carried on in a straight line, 1 mark for ray parallel to the axis bending at the lens and passing through principal focus, 1 mark for image drawn at the point where the rays meet.]

1.2 It is a real image ***[1 mark]***. The light rays come together to form the image ***[1 mark]***.

A quick test between virtual and real images — you can project a real image onto a piece of paper, but you can't do the same for a virtual image.

2.1

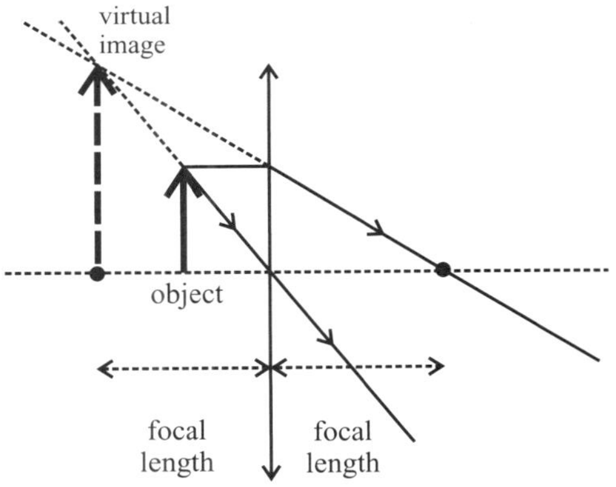

[1 mark for light ray continued in a straight line through the middle of the lens and traced back, 1 mark for ray parallel to the axis bent towards the principle focus and traced back, 1 mark for image drawn at point the two rays meet, 1 mark for image labelled as a virtual image.]

2.2 Any two from: The new image is a real image while the original is virtual. / The new image is on the opposite side of the lens to the original image. / The new image is the same size as the object while the old image was larger. / The new image is inverted while the old image was the same way up. ***[2 marks — 1 mark for each correct answer]***

Page 95 — Concave Lenses and Magnification

1.1 A ***[1 mark]***, C ***[1 mark]***

Concave lenses always bend light away from the axis — except for rays which pass through the centre of the lens, which pass through unaltered.

1.2

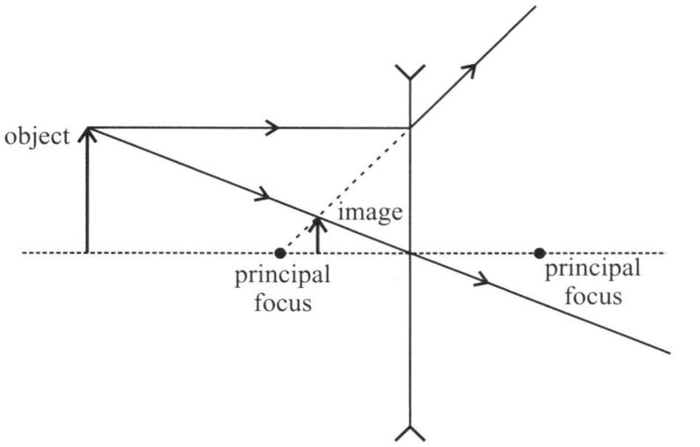

[1 mark for ray drawn from top of object parallel to axis, diverging at the lens so that it is traced back to principal focus, 1 mark for ray drawn from top of object through the centre of the lens, 1 mark for image drawn and labelled at the point where the rays meet.]

2

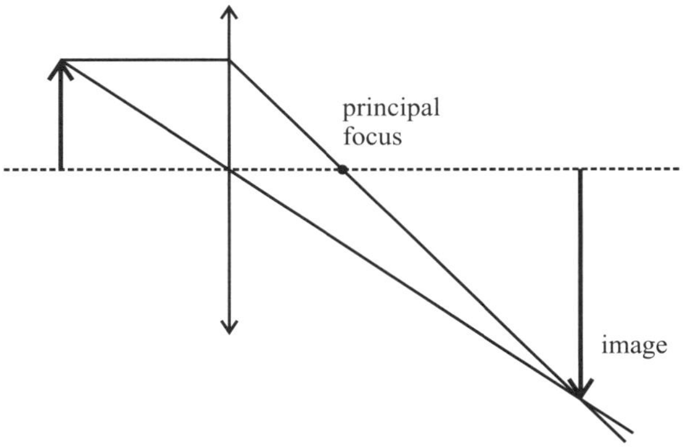

[1 mark for ray through middle of the lens carried on in a straight line, 1 mark for ray parallel to the axis bending at the lens and passing through principal focus.]

Image height is 40 mm (accept between 40 and 45 mm) ***[1 mark]***

So magnification = image height ÷ object height

= 40 ÷ 20 ***[1 mark]***

= **2** (accept between 2 and 2.5) ***[1 mark]***

Pages 96-97 — Visible Light

Warm-up

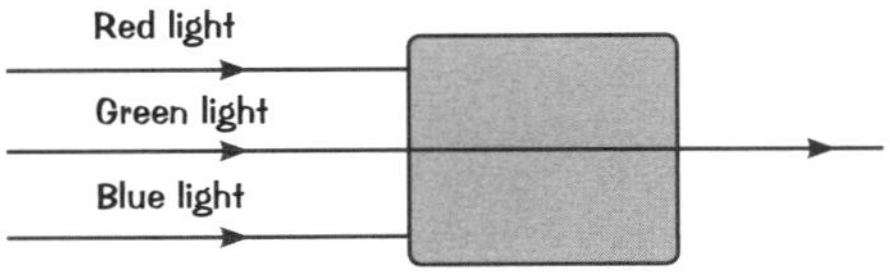

The green light ray should continue in a straight horizontal line on the other side of the block. The red and blue rays should not continue past the block.

1.1 Opaque objects do not transmit light. All light which hits them is either absorbed or reflected ***[1 mark]***.

1.2 The white football reflects all wavelengths/frequencies of visible light equally ***[1 mark]***, so it appears white.
The red football only reflects the wavelengths/frequencies corresponding to red light (it absorbs all other wavelengths/ frequencies) ***[1 mark]***.

1.3 The red filter is only letting red light pass through it ***[1 mark]***.
It absorbs all other colours of light from the white ball ***[1 mark]***.

1.4 The green filter only lets green light pass through ***[1 mark]***. Since the white football is reflecting all colours of light, it appears green ***[1 mark]***. The red football looks black because it is only reflecting red light, which is absorbed by the green filter ***[1 mark]***.

2.1 opaque ***[1 mark]***

A transparent object doesn't absorb visible light.

2.2 The object is blue ***[1 mark]***.

The dip corresponds to light of wavelength 470 nm being reflected.

2.3

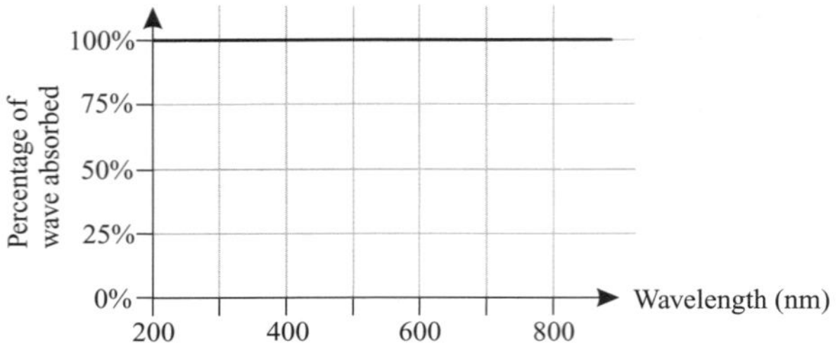

[1 mark for horizontal line at 100% absorption]

2.4

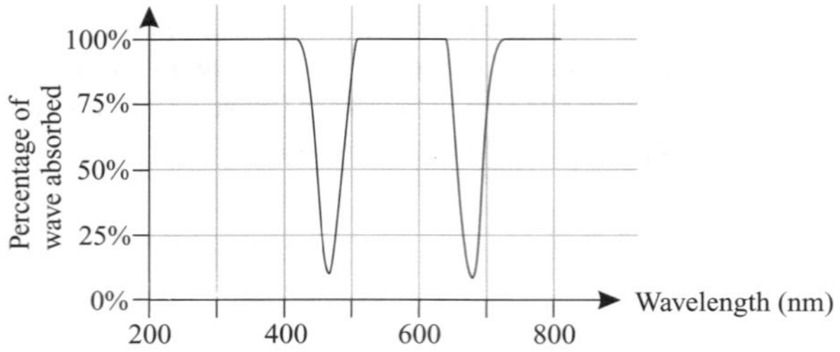

[1 mark for 100% absorption for all wavelengths apart from red and blue, 1 mark for less absorption at 470 nm, 1 mark for less absorption at 680 nm.]

Pages 98-99 — Infrared Radiation and Temperature

1.1 All objects emit and absorb infrared radiation ***[1 mark]***.

1.2 The temperature of the object is constant ***[1 mark]***.

1.3 The temperature of the object would decrease ***[1 mark]***.

2.1 Matte black ***[1 mark]***

2.2 Shiny white ***[1 mark]***

2.3 E.g. use a radiation detector to measure the emitted radiation / use a ruler to make sure he measures the radiation emitted from each side from the same distance ***[1 mark for any sensible suggestion]***

3.1 Any three from: e.g using the same mass of water in each can / using the same equipment for each can / starting measurements at the same temperature for each can / using cans that are the same size and shape / using cans that are made from the same material ***[3 marks]***.

Each of these make sure that the rate of change of temperature is only affected by the paint on the can, not any other properties of the cans, the water, or the experimental set-up. This ensures that it is a fair test, and so the experiment will produce valid results.

3.2 E.g. the water in can A / the can painted with matt navy blue paint will cool fastest ***[1 mark]***. This is because dark and matt surfaces are better emitters of infrared radiation than light and shiny/glossy surfaces ***[1 mark]***.

3.3 E.g.

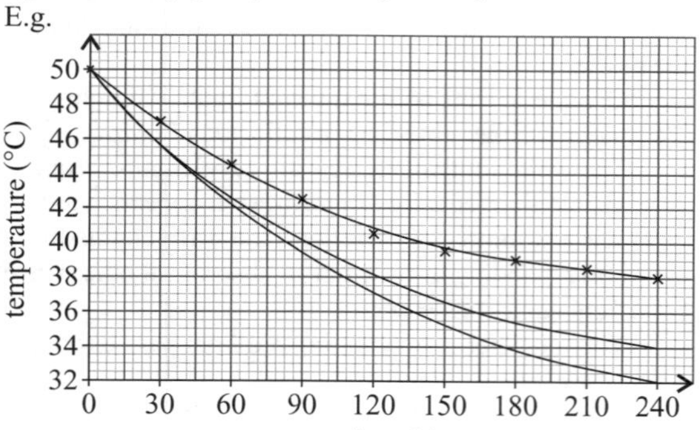

[1 mark for all points drawn correctly, and 1 mark for a smooth curve of best fit which passes through or close to all the points]

Page 100 — Black Body Radiation

1.1 An object that absorbs all of the radiation that hits it ***[1 mark]***.

1.2 It has gotten cooler ***[1 mark]***.

1.3 The radiation emitted covers a large range of wavelengths ***[1 mark]***.

2 How to grade your answer:

Level 0: There is no relevant information. ***[No marks]***

Level 1: There is a brief explanation of how the Earth absorbs radiation emitted by the Sun. ***[1 to 2 marks]***

Level 2: There is an explanation of how the Earth emits radiation and absorbs radiation emitted by the Sun and how this affects the Earth's temperature at different times of the day. ***[3 to 4 marks]***

Level 3: There is a detailed explanation of how the Earth emits radiation and absorbs radiation emitted by the Sun and how the balance between these at different times of the day keeps the Earth's temperature constant. ***[5 to 6 marks]***

Here are some points your answer may include:

During the day, the half of the Earth which is facing the Sun is hit by radiation emitted by the Sun.

Some of this radiation is absorbed by the atmosphere and the Earth's surface.

Because of this, the amount of radiation absorbed during the day is greater than the amount that is emitted.

This causes an increase in local temperature.

The half of the Earth which is facing away from the Sun has no radiation from the Sun hitting it — it is night time.

This half of the Earth absorbs very little radiation, but emits radiation at its usual rate.

So at night time radiation is emitted at a much higher rate than it is absorbed.

This causes a decrease in local temperature.

Throughout each full cycle of day and night, one half of the Earth will be increasing in temperature and the other half will be decreasing in temperature.

Overall, these local temperature changes balance out, and so the average temperature of the Earth remains roughly constant.

Page 101 — Sound Waves

1.1 20 Hz to 20 kHz ***[1 mark]***.

1.2 The eardrum vibrates when sound waves vibrate the air inside the ear ***[1 mark]***, passing these oscillations onto the rest of the ear ***[1 mark]***.

2.1 A child speaks and produces sound wave. The particles in the air vibrate back and forth (creating compressions and rarefactions) as the sound wave travels through the air to the end of the pot ***[1 mark]***. When the sound wave hits the pot, the air particles hitting the base of the pot cause it to move back and forth (vibrate) ***[1 mark]***. This causes particles in the end of the string tied to the pot to vibrate ***[1 mark]***. The particles in the string vibrate and transmit the wave along the string ***[1 mark]***. When the vibrations reach the other end of the string, they are transmitted to the base of the second pot. This causes the surrounding air particles to vibrate, generating a sound wave which is heard by the second child ***[1 mark]***.

2.2 The frequency stays the same ***[1 marks]*** and the wavelength increases ***[1 marks]***.

Page 102 — Ultrasound

1.1 Vibrations/sound waves with frequencies that are too high for humans to hear ***[1 mark]***.

1.2 30 kHz ***[1 mark]***, 30 MHz ***[1 mark]***

30 Hz is within the human hearing range, so cannot be ultrasound. 30 mHz is outside our hearing range, but its frequency is too low — ultrasound is a high frequency sound wave. Remember that 'm' stands for milli- (× 10^{-3}) while 'M' stands for mega (× 10^{6}).

2 Pulses of ultrasound are directed towards the foetus ***[1 mark]***. When they reach the boundary between the fluid of the womb and the skin of the foetus, they are partially reflected ***[1 mark]***. The reflections are detected and their timings and distributions are used to produce a video image ***[1 mark]***.

3.1 30 ms ***[1 mark]***

Measure from the start of the first peak to the start of the second peak.

3.2 $s = vt$

Distance = 1500 × 0.030 ***[1 mark]*** = 45 m ***[1 mark]***

However, this is twice the distance between the submarine and the ocean floor.

So the distance to the ocean floor = 45 ÷ 2 = **22.5 m** ***[1 mark]***

Page 103 — Exploring Structures Using Waves

Warm-up

Is a transverse wave — S-waves

Can pass through a liquid — P-waves

Can pass through a solid — Both

1.1 As there are no S-waves at C, something is stopping them ***[1 mark]***. S-waves cannot pass through a liquid so it is likely that part of the interior of the Earth is in a liquid state ***[1 mark]***.

1.2 At both points the waves pass between a solid and a liquid medium ***[1 mark]***. They travel at different speeds in solids and liquids, so they experience a sudden change in velocity ***[1 mark]***.

Topic 7 — Magnetism and Electromagnetism

Pages 104-105 — Permanent and Induced Magnets

Warm-up

non-contact

1.1 A region in which a magnet or magnetic material will experience a force ***[1 mark]***.

1.2 Any two of e.g. iron/steel/nickel/cobalt ***[2 marks]***

1.3

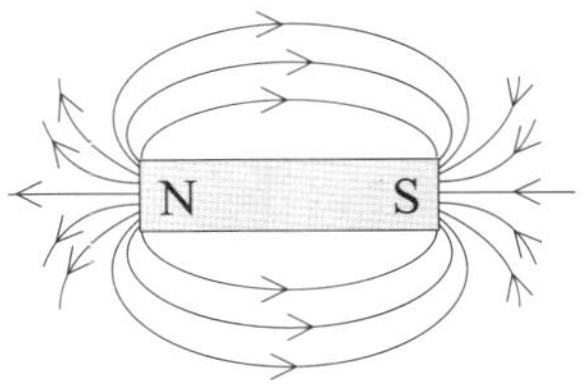

[2 marks in total — 1 mark for correct shape, 1 mark for arrows pointing from north to south]

1.4 The correct statements are:

The closer together the magnetic field lines, the stronger the magnetic field ***[1 mark]***.

Magnetic field lines point from the north pole to the south pole of a magnet ***[1 mark]***.

2.1 The block of cobalt becomes an induced magnet when it is placed in the magnetic field of the bar magnet ***[1 mark]***, which causes a force of attraction between the paperclip and the cobalt ***[1 mark]***

2.2 When the bar magnet is removed, the cobalt will quickly demagnetise ***[1 mark]***, so the paperclip will become unstuck ***[1 mark]***.

3.1 How to grade your answer:

Level 0: There is no relevant information. ***[No marks]***

Level 1: There is a brief description of how the compass should be used. ***[1 to 2 marks]***

Level 2: There is a good description of the method used to determine the magnetic field, including the effect on a compass when placed in a magnetic field. ***[3 to 4 marks]***

Here are some points your answer may include:

The needle of a compass points in the direction of the magnetic field it is in.

Put the magnet on a sheet of paper.

Move the compass along the field lines of the horseshoe magnet.

Mark the direction of the compass needle at each point.

Join up the marks to create a diagram of the magnetic field lines.

3.2 E.g. it would point (to geographic) north ***[1 mark]*** because it is aligning itself with the magnetic field of the Earth ***[1 mark]***.

Pages 106-107 — Electromagnetism

1.1

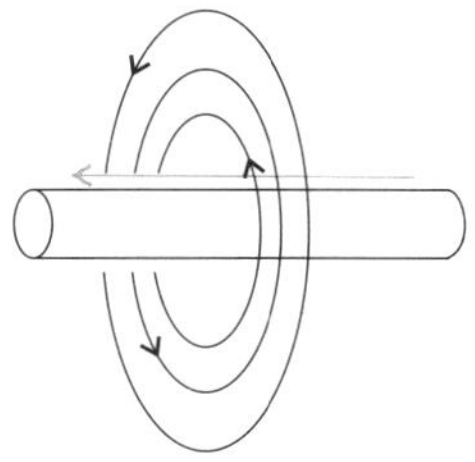

[2 marks in total — 1 mark for correct shape, 1 mark for correct direction]

You can work this out using the right-hand thumb rule — point your right thumb in the direction of the current and your curled fingers will show the direction of the field lines. Bingo.

1.2 The direction of the field will also be reversed ***[1 mark]***.

1.3 Increase the current ***[1 mark]***.

2.1 E.g. a permanent magnet always has a magnetic field, but an electromagnet can be controlled (turned on and off) by an electric current ***[1 mark]***.

2.2 E.g. the magnetic field is strong ***[1 mark]*** and uniform ***[1 mark]***.

2.3 If the current is stopped, there will no longer be a magnetic field around the solenoid ***[1 mark]***.

3.1 E.g. put a block of iron in the middle of the solenoid ***[1 mark]***.

3.2 Repelled ***[1 mark]***, because the direction of the current means that the left-hand end of the solenoid acts as a north pole ***[1 mark]***, and like poles repel ***[1 mark]***.

4 How to grade your answer:

Level 0: There is no relevant information. ***[No marks]***

Level 1: There is a brief explanation of how the moving hammer strikes the bell. ***[1 to 2 marks]***

Level 2: There is some explanation of how the electromagnet causes the hammer to move. ***[3 to 4 marks]***

Level 3: There is a clear and detailed explanation of how the circuit works. ***[5 to 6 marks]***

Here are some points your answer may include:

When the switch is closed, current will flow in the circuit.

The electromagnet will 'switch on' and become magnetised.

This will attract the iron, which will swing the arm on the pivot and cause the hammer to ding the bell.

When the arm pivots, the contacts will move apart from each other, breaking the circuit.

The current will stop flowing, the electromagnet will 'switch off', becoming demagnetised.

The iron will no longer be attracted to the electromagnet, so the arm will swing back to its original position.

This will re-complete the circuit, and the process will start again.

The result is that the bell will continue to ring until the switch is opened again.

Page 108 — The Motor Effect

1.1 It will move towards you, out of the paper ***[1 mark]***.

Use Fleming's left-hand rule here. Point your first finger in the direction of the field (i.e. from the north pole to the south pole of the magnets). Point your second finger in the direction of the current (shown in the diagram). Your thumb will then show the direction of motion of the wire.

1.2 E.g. the motor effect *[1 mark]*, caused by the magnetic field of the current-carrying wire interacting with the magnetic field of the permanent magnets (which results in a force) *[1 mark]*.

1.3 The magnetic flux density *[1 mark]*. The current flowing through the wire *[1 mark]*. The length of the wire in the magnetic field *[1 mark]*.

2 $F = BIl$, so $B = F \div Il$ *[1 mark]*
$B = 1.2 \div (0.4 \times 0.75)$ *[1 mark]*
$= 1.2 \div 0.3 =$ **4 T**
[1 mark for correct value, 1 mark for correct unit]

Page 109 — Electric Motors and Loudspeakers

1 An alternating current is passed through a coil of wire. The coil is surrounded by a **permanent magnet** and attached to the base of a paper cone. When the coil carries a current, it experiences a **force**, so the paper cone moves. This allows variations in **current** to be converted into variations in **pressure** in sound waves. *[3 marks for all correct, otherwise 2 marks for 3 correct, 1 mark for 2 correct]*

2.1 clockwise *[1 mark]*

2.2 E.g. the interacting magnetic fields (of the coil and the magnets) causes a force on each arm of the coil *[1 mark]* in the opposite direction (which causes the coil to rotate) *[1 mark]*.

2.3 E.g. swap the contacts every half turn (e.g. using a split-ring commutator) to reverse the direction of the current *[1 mark]*. This swaps the direction of the forces for each arm and keeps the direction of rotation constant *[1 mark]*.

Page 110 — The Generator Effect

1 Both statements A and B are true *[1 mark]*.

2.1 As the bicycle wheel turns, the generator wheel on the device is turned. This causes the magnet to rotate *[1 mark]*. The coil of wire experiences a change in magnetic field, which induces a potential difference *[1 mark]*. The wires to the lamp form a complete circuit, and so a current is induced *[1 mark]*.

2.2 E.g. By pedalling faster *[1 mark]*.

2.3 The direction that opposes the changing magnetic field caused by the rotating magnet *[1 mark]*.

Page 111 — Generators and Microphones

Warm-up

Alternators use slip rings and brushes and generate ac.
Dynamos use a split-ring commutator and generate dc.

1 The diaphragm is attached to a coil of wire, which is surrounded by (and wrapped around) a permanent magnet *[1 mark]*. When the sound wave hits the diaphragm, the diaphragm moves. This in turn causes the coil of wire to move relative to the magnet *[1 mark]*, which induces (a potential difference, and so) a current (an electrical signal) *[1 mark]*.

2 E.g.

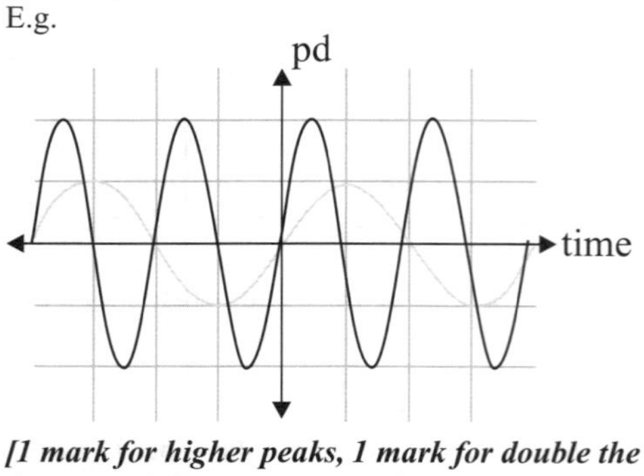

[1 mark for higher peaks, 1 mark for double the initial frequency/twice as many peaks]

Pages 112-113 — Transformers

1 D, A, C, B *[1 mark]*

2.1 $n_p = 12$, $V_p = 240$ V, $V_s = 80$ V, $\frac{V_s}{V_p} = \frac{n_s}{n_p}$
$n_s = \frac{V_s n_p}{V_p}$ *[1 mark]*
$= (80 \times 12) \div 240$ *[1 mark]* $=$ **4** *[1 mark]*

2.2 step-down *[1 mark]*

There are fewer turns on the secondary coil, and the output pd is less than the input pd.

3.1 $V_p = 12$ V, $n_p = 30$, $n_s = 40$, $\frac{V_s}{V_p} = \frac{n_s}{n_p}$
$V_s = \frac{n_s V_p}{n_p}$ *[1 mark]* $= (40 \times 12) \div 30$ *[1 mark]*
$=$ **16 V** *[1 mark]*

3.2 $V_s \times I_s = V_p \times I_p$ so $I_s = (V_p \times I_p) \div V_s$ *[1 mark]*
$I_s = (30 \times 20) \div 40$ *[1 mark]*
$=$ **15 A** *[1 mark]*

3.3 E.g. to make transferring electricity more efficient / to reduce energy losses when transferring electricity *[1 mark]*

4.1 E.g. if the exposed wire came into contact with the iron core, it could cause electricity to flow through the core, leading to inaccurate results *[1 mark]*.
The exposed wire could cause an electric shock *[1 mark]*.

4.2 E.g.

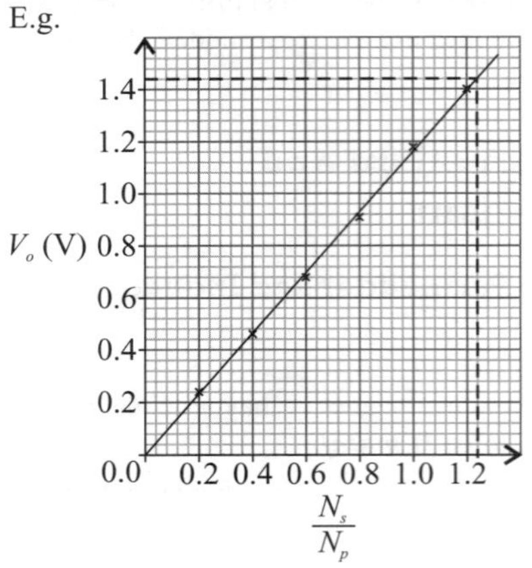

gradient $= \frac{\text{change in } y}{\text{change in } x} = \frac{1.44 - 0}{1.24 - 0}$ *[1 mark]*
$= 1.1612...$
$=$ **1.2 V (to 2 s.f.)** *[1 mark]*

4.3 The results do agree with this relationship. E.g. rearranging the relationship to $V_o = V_i \frac{N_s}{N_p}$ and comparing it to the equation of a straight line, it can be seen that a graph of V_o against $\frac{N_s}{N_p}$ should give a straight line through the origin, with a gradient equal to V_i *[1 mark]*. The graph in Figure 2 does pass through the origin *[1 mark]*, and it has a constant gradient which is equal to 1.2 V to 2 significant figures, which is equal to V_i, so it does agree with the relationship *[1 mark]*.

Topic 8 — Space Physics

Pages 114-115 — The Life Cycle of Stars

1.1 A cloud of dust and gas (in space) *[1 mark]*

1.2 Gravitational force *[1 mark]*

2 In the following order: dust and gas / nebula, protostar, main sequence *[1 mark]*, red super giant *[1 mark]*, supernova *[1 mark]*
Bottom boxes: neutron star (once, in either box) *[1 mark]*
black hole (once, in either box) *[1 mark]*.

3.1 As a protostar ages, its **temperature** / **density** and **density** / **temperature** increase. This causes particles to **collide** with each other more often. When the temperature gets hot enough, **hydrogen** nuclei fuse together and create **helium** nuclei. This process is known as nuclear fusion.
[3 marks for all five correct, otherwise 2 marks for three or four correct, 1 mark for one or two correct]

3.2 The outward pressure/expansion due to nuclear fusion ***[1 mark]*** balances the inwards force due to gravitational attraction ***[1 mark]***.

3.3 It keeps the star a steady size ***[1 mark]*** and keeps the core hot ***[1 mark]***.

4 When a star with a mass much greater than the Sun stops being a red supergiant, it expands and contracts several times until it finally explodes in a supernova ***[1 mark]***. This leaves behind a very dense core, called a neutron star ***[1 mark]*** or, if the star was massive enough, a black hole ***[1 mark]***.

Pages 116-117 — The Solar System and Orbits

Warm-up
Planet: Neptune, Venus, Earth
Dwarf Planet: Pluto
Natural Satellite: The Moon
Artificial Satellite: Hubble Space Telescope, Communications satellite

1.1 The Sun

1.2 The Milky Way galaxy ***[1 mark]***

2.1 The Sun ***[1 mark]***
A planet ***[1 mark]***

2.2 Gravity ***[1 mark]***

2.3 Similarity: e.g. they both have (almost) circular orbits ***[1 mark]***. Difference: e.g. moons orbit planets, planets orbit the Sun ***[1 mark]***.

3.1

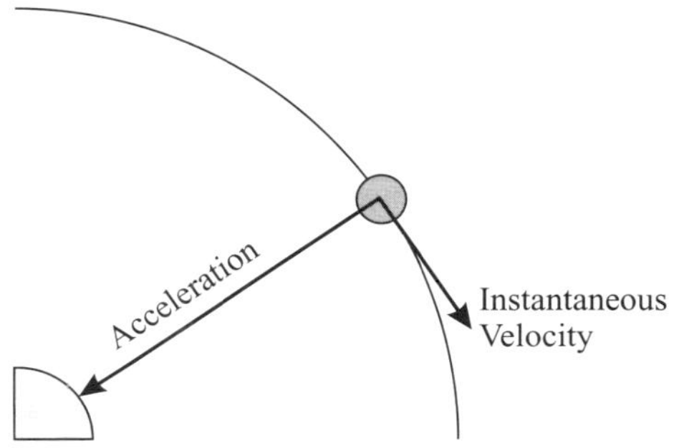

Acceleration: An arrow pointing from the planet to the Sun ***[1 mark]***.
Instantaneous Velocity: An arrow at a tangent to the orbit at the planet (as illustrated or in opposite direction) ***[1 mark]***.

3.2 How to grade your answer:
Level 0: There is no relevant information. ***[No marks]***
Level 1: There is a brief explanation of why centripetal acceleration does not change the speed of the planet. ***[1 to 2 marks]***
Level 2: There is some explanation of why the planet's velocity changes but the speed does not. ***[3 to 4 marks]***
Level 3: There is a clear and detailed explanation of why the acceleration changes the velocity of the planet, but not its speed. ***[5 to 6 marks]***
Here are some points your answer may include:
The acceleration acts along the radius of the orbit, towards the centre.
This means it acts at right angles to the planet's speed (instantaneous velocity).
Acceleration that is perpendicular to the direction of motion does not affect the speed of the motion, it just changes the direction.
Therefore, the speed of the planet is not changed by the acceleration.
Velocity is a vector quantity, with magnitude and direction.
The planet's velocity is constantly changing because its direction is constantly changing.
The acceleration causes the planet to move on a circular path.
Circular motion means that the object experiences changing velocity (i.e. acceleration) but not changing speed.

4 Satellite A is orbiting faster than satellite B ***[1 mark]***. The closer the satellite is to the Earth, the stronger the gravitational force on the satellite is ***[1 mark]***. This means a larger instantaneous velocity is needed to balance it, so satellite A will need to orbit the Earth faster to remain in a stable orbit ***[1 mark]***.

Pages 118-119 — Red-shift and the Big Bang

1.1 The universe started off hot and dense. ***[1 mark]***
The universe is expanding. ***[1 mark]***

1.2 E.g. dark matter/dark mass/dark energy ***[1 mark]***

2.1 E.g. Galaxies are moving away from each other ***[1 mark]***. More distant galaxies are moving away faster ***[1 mark]***.

2.2 They are held together by gravity ***[1 mark]***.

2.3 Recent observations of distant supernovae indicate that the speed at which distant galaxies are receding has **increased**. This suggests that the expansion of the universe is **accelerating**.
[1 mark for each correct]

3.1 The light's wavelength has increased / is shifted towards the red end of the spectrum ***[1 mark]***.

3.2 Tadpole galaxy ***[1 mark]***. It is the furthest away ***[1 mark]***, so it is travelling away fastest ***[1 mark]***, so it has the greatest red-shift.

3.3 It will have increased ***[1 mark]***. The universe is expanding, so the galaxy will be further away ***[1 mark]*** and will be travelling away faster ***[1 mark]***. So a greater red-shift will be observed.

3.4 Any value between (but not including) 12 million light years and 37 million light years ***[1 mark]***.

Mixed Questions

Pages 120-130 — Mixed Questions

1.1 E.g. a permanent magnet produces its own magnetic field ***[1 mark]***. An induced magnet is a material that on becomes magnetic when it is put in a magnetic field ***[1 mark]***.

1.2

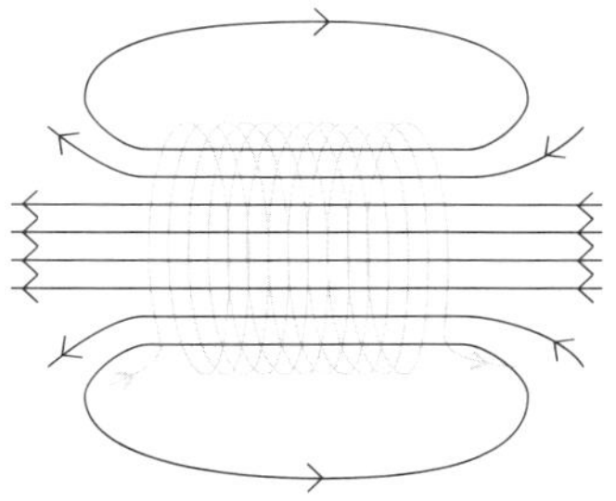

[1 mark for field lines pointing in the correct direction, 1 mark for drawing straight, parallel field lines inside the coil, 1 mark for drawing the field outside the coil]

2.1 E.g. nuclear fallout from nuclear weapons testing / nuclear accidents ***[1 mark]***.

2.2 Radioactive decay is where a nucleus releases radiation to become more **stable**. It is a **random** process, which means you **cannot** predict which individual nucleus in a sample will decay next. ***[2 marks for all correct, otherwise 1 mark for two correct]***

2.3 E.g. The rate of decay of a source of unstable nuclei/a radioactive source ***[1 mark]***.
It is measured in becquerels/Bq ***[1 mark]***.

2.4 E.g. the time taken for the activity of a sample to halve ***[1 mark]***.

3.1 three-core cable ***[1 mark]***

3.2 Live — **brown** — **230** ***[1 mark]***
Neutral — blue — **0** ***[1 mark]***
Earth — **green and yellow** — 0 ***[1 mark]***

3.3 Energy is transferred **electrically** from the mains supply to the **kinetic** energy store of the fan's blades. ***[1 mark for each correct answer]***

3.4 Energy transferred = Power × Time = 30 × (30 × 60) ***[1 mark]*** = **54 000 J** ***[1 mark]***

4.1 C ***[1 mark]***

4.2 $V = IR$ ***[1 mark]***

4.3 $R = V \div I$ ***[1 mark]*** = 240 ÷ 1.2 ***[1 mark]*** = **200 Ω** ***[1 mark]***

5.1 sound waves, P-waves ***[1 mark for both correct]***

5.2 $T = 1 \div f = 1 \div 40$ ***[1 mark]*** = 0.025 s
0.025 × 1000 ***[1 mark]*** = **25 ms** ***[1 mark]***

5.3 $v = f\lambda$ ***[1 mark]***

5.4 $v = 40 \times 0.6$ ***[1 mark]*** = **24 m/s** ***[1 mark]***

6.1

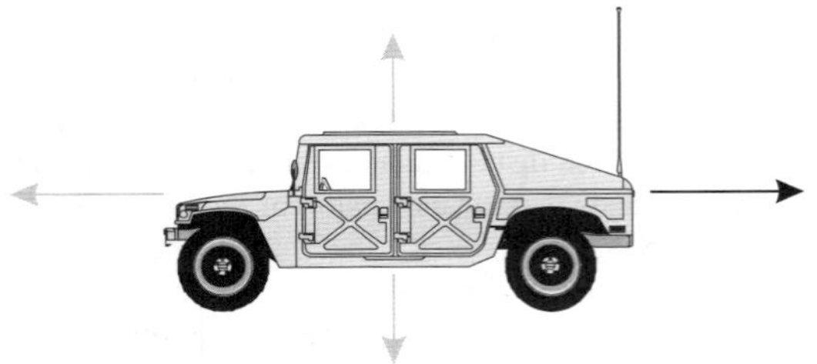

[1 mark for an arrow in the right direction, 1 mark for it being the same length as the driving force arrow]

6.2 $s = vt$ ***[1 mark]***

6.3 $s = 5.0 \times 30$ ***[1 mark]*** = **150 m** ***[1 mark]***

6.4 $E_k = ½mv^2$
$E_k = ½ \times 0.50 \times 5.0^2$ ***[1 mark]*** = **6.25 J** ***[1 mark]***

6.5 Efficiency = Useful output energy transfer ÷ Total input energy transfer ***[1 mark]***

6.6 0.65 = Useful output energy transfer ÷ 1200
Useful output energy transfer = 0.65 × 1200 ***[1 mark]*** = **780 J** ***[1 mark]***

7.1 The pressure of the water exerts a force on the submerged sides of the cube ***[1 mark]***. This leads to a resultant force upwards called upthrust ***[1 mark]***, which is equal to the weight of the displaced water ***[1 mark]***. The cube is less dense than water, so it can displace enough water that the upthrust equals its weight (so it floats) ***[1 mark]***.

7.2 $\rho = m \div v$ ***[1 mark]***

7.3 Volume of water displaced = volume of the cube submerged
Volume = 0.1 × 0.1 × 0.07 = 0.0007 m^3 ***[1 mark]***
$m = \rho \times v$ ***[1 mark]*** = 1000 × 0.0007 ***[1 mark]*** = **0.7 kg** ***[1 mark]***

8 Calculate the energy to raise the temperature of the water:
$E = mc\Delta\theta = 1.2 \times 4.2 \times 90$ ***[1 mark]*** = 453.6 kJ ***[1 mark]***
Energy needed to completely evaporate the water:
$E = mL = 1.2 \times 2300$ ***[1 mark]*** = 2760 kJ ***[1 mark]***
453.6 + 2760 = 3213.6 kJ = 3200 kJ **(to 2 s.f.)** ***[1 mark]***

9.1 increasing acceleration ***[1 mark]***
steady speed ***[1 mark]***
constant acceleration ***[1 mark]***

9.2 Acceleration = gradient of the graph ***[1 mark]***
Acceleration = $\Delta v \div \Delta t = (7 - 4) \div (7 - 5)$ ***[1 mark]***
= 3 ÷ 2 = **1.5 m/s²** ***[1 mark]***

9.3 $F = ma$
So $a = F \div m$ ***[1 mark]*** = (–)440 ÷ 83 ***[1 mark]***
= (–)5.30... m/s²
So deceleration = **5.3 m/s²** ***[1 mark]***

Remember, force is a vector quantity. It's negative here because it's acting in the opposite direction to the motion of the cyclist. That's what gives you a negative acceleration (deceleration).

9.4 Distance travelled whilst reacting (thinking distance):
Assume a 0.5 s reaction time (accept 0.2-0.9 s) ***[1 mark]***
From the graph, the cyclist's speed is 7 m/s, so:
$s = vt = 7 \times 0.5 = 3.5$ m (accept 1.4-6.3 m) ***[1 mark]***
Distance travelled whilst braking (braking distance):
$v^2 - u^2 = 2as$
$u = 7$ m/s, $v = 0$, $a = -5.3$ m/s
$s = (v^2 - u^2) \div 2a = (0^2 - 7^2) \div (2 \times -5.3)$ ***[1 mark]***
= –49 ÷ –10.6 = 4.62... m ***[1 mark]***
Stopping distance = thinking distance + braking distance
= 3.5 + 4.62... = 8.12... m = 8.1 m
(accept 6.0-11.0 m)
Stopping distance is less than 12 m, so the cyclist won't hit the car ***[1 mark]***.

10.1 $p = F \div A$ ***[1 mark]***

10.2 $F = p \times A$ ***[1 mark]*** = 1200 × 0.005 ***[1 mark]*** = **6 N** ***[1 mark]***

10.3 $p = h\rho g$ so
$\rho = p \div hg$ ***[1 mark]*** = 2850 ÷ (0.15 × 10) ***[1 mark]***
= **1900 kg/m³** ***[1 mark]***

10.4 How to grade your answer:
Level 0: There is no relevant information. ***[No marks]***
Level 1: There is a brief explanation of how increased density means an increase in the number of collisions in a given time, which leads to an increase in pressure. ***[1 to 2 marks]***
Level 2: There is a clear explanation of how increased density means an increase in the number of collisions in a given time and an increase in the weight above a surface at a given depth. There is a brief description of how both of these cause an increase in pressure. ***[3 to 4 marks]***
Here are some points your answer may include:
The new liquid is denser than water, so there are more particles in a given volume for the new liquid.
This means there are more collisions for a given area in a given time.
This means that there is a higher pressure for a surface in the new liquid.
There are also more particles above a surface at a given depth in the new liquid.
This means the weight of the particles above a given depth is larger for the new liquid than for water.
So the pressure is higher.

11.1 E.g.

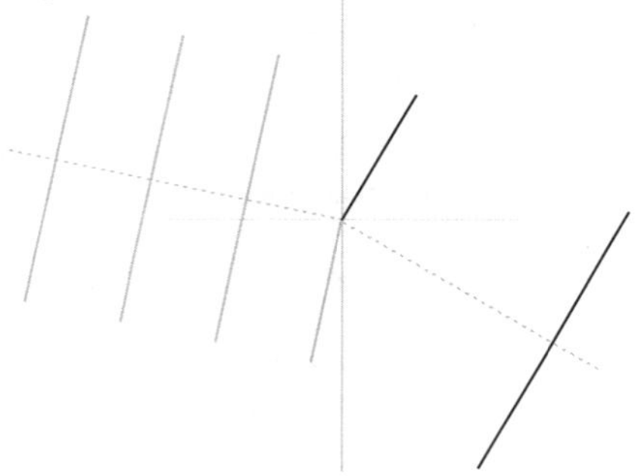

[1 mark for wave fronts correctly changing direction, 1 mark for wave fronts being spaced further apart]

11.2 How to grade your answer:
Level 0: There is no relevant information. ***[No marks]***
Level 1: There is a brief description of how the speed of different parts of the wave front change between air and diamond. ***[1 to 2 marks]***
Level 2: There is a good description of how different parts of a wave front travel at different speeds when crossing a boundary. There is some description of how this results in refraction. ***[3 to 4 marks]***

Level 3: There is a detailed explanation of how the difference in speed for different parts of a wave front results in a difference in distance travelled. There is a clear description of how this results in refraction when crossing a boundary at an angle. ***[5 to 6 marks]***

Here are some points your answer may include:
Light travels faster in air than it does in diamond.
When the light ray crosses the boundary between diamond and air at an angle, it means different parts of the wave front cross the boundary at different times.
The parts of the wave front that have crossed the boundary travel faster than the rest of the wave front that is still travelling through the diamond.
Distance = speed ÷ time.
So in the time it takes the entire wave front to cross over the boundary, the parts of the wave front that have spent more of that time travelling through air have travelled further.
This difference in distance travelled between points along the wave front causes the ray to bend (refract) away from the normal.

12.1 E.g.

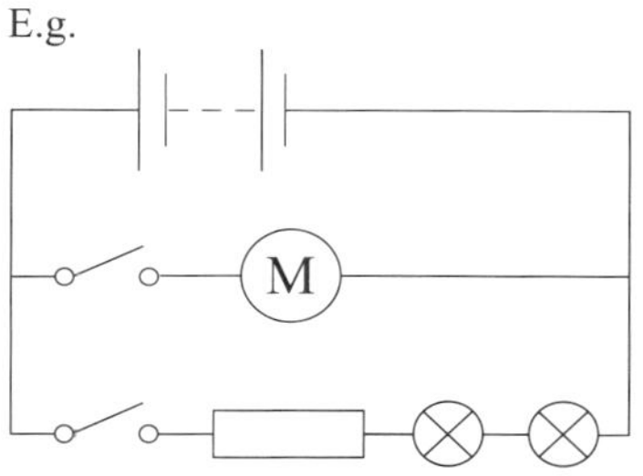

[2 marks for all circuit symbols correctly drawn, otherwise 1 mark for 4 symbols correctly drawn. 1 mark for filament lamps and resistor in series with each other, 1 mark for motor in parallel with other components, 1 mark for correct placement of switches]

12.2 $E = QV$ and $Q = It$ so $E = VIt$ ***[1 mark]***
$E = 6.0 \times 70.0 \times 10^{-3} \times (15 \times 60)$ ***[1 mark]*** = 378 J
$\Delta E = mc\Delta\theta = 0.0250 \times 120 \times 6$ ***[1 mark]*** = 18 J
378 – 18 ***[1 mark]*** = **360 J** ***[1 mark]***

12.3 E.g. he could lubricate the parts within the motor ***[1 mark]***. This would reduce friction and the amount of energy being wasted/dissipated to the thermal energy store of the motor ***[1 mark]***.

13.1 $V_p \div n_p = V_s \div n_s$
So $V_s = (25\,000 \div 1400) \times 21\,000$ ***[1 mark]***
= 375 000 V ***[1 mark]***
(For a 100% efficient transformer, power in = power out, so:)
$V_pI_p = V_sI_s$
$I_s = (25\,000 \times 4100) \div 375\,000$ ***[1 mark]***
= 273.3... = **270 A (to 2 s.f.)** ***[1 mark]***

13.2 Power transferred out of the generator = power transferred to the step-up transformer
Power output of generator = VI
= 25 000 × 4100
= 1.025×10^8 W ***[1 mark]***
Power input of generator
$P = E \div t$
= $(34.92 \times 10^9) \div 60$ ***[1 mark]***
= 5.82×10^8 W ***[1 mark]***
Efficiency = useful power output ÷ total power input
= $1.025 \times 10^8 \div 5.82 \times 10^8$ ***[1 mark]*** = 0.1761...
= **18% (to 2 s.f.)** ***[1 mark]***

13.3 In the national grid, energy is transferred electrically to the thermal energy stores of the wires ***[1 mark]*** (this is an unwanted energy transfer). This transfer occurs because a moving charge does work against resistance ***[1 mark]***, and work causes a transfer of energy ***[1 mark]***. Current is the rate of flow of charge ***[1 mark]***, so reducing the current reduces the work done and the energy transferred to thermal energy stores ***[1 mark]***.

14.1 How to grade your answer:
Level 0: There is no relevant information. ***[No marks]***
Level 1: There is a brief description of how a fission reaction occurs, limited to the splitting of a large unstable nuclei into two smaller nuclei. ***[1 to 2 marks]***
Level 2: There is a clear description of how a forced nuclear fission reaction occurs. There may be some mention of control rods. ***[3 to 4 marks]***
Level 3: There is a clear and detailed description of how a forced nuclear fission reaction occurs. There is a mention of the energies of the fission products and a clear description of how control rods are used to control the energy produced by a fission reactor. ***[5 to 6 marks]***

Here are some points your answer may include:
A neutron is absorbed by a radioactive isotope.
This causes it to become more unstable, so it decays.
It splits into two new, lighter elements that are roughly equal in size.
It also releases two or three neutrons.
All of these products have energy in their kinetic energy stores.
Any excess energy is transferred away by gamma rays.
This energy is used to generate electricity.
The neutrons released by an isotope decaying go on to be absorbed and cause more decays / create a chain reaction.
The control rods are lowered into the reactor to absorb neutrons, which reduces the amount of decaying nuclei / which reduces the rate of fission.
This slows down the rate that energy is released.
This reduces the output power (rate of energy transfer) of the power plant.

14.2 How to grade your answer:
Level 0: There is no relevant information. ***[No marks]***
Level 1: There is a brief explanation of the safety implications of storing nuclear waste. ***[1 to 2 marks]***
Level 2: There is some explanation of the safety implications of storing nuclear waste with some reference being made to half-life. ***[3 to 4 marks]***
Level 3: There is a clear and detailed explanation of the safety implications caused by storing nuclear waste and of the precautions needed, including a reference to the penetrating and ionising power of the radiation produced and the half-life of the waste. ***[5 to 6 marks]***

Here are some points your answer may include:
The caesium has a half-life of 30 years, so it will take 30 years for the activity of the waste to halve.
This means that the surrounding area will be exposed to radiation for a long time.
The gamma rays released by the waste can travel a large distance before ionising an atom.
This means that a large area surrounding the nuclear waste will be irradiated.
Exposure to nuclear radiation is harmful to humans.
It can kill cells or cause gene mutations which can lead to cancer.
So nuclear waste should be stored far away from humans and other living creatures.
Shielding should also be put around the storage sites of nuclear waste to reduce irradiation.

Equations List

Here are some equations you might find useful when you're working through the book.

Topic 1 — Energy

$E_e = \frac{1}{2}ke^2$	elastic potential energy = 0.5 × spring constant × (extension)^2
$\Delta E = mc\Delta\theta$	change in thermal energy = mass × specific heat capacity × temperature change

Topic 3 — Particle Model of Matter

$E = mL$	thermal energy for a change of state = mass × specific latent heat
pV = constant	pressure × volume = constant (for gases)

Topic 5 — Forces

$p = h\rho g$	pressure due to a column of liquid = height of column × density of liquid × gravitational field strength (g)
$v^2 - u^2 = 2as$	(final velocity)^2 – (initial velocity)^2 = 2 × acceleration × distance
$F = \frac{m\Delta v}{\Delta t}$	force = $\frac{\text{change in momentum}}{\text{time taken}}$

Topic 6 — Waves

period = $\frac{1}{\text{frequency}}$
magnification = $\frac{\text{image height}}{\text{object height}}$

Make sure you understand all the equations on this page, and you're happy using and rearranging them.

Topic 7 — Magnetism and Electromagnetism

$F = BIl$	force on a current-carrying conductor (at right-angles to a magnetic field) = magnetic flux density × current × length
$\frac{V_p}{V_s} = \frac{n_p}{n_s}$	$\frac{\text{potential difference across primary coil}}{\text{potential difference across secondary coil}} = \frac{\text{number of turns in primary coil}}{\text{number of turns in secondary coil}}$
$V_pI_p = V_sI_s$	potential difference across primary coil × current in primary coil = potential difference across secondary coil × current in secondary coil